D1432314

The Rose in the Steel Dust

THE
ROSE IN THE
STEEL DUST

AN EXAMINATION OF THE
CANTOS OF EZRA POUND

by

WALTER BAUMANN

UNIVERSITY OF MIAMI PRESS
Coral Gables, Florida

Hast 'ou seen the rose in the steel dust
(or swansdown ever?)
so light is the urging, so ordered the dark petals of iron
we who have passed over Lethe.

(End of Canto LXXIV).

Quotations from Ezra Pound's poetry and prose are reprinted here by permission of Messrs. Faber and Faber,
London, and New Directions Publishing Corp., New York.

PREFACE

The approach to Ezra Pound's *Cantos* in this book is in so far new as the greater part of it is a line for line interpretation of two of the key Cantos. Not that these two Cantos, IV and LXXXII, have hitherto gone unnoticed, but no one has as yet supplied much more than simple annotations or a characterization of the main themes. Thus a study in which they are taken as nodes, and in which they and the whole of the *Cantos* are further informed by a treatment of the role of the Odysseus figure, may perhaps help to fill a few of the blanks on the map of the Poundian universe which a good many critics have, especially in the past fifteen years, been labouring to plot.

My debts to previous students of Pound are, of course, enormous. Whenever I found that their formulations could hardly be bettered I have admitted them into my text in their own words. In particular I acknowledge my indebtedness to Hugh Kenner's pioneering criticism. In fact, Kenner has — quite unconsciously — left a further mark on this book, for I did not realize when I chose the title that he had published part of what was to make up his *Poetry of Ezra Pound* as 'The Rose in the Steel Dust' (*Hudson Review*, III, 66–124). I apologize for this clash, but I cannot bring myself to give my study a different title, since the image of the rose is too significant. I let it stand also in recognition of the fact that, although more recent criticism has tended to move away from Kenner's position, his reading of the *Cantos* still affords some of the most ingenious insights, however difficult to share they may seem at first.

For the guidance, suggestions and help I was offered during the preparation of this study I wish to thank, first of all, Prof. Heinrich Straumann of Zurich University under whose supervision it was written and who showed himself a sympathetic listener whenever the problems presented by such an undertaking were laid before him; the staff of King's College Library, Aberdeen, who obliged me on many occasions by supplying me with material through inter-library loans; also the staff of the British Museum Library for providing me with a number of special items.

Among the major stimuli I received I should like to mention the many hours spent in Aberdeen discussing Pound with Dr. Carlos Pujol,

Barcelona. A special word of thanks is due to Prof. Max Wildi, Zurich, who first introduced me to the subject, and whose inspiring enthusiasm made me want to know more. Above all, however, I am deeply grateful to my wife, who encouraged me throughout, read the drafts, suggested various stylistic alterations and, together with my mother-in-law, typed out the MS.   W. B.

CONTENTS

8

NOTE ON REFERENCES

Unless an additional note is called for, all quotations from Pound's works are identified in brackets set in the text.

Quotations from the *Cantos* are given by Canto number (in Arabic numerals) and page number, separated by colon. With Cantos I–LXXI and LXXIV–LXXXIV *(Pisan Cantos)* the figure after the colon indicates the page number(s) in the 1948 New Directions editions, in which the pagination of the individually published instalments has been preserved; the figure after the oblique refers to the page number(s) of the 1954 Faber edition, which is numbered straight through. With *Section: Rock-Drill* (Cantos 85–95) and *Thrones* (Cantos 96–109) only one page reference is given, since both the New Directions and Faber volumes were printed by offset from the Italian first editions, and the pagination is identical (V. Gallup, A61, A70 & A77).

For the short titles of Pound's other works see the Bibliography.

All other references are in the Notes. For the main works on Pound, identified by author's name only, see also the Bibliography.

Introduction

THE FAME OF THE *CANTOS*

Ever since February 1949, when the *Pisan Cantos* was awarded the Bollingen Prize for poetry, the *Cantos* of Ezra Pound has been the subject of heated controversy wherever modern literature is discussed. Whereas appreciation of the works of Joyce and Eliot, his two outstanding friends and contemporaries, has become a matter of course, Pound's colossal poem is still a stumbling block of literary criticism, and many recognized critics even tend to discard it as a failure. Nevertheless, the publication of every further instalment of this work in progress which has still no actual title causes a new wave of enthusiasm – and disapproval.

Hardly had the readers of the Chicago magazine *Poetry* been presented with the first samples of what was to become Pound's life-work, when an anonymously published pamphlet on *Ezra Pound: His Metric and Poetry* declared at the end: 'We will leave it as a test: when anyone has studied Pound's poems *in chronological order*, and has mastered *Lustra* and *Cathay*, he is prepared for the Cantos – but not till then.' [1]

The writer of the pamphlet appears quite convinced that this new poem, referred to as the 'Cantos', will deserve all the reader's attention, whereas Pound's earlier poems will be of interest chiefly as a preparation for it, and that the popularity of the author of *Lustra* and *Cathay* should be transferred to the poet of the *Cantos*.

The man who was trying to effect this change of literary opinion turned out to be none other than T. S. Eliot, who, it can be assumed, was thus repaying a debt to the young compatriot through whom he had obtained his first audience. But Eliot was actually too early with his claim for the *Cantos*, since what was published in *Poetry* in 1917 proved to be a false start. Eliot must have based his opinion on Pound's own words, a trace of which survives in a letter to Harriet Monroe, the editor and founder of *Poetry*: 'My next contribution will probably be a 40 page fragment from a more important opus.' (*Letters*, p. 130). Another indication of Pound's original intentions is contained in a letter to the art collector John Quinn, his friend and patron: '. . . then work on a new long poem (really LONG, endless, leviathanic).' (p. 157).

It was not until 1924–1925 that the *Cantos* was really launched, with *A Draft of XVI Cantos*. Appearing in the Paris of the Lost Generation, it was in line with the rest of the so-called avant-garde literature of the period. The 1919 bibliophile edition of an early version of Canto IV and its inclusion with the three following Cantos in *Poems 1918–21* may have reminded Pound's intimates of his plan. But in the meantime it was his critical prose, his translations and above all *Homage to Sextus Propertius* (1919) and *Hugh Selwyn Mauberley* (1920) which, from 1917 to 1925, added to his reputation. In fact, when Pound was offered the *Dial* Award for 1927 he found it necessary to write in reply: 'It is impossible for me to accept an award except on Cantos or on my verse as a whole.' (*Letters*, p. 288). He could not have made it clearer that he wanted to be known as a poet, as 'scriptor cantilenae' (24:112/117 etc.) first and last. Unfortunately, he has only himself to blame for the fact that, especially since World War II, he goes more frequently under other descriptions. Ask the average American, and he will answer: *We call him the traitor.*

From 1925 to 1940 the *Cantos* appeared fairly regularly, with an average yearly increase of something over twenty pages. Their critical estimation was mainly the concern of fellow poets. The leading critic was still T. S. Eliot with his 'conviction that [Pound's] verse has steadily improved, and that the Cantos are the most interesting of all'.[2] In 1932 F. R. Leavis became the leader of those who considered *Hugh Selwyn Mauberley* to be Pound's poetic peak. Edith Sitwell and R. P. Blackmur may be said to have initiated analytical criticism of the *Cantos*. W. B. Yeats's *Packet for Ezra Pound*, which records Pound's description of one structural principal of the *Cantos*, was only taken up with profit after World War II, though it had already been quoted by Alice Steiner Amdur in 1936.[3]

Despite these attempts at criticism of the *Cantos*, the poem remained overshadowed by Pound's other merits and activities. After the Big Slump the devoted reader was kept busy with Pound's tracts on economics, such as the *ABC of Economics* (1933) and *Jefferson and/or Mussolini* (1935), and by the various volumes of his critical prose. And when Pound started broadcasting for Fascist Italy during the War, seeming to be another Lord Haw Haw, the *Cantos* became a highly suspicious piece of literature. Pound himself stopped work on them, and had it not been for the *Pisan Cantos*, which persuaded the fellows in American Letters of the Library of Congress that Pound's poetic powers had not suffered through his political alignment, the 1950's would hardly have seen a revival of the poet of the *Cantos*.

T. S. Eliot said, in his much-quoted *Dial* article of 1928: 'Pound has had, and has an immense influence, but no disciples . . . and I think that the reason is this: that influence can be exerted through form, whereas one makes disciples only among those who sympathize with the content.'

As far as the writing of poetry is concerned, Eliot's statement is still, on the whole, valid: Pound's influence is felt as a certain undercurrent in modern verse-forms, but there is hardly any poet who has whole-heartedly taken up Pound's message. Yet there exists a species of Poundians for whom Pound's word has become gospel. A. Alvares, recording his visits to St. Elizabeth's Hospital in Washington, where Pound was interned for almost thirteen years, furnishes an instructive picture of them: 'He was surrounded by his disciples and was talking politics. They were pumping him on currency reforms, "Commy plots" and the use of dope for political ends.' (*Observer*, March 6, 1960).

These followers, squatting round their latter-day Confucius in the hospital's park, can easily be ridiculed. But even some of the chiefly literary-minded Poundians are not altogether free from certain sectarian motives in their writings on Pound's poetry. It is certainly only natural that those who find it worthwhile to study and commentate Pound's work cannot help being under his spell to some extent.

CRITICISM OF THE *CANTOS*

To find some of the reasons for the predominance of negative criticism of the *Cantos* is one of the objects of the present study. In spite of the increasing number of Pound exegetes, especially in America, it is only too obvious that the literary world as a whole has lost patience with Pound — a state of affairs which is unlikely to change. There is a sufficient quantity of other twentieth-century poetry still waiting to be appreciated and properly understood, and much of it seems far more rewarding than Pound's exasperating obscurities, which are, in the eyes of many critics, obscurities of the wrong kind.

The trouble with most of the negative criticism is that it dismisses Pound's *Cantos* before even its basic scope is taken into consideration, and this is quite understandable, since it can only be gauged after long and detailed study, which is rendered all the more difficult by the numerous provocations to which one is exposed on practically every page. It scarcely surprises us, therefore, that such temperamental persons as

Robert Graves[4] cannot be considered fair judges of so provocative a work as Pound's *Cantos*. It is, on the other hand, typical that Pound, a man of little or no patience himself, finds *Finnegans Wake*, that other work demanding assiduous study, just as unreadable as Joyce found the *Cantos*.

On April 9, 1958, ten days before Pound's release from St. Elizabeth's, a leading article in the London *Times* began: 'American public opinion is being stirred up into one of its periodical fits of emotional injustice.' Such an attitude is of course prejudicial to any sort of understanding of Pound's poetry. The only way to be just to the *Cantos*, then, is through conscious disengagement. Both extreme enthusiasm and utter antipathy make impossible the task of establishing a satisfactory exposition. But since provocation is one of Pound's intentions, since avowal and disavowal are part of the very principle of the poem,[5] a dispassionate attitude can hardly be maintained. All that can be attempted is to detach oneself from the emotional tensions created in one by the reading of the *Cantos*, the corresponding prose and the information about Pound's political activities. This does not, however, by any means imply that Pound is to be excused on every possible count.

THE *CANTOS* AS A MIRROR OF POUND THE MAN

Now that the first full biography of Pound has appeared,[6] there is, together with what is to be learned from the increasing number of books of memoirs by those who knew him, quite enough material available for a preliminary consideration of Pound's personal involvement in the *Cantos*. In one sense the *Cantos* is very autobiographical, in another it could not be more impersonal, in accordance with Eliot's definition in his famous 'Tradition and the Individual Talent' (1919).

In this study special attention will be paid to the two seemingly contradictory 'Faces of Ezra Pound' (Alvares), the man of letters and lover of beauty over and against the economic and political propagandist and agitator. It will generally be seen that the *Cantos* is to a great extent a mirror of this often eccentric personality. A really exhaustive treatment of the biographical background is, on the other hand, not yet possible. There is need for a biography of Pound (similar to Ellmann's *James Joyce*) to supply even more detailed information. At present many incidents in Pound's life which are of importance for the understanding of certain passages of the *Cantos* can be only imperfectly reconstructed, mostly by guesswork. There will be such guesses in this study, too, but it is hoped that once all the material is available they will not be proved entirely wrong.

A WORD ABOUT METHODS

Allen Tate concluded his review of *A Draft of XXX Cantos* on a mildly ironic note : 'And the thirty *Cantos* are enough to occupy a loving and ceaseless study — say a canto a year for thirty years, all thirty to be read every few weeks just for the tone.'[7] Whether 'loving' or not, 'ceaseless study' of one Canto at a time is the answer to the rather formidable wealth of material in any of the Cantos. The hasty and uninitiated reader may be struck by certain passages of poetic intensity, but he cannot pierce the complex, if not complicated, surface and acquire a sufficiently disentangled vision of the core of this poem. Thorough penetration of a small but representative portion of the text can alone surmount this acute difficulty, and since criticism of the *Cantos* has become mainly textual, some generalizations not based on the immediate text have been refuted, even some of T. S. Eliot's. Moreover, this approach is of great practical value, as it facilitates the correct reading of the work.

The *Cantos* is so full of details which are at first sight utterly incoherent that it has been called a rag-bag. Pound is, however, so fanatical in his juxtaposition of a 'sufficient phalanx of particulars' (74 : 19/469) that to shed light on such obscure passages must be the primary task of any detailed study of this extraordinary literary composition. Since the publication of the *Annotated Index to the Cantos of Ezra Pound* (1957) the commentator's work has certainly been made easier, but those annotations which are merely compiled from standard works of reference are often of little or no use. The fragments of learning in Pound's *Cantos* are, more often than not, taken from obsolete sources, a good many of which are now, mostly through Pound's own agency, fortunately better known. The compilation of an exhaustive commentary, however, still involves a great many shots in the dark. What one of the commentators of Browning's *Sordello* discovered, that no amount of editing was really enough,[8] is even more true of the *Cantos*, especially since *Sordello* constitutes one of Pound's models. Nevertheless, inspired source-hunting in the study of Pound can reveal highly significant shades of meaning and must be pursued with diligence.

Though the single Canto is in some measure a separate unit, it is futile to isolate it from the rest. 'Discussing that immense poem' with Yeats, Pound once hinted at an analogy with a Bach fugue,[9] but this is only one of the many analogies proposed by Pound and others. For the moment it suffices to say that a certain underlying coherence can be observed to run through the whole of the *Cantos*. One of the most useful analogies that can be suggested is perhaps that of 'the rose in the steel dust'

(74 : 27/477), and this is used as the title of the present study, since it may serve as a very apt metaphor for the whole of Pound's work and of Pound the man and poet.

Most passages, and a great number of single lines in each Canto, are linked up with echoes and variations in other Cantos and fairly often have their counterparts in Pound's prose. An attempt at overall interpretation must therefore bring all these cognate passages and utterances to bear upon each other. This phenomenon of the mutual supplementation of passages from various writings of the same author, is, of course, a critical commonplace. But with Pound it will be seen to have particularly significant function. It is therefore never very enlightening to commentate one Canto alone: only as the basis of a total interpretation does the single Canto come properly alive.

Though Pound's craftsmanship would on its own fill more than a volume, a separate discussion of technique is not attempted here. Eliot's statements about the unity of form and content seem to be particularly true in the case of Pound.[10] The character of this in Pound's work is, however, highly disputable. Yeats found 'more style than form' in the *Cantos*, particularly because in his eyes 'form must be full, sphere-like, single' and not 'constantly interrupted'.[11]

It may be added that if style is a more appropriate word than form, Pound employs not one but several styles, very largely depending on the subject-matter. Therefore the discussion of the technique used in a given passage must necessarily be based on the discussion of the subject treated.

Part One

TOWARDS THE IDEAL CITY

Perhaps as the poem goes on I shall be able to make various things clearer. Having the crust to attempt a poem in 100 or 120 cantos long after all mankind has been commanded never again to attempt a poem of any length, I have to stagger as I can.

(To Felix E. Schelling on July 9, 1922).

It was not until 1924 that Pound decided on the definitive form and content of Cantos I, II and III. Canto IV, however, has not, apart from the end, undergone any drastic changes. The fact that Pound found it worthy of being recited on the first Caedmon record[12] shows that he considers it, together with the final version of Canto I, as a special achievement. And as it is the first Canto to survive Pound's search for the appropriate form, it is a suitable point of departure.

A detailed analysis of the 25 different elements which go to make up the 128 lines of Canto IV yields, once all the references have been established, a particularly instructive insight into Pound's preoccupation with the mythical aspects of his vision of the world.

For the sake of reference I have made a plan of Canto IV, in which each separate passage appears under some apt heading.[13] To give the exploring mind a few pointers, it seems desirable to interpolate some reflections on the formulation of the theme or themes of Canto IV. Hugh Kenner calls it 'fatal passion', and considers all the Cantos from II to VII as one group, headed summarily 'PASSION, Myths, metamorphosis, modes of love and violence'.[14] Sister M. Bernetta Quinn sums up this theme, together with related ones in other Cantos, as 'beauty is extremely hard to possess' and 'nothing truly good comes from violence'.[15] R. P. Blackmur, in his somewhat impatient essay, 'Masks of Ezra Pound', supplies an abstract characterization of the treatment of the subject-matter of Canto IV and others : he styles it an 'anthropological identification of different materials.'[16]

Since the appearance of the *Pisan Cantos* (1948) and the publication in 1950 of Pound's pamphlet *Patria Mia,* serialized in the *New Age* in 1912 and then lost for all those years, the aspect under which Canto IV is mainly considered here, that of the Ideal City, adds greatly to its significance in Pound's work as a whole, as this theme is thrown into prominence by the later writings. Although there is no sequence of events in our Canto, we shall discover a progression of values, a moving away from baser passions towards the contemplation of spiritual beauty, towards the sphere in which the well-ordered state becomes a spiritual reality. Seen in this light, the theme can be restated as metamorphoses in different strata of love *and* civilization, as they affect a set of archetypal persons.

Thus in Canto IV Pound reviews the march of civilization from the passion which destroys men and cities to the affection which is in harmony with the great mysteries of this world and leads men to the Ideal City. From the point of view of this dualism metamorphosis is, to a certain extent, the intervention of divine justice.

ANCIENT BLOOD FEUD

Taking the first line, 'Palace in smoky light', whose exact relation to the following lines is hardly discernible, as an upbeat, we can say with Blackmur that 'Canto IV begins with an apostrophe to burning Troy':[17]

> Troy but a heap of smouldering boundary stones   (1. 2).

Pound's image of the destroyed city seems to emulate both Virgil and Dante. Virgil's '... et omnis humo fumat Neptunia Troia'[18] may have prompted Pound's highly evocative 'smouldering', whereas Dante, who, working from the *Aeneid*, introduced the concrete image of hollows formed by fragments of masonry, may have led him to the still more concrete image of 'boundary stones'.[19] Moreover, the addition of the word 'heap' with Pound stresses the idea that the beholder of the fallen city cannot recognize even the barest outline of the former splendour, and the word has a similar effect as in Eliot's :

> ... for you only know
> A heap of broken images ...[20]

Virgil's 'superbum Ilium'[21] must have caused Dante to list the fall of Troy as the thirteenth instance of punished pride,[22] to which he refers a number of times. Pound likewise reminds the reader of the example of proud Troy', identifying it with the fate of other castles and towns,[23] particularly in :

> and at Ho Ci'u destroyed the whole town
> for hiding a woman ...   (84 : 116/573).

In Pound's eyes, however, Troy fell not so much because of pride, but because of what Homer made the old Trojan leaders utter when they were watching Helen climbing the battlements.[24] This is at the same time the only Iliadic passage, apart from single phrases, which Pound considered to be fit material for the *Cantos* :

> ... murmur of old men's voices :
> 'Let her go back to the ships,
> Back among Grecian faces, lest evil come on our own,
> Evil and further evil, and a curse cursed on our children,
> Moves, yes she moves like a goddess
>
>   . . .
>
> And doom goes with her in walking'   (2 : 6/10).

Seen in the context of Canto II, where it is in juxtaposition to the story of the metamorphosis of the Tyrrhenian pirates (told as an obvious instance of punishment for non-recognition of a god),[25] Pound's powerful adaptation of the old men's wisdom is undoubtedly meant to show the real cause of Troy's downfall. Had the fighting Trojans been warned by Helen's godlike and daemonic nature, had they recognized in her Κύθηρα δεινά,[26] the fearful aspect of Aphrodite, whose likeness she was, they might have been spared the final catastrophe.

The theme of Helen of Troy attains its characteristic dimension only through a set of puns from a chorus in Aeschylus' *Agamemnon*, the discussion of which belongs more appropriately to Part Three of this study. All that need be known here is skilfully brought out in H. Weir Smyth's translation of the Aeschylean passage in question : 'who named that bride of the spear and source of strife with the name of Helen? For, true to her name, a Hell she proved to ships, Hell to men, Hell to city'.[27]

The image of burnt Troy at the beginning of Canto IV may also be said to have a temporal significance. The time before was a period of greedy passion, which of necessity violated the laws of nature, and the time after it is to be a period of 'vengeances reavenged',[28] a period when the blood feud is to take its course. In the following Canto Agamemnon's death-cry resounds, although it is brought forward in time to Renaissance Italy (V. 5 : 19/23), and we shall see in Part Three that the doom of a variety of persons is identified with the archetypal doom of the house of Atreus.

After the image of sacked Troy, which we now see to function more as part of one of those elaborate echo-patterns ranging over the whole of the *Cantos* than as part of Canto IV, the apostrophe is continued in the opening epithet of Pindar's second Olympian ode, here transliterated as 'ANAXIFORMINGES'. Greek scholars like F. Peachy[29] speak of it as a 'unique epithet', but Pound commented in the *Egoist* of March-April 1919: 'Pindar is a *pompier* and his Ἀναξιφόρμιγγες ὕμνοί etc. ought to be sent to the dust-bin ...'[30]

Since Pound has never ceased to voice his distaste for Pindar's rhetoric, the motive which led to the inclusion of the epithet in Canto IV can only be scorn, just as the stanza in *Mauberley* where lines 2 and 3 of the same ode are parodied is intended to render audible a brassy hollowness and stiltedness (V. *Personae*, p. 199).

Pound's aim in using the Pindaric 'ANAXIFORMINGES' is only too apparent from its juxtaposition with the name of the bride who receives fatherly praise in Catullus' *Carmen* LXI, Vinia Aurunculeia. This juxtaposition epitomizes the necessary choice of both manner and matter of this very Canto. Pointing out the classical authors 'who matter' (*Letters*, p. 138) in a series of letters to Iris Barry, Pound put lines 2 and 3 of Pindar's ode side by side with the end of the fifth stanza of Sappho's 'Hymn to Aphrodite', to illustrate the different rhythms. Pindar's is rudely condemned, whereas Sappho's, and with hers those of Catullus and Propertius, are erected as touchstones for young poets.

Pindar, in the first stanza of his ode, enumerates three possible subjects :

> Hymns that are lords of the lyre,
> What god, what hero, what man
> shall we sing of? [31]

The two lines at the beginning of Canto IV could very well lead on to any of these subjects. But if 'Aurunculeia' is correctly interpreted as the answer to what must be, at another level, a typically Poundian one-word ellipsis of the Pindaric context, we must conclude that Pound is announcing that a fourth matter is mainly to be sung of. We are even tempted to extend the answer to 'My genius is no more than a girl', a crucial line in *Homage to Sextus Propertius*. [32] Pindar and his lyre are dismissed from the *Cantos* once and for all, and the family-name of the bride made immortal in one of the finest extant classical epithalamia, which is further recalled in lines 82—88 of this Canto and also in Canto V, indicates, by means of metonymy, that Pound's subject here is above all that of Sappho, Catullus, Propertius and Ovid : the ways of love and woman.

But Vinia Aurunculeia is destined for a serene life, for what we shall see embodied in the pines of Takasago : conjugal loyalty. As we shall realize presently, Vinia forms a contrast to the less fortunate women who are evoked in the course of the Canto, and who experience to the full the cruelty of love.

Line 4, the end of the initial apostrophe, represents that point in Ovid's account of the Cadmus myth where Athene suddenly summons the hero and appears to him, commanding him to sow in a ploughed furrow the teeth of the dragon he killed. [33] Thus guided by Athene, Cadmus obtains the helpers, the Spartoi, to build the Cadmeia, the acropolis of Thebes.

This line must be looked upon, in the first place, as a contrast to line 2 : Troy has fallen because Helen's nature and many divine principles have been violated; the Cadmeia arises because the divine instructions are followed. The acceptance of divine guidance, and the repulsion of it, form, as Emery points out, the unifying theme of the beginning of Pound's poem.[34] Accordingly Pentheus, who rejects the cult of Dionysus, is exhorted to listen to Tiresias and to Cadmus, his grandfather, or else he will be destroyed (V. 2 : 9/13).

The autochthonism as contained in the Cadmus legend becomes part of the mysteries contemplated by Pound in the *Pisan Cantos*. In Canto XXVII, however, 'Tovarisch' (Russian for 'comrade'), who apparently represents the masses stirred up to revolution, speaks as one sprung from the teeth sown by Cadmus, but not rising to be among the builders of the City, as he returns to the earth, a mere victim of strife.[35] Be it in the American War of Independence (V. 62 : 88/358) or in World War II (V. 74 : 8/456), he is the eternal cannon-fodder, or, in times of peace, belongs to the 'exploited proletariat'.[36]

When Pound wrote in Pisa : 'the forms of men rose out of $\gamma \acute{\epsilon} \alpha$'[37] he was voicing his desire that new city-builders and not blind warriors should come up again, now that Mussolini's Rome had fallen. The African folksong about Wagadu, the spirit of strength, whom Pound, in his preoccupation, makes a city-builder, together with the city of Deioces, Ecbatana,[38] unites with the earth-born founders of Thebes into one vision of the city to be rebuilt 'now in the heart indestructible' (77 : 43/494). Yet since the mysteries of the earth were particularly dear to Pound's heart in Pisa, the Cadmus legend also left its mark on the city-image of the 'HUDOR' Canto :

> The roots go down to the river's edge
> and the hidden city moves upward (83 : 608/565).

That on the other hand Pound assumes the Phoenician-Semitic origin of Cadmus is evident from the epithet 'Golden Prows' and from Canto XXVII :

> That he came with the gold ships, Cadmus (132/137).

Ovid, too, accepted this genealogy,[39] but its modern champion was Victor Bérard,[40] whose theories may have influenced Pound in making Cadmus a sailor-hero, the forefather, so to speak, of Odysseus and Hanno, the Carthaginian commander, both of whom we shall consider as Poundian archetypes in Part Two. This somewhat lengthy discussion of the opening four lines is thus justified, since they contain in a nutshell all the major themes of the Canto.

What follows in lines 5—12 is the first of the three pieces of nature lyric within this Canto. Primarily they show the light-process at different times of the day, so that we shall refer to them as the Dawn Lyric, the Noon Lyric (ll. 68—80) and the Evening Lyric (ll. 103—109). At the same time they are 'metaphors . . . for certain emotional colours . . .' by means of which Pound is eager to 'assert that the Gods exist' (Guide, p. 299). In the context of Canto IV they also have a structural significance and may be said to serve as a frame for allusions to various mythical events. The Dawn Lyric reads :

> The silver mirrors catch the bright stones and flare,
> Dawn, to our waking, drifts in the green cool light;
> Dew-haze blurs, in the grass, pale ankles moving.
> Beat, beat, whirr, thud, in the soft turf
>   under the apple trees,
> Choros nympharum, goat-foot, with the pale foot alternate;
> Crescent of blue-shot waters, green-gold in the shallows,
> A black cock crows in the sea-foam.

The most impressive feature of these lines is the way in which they render the setting in motion of nature by the arrival of the first light of morning : as the primary impulse a flare on the surface still charged, as it were, with the moon's silvery reflection, then the drifting in of the rosy glow of dawn on its complementary 'green cool light', followed by the movement in the grass which suddenly reveals itself to be the very pulse of life in the onomatopoeic 'Beat, beat, whirr, thud . . .'

As in most other passages in the *Cantos* in which Pound speaks of light the mood is objectified by visions of 'elemental creatures' (*Pavannes*, p. 96) and gods. This is rooted in literal acceptance of certain mythopoetic tenets of Neoplatonism. Of the early Cantos, the opening lines of Cantos V and XXIII are steeped in Iamblicus' conception of the light of heaven as the Neoplatonic One — 'God's fire' (23 : 107/111) with Pound — 'from which all things emanate', and in Porphyry's conviction that 'Omnis Intellectus Est Omniformis',[41] a concise version of which is found in the lines :

> 'Et omniformis' : Air, fire, the pale soft light.
>   . . .
> The fire? always, and the vision always (5 : 17/21).

In Pound's 'RELIGIO or, The Child's Guide to Knowledge' (his mock-catechism) one of the answers states that 'when the states of mind take

24

form' a god is manifest, the god being himself 'an eternal state of mind' (*Pavannes*, p. 96).

In line 8 the onomatopoeic registration of the first stirrings of morning is a mere mimicry of sense perception. Only the re-discovery of what exists permanently 'in the record of human experience' — the 'elements of dawn and magnificence in Greece', 'perceived by the mind's eye' — grants Pound the vision of 'intelligible form'.[42] Here the form is a ritual dance, the rhythmic pattern of which is formed by the 'goatfoot, with the pale foot alternate'. The fact that it is the rather coarse and promiscuous goat-footed companions of Zagreus-Dionysus who tread out the dance with the delicate and chaste pale-footed companions of Artemis, 'the goddess of the fair knees' (17 : 76/80), unites in one vision the truth that any rhythmic pattern hangs between order and chaos.[43]

As the *Cantos* progresses, ritual dances become a more and more essential feature of Pound's view of civilization. In Canto XVII, where the linguistic hybrid 'choros nympharum' is again superimposed (77 / 81), the uninhibited, dynamic dance marks, in its reminiscence of most ancient Greece, a sharp contrast with the magnificent but fatal petrifaction of the essence of the sea in the marble of Venice, and we find a particularly striking example in the Lynx Song of the *Pisan Cantos* (79 : 65—70/ 520—525), one of the most sustained ritual passages in the *Cantos*, the end of which celebrates that goddess who is 'lighter than air', yet 'terrible in resistance'. So too the Dawn Lyric in our Canto contains portents of her who 'was born of sea-foam' (79 : 70/525). Apple trees (Cf. l. 9) are, after all, sacred to her : we are, as in Canto LXXIX, in a 'garden of Venus' (67/521).

Yet although our eyes are turned to the sea, her 'native element',[44] Aphrodite does not reveal herself at this point, contrary to her appearance to Odysseus-Pound after the voyage to Hades in Canto I. Instead of seeing 'waves taking form' (23 : 109/114), we hear 'a black cock crow ... in the sea-foam'. This obviously sexual image must be intended to recall the sinister side of Aphrodite's origin, the outcome of Uranos' castration by Kronos.

It is quite probable that the conception behind Pound's image is inspired by Swinburne, that other revolutionary neo-pagan, whose impact on Pound will later concern us on several occasions. Admittedly, Pound's Aphrodite is predominantly 'the archetype of what comes out of the flux', 'something formed and permanent, ... a conquest over chaos',[45] but, as we have already observed in the discussion of her likeness, Helen, Pound is not blind to her double nature, so that Swinburne's 'evil blossom ... born / Of sea-foam and the frothing of blood', 'a perilous goddess',

25

'Aphrodite, a mother of strife',[46] aptly illustrates part of Pound's intention. Opening 'with the first pale clear of the heaven' (17 : 76/80), in which the poet discovers, though only partially, the manifestation of eternal states of mind, our Dawn Lyric thus ends with the evocation of the sinister aspect of love, unbounded passion, which above all causes violence and even bestial cruelty. It is perhaps not accidental that the stretch of sea on which the light of morning displays its ever-increasing brightness is crescent-shaped. It was a sickle-sword with which Kronos took vengeance on his father, so that the allusion to this dreadful weapon may point forward to the slaughters now to be referred to.

The unifying motif of lines 13—31 is the cry of the swallows. As will be seen in Part Three, the discovery of an equivalent in art to the song of birds is one of Pound's main preoccupations in the *Pisan Cantos*. In Canto IV such an equivalent is found in the onomatopoeic qualities of one of the names mythologically associated with the origin of the swallow. It is in this connection that the theme of metamorphosis is introduced.

ITYLUS

At the time of Pound's arrival in London, and for some years after, the name of Itylus was still closely linked with Swinburne's magnificent 'Swallow, my sister, O sister swallow',[47] and is, in our Canto, first heard 'in the low drone' (l. 15) of an old man whom the poet depicts as being seated beside what must be a deathbed :

> Ityn!
> Et ter flebiliter, Itys, Ityn! (ll. 16—17).[48]

In making the old mourner's lament echo a line from Horace, Pound apparently wants to draw a parallel between the metamorphoses ocurring in the myth in question and the metamorphosis which the myth itself underwent in its literary tradition.

In his ode on 'The Delights of Spring', from which Pound is borrowing here, Horace presents an 'ill-fated' bird as 'making tearful moan for Itys', the child who was butchered by his own mother, Procne, for the sake of bestial revenge on Tereus, her husband, who had raped her sister Philomela :

> nidum ponit, *Ityn flebiliter* gemens,
> infelix avis et Cecropiae domus
> aeternum opprobrium, quod male barbaras
> regum est ulta libidines.

This bird, Horace comments, is the 'everlasting disgrace of the Cecropian house, for that she avenged too cruelly the barbarous lust of kings'. [49] Whatever Horace's reasons for using the general term 'infelix avis' instead of naming the bird, the swallow, an unmelodious songster, is a more expressive form for a jealous wife and cruel mother than the tuneful nightingale. [50]

Adapting Horace, Pound introduces a pun on the adverbial suffix '-iter' and the numeral 'ter'; it becomes almost an internal rhyme through the addition of the seemingly superfluous 'et'. 'Shedding threefold tears' ('ter flebiliter') applies both to the mourner, whom we may assume to be Procne's father, Pandion, and to Procne-become-swallow, for Pandion grieves for two daughters and a grandchild, and Procne for a sister, a husband and a son.

By line 18 the vision of Pandion beside the couch with the elaborately carved feet has faded, and we find ourselves in the presence of a woman committing suicide :

> And she went toward the window and cast her down.

But Pandion's daughter (metamorphosed and multiplied) is still there :

> 'All the while, the while, swallows crying : (l. 19).

They are, in fact, crying the same thing as that archetypal swallow Procne. Pound's colon after 'crying' makes it quite clear that 'Ityn' (l. 20) records the actual cry. What has happened in his mind can be called an identification of the slaughtered child's name with the sound produced by the swallows.

It is only in the following line that Pound gives some indication as to the woman's identity :

> 'It is Cabestan's heart in the dish' (l. 21).

According to Provençal tradition this dish was placed before Lady Soremonda by her husband, Raymond de Château Roussillon, who in his boundless jealousy had killed Guillem da Cabestan (fl. 1196), his wife's troubadour lover. To the triumphant Raymond's consternation, however, his wife adopted the attitude of a tragic heroine and declared, when she had unwittingly eaten of her lover's heart :

> 'No other taste shall change this.' (l. 23) [51]

The fundamental identity of Procne's crime with this particular bestiality sprung from the almost pagan life of Troubadour Provence lies

27

in the jealous act of serving up human flesh. But whereas Tereus thinks only of violent revenge when he is told that he has eaten his son's flesh, so that the gods have to intervene to prevent further horrors, Soremonda, a defenceless woman, manifests, in her decision to commit suicide, a high degree of nobility. This difference in spirit seems to be reflected in the 'sculpturesque imagery'[52] of both scenes. Barbaric alliterations stress the unnaturalness of the Chimera adorning the incestuous bed, whereas the window from which Soremonda throws herself is of smooth-cut stone, and the alliterations in line 27 are, significantly, spirants and not stops as in line 13 :

> Firm even fingers held the firm pale stone.

This highly-balanced line reflects the dignity with which she stands on the brink of certain death.

There is a curious arrestation of clock-time in the rendering of this scene, Soremonda's fall from the window, depicted in lines 28—30, being deliberately announced as early as line 18. The psychological expansion of time, the shrieking of the swallows, which is imagined to continue, and the fragments of dialogue, which become, as it were, the circling inner utterance of her agonized mind, may indeed remind us of cinematographic montage, particularly of that on the sound-track.[53]

The actual fall is presented with camera-like precision :

> Swung for a moment,
> and the wind out of Rhodez
> Caught in the full of her sleeve. (ll. 28—30)

To the poet, however, that which gives itself over to the air is no longer a real person. Soremonda's sleeve catches on the wind 'out of Rhodez':[54] she literally takes wing and fades in the current of air. Cinematographically speaking, the shot fades out, but the sound-track still provides the background :

> 'Tis, 'Tis. Ytis! (l. 32)

Considering that swallows are frequently seen flying round Provençal castles and towers, Pound's primary inspiration for the whole Itylus-Cabestan passage probably goes back to one of his journeys in that region, especially since we know from the history of 'In a Station of the Metro' that Pound's mind works in this way.[55]

Thus we see that Pound, in writing this passage, revived, as it were, ancient aetiology, which was always at work in animal sagas. The onomatopoeic notation of the cry (l. 32) can thus be taken to strengthen the likelihood that the way the sound was perceived gave rise to the name 'Itys', so that the identification which we found in line 20 brings out the very node of this myth.[56] But the swallows' finale, ''Tis, 'Tis...' (l. 32), is at the same time, as Eva Hesse points out,[57] an answer to :

'It is Cabestan's heart in the dish? (l. 22)

'The important thing about the reference [to Soremonda's suicide]', says Blackmur, 'is that it completes the reference to the myth of Itys with which the Cabestan material is prefaced and concluded.'[58] Though we have already implicitly treated this mutual supplementation, some clarifying discussion is still needed, especially as to why Pound chose the story of Cabestan and Soremonda. The choice of stories in which human flesh is eaten is, in the first place, extremely limited, but, full of the 'spirit of romance', and wont to see parallels in the poetry of the troubadours (and consequently in Provençal love-affairs) with Greek paganism,[59] Pound, having travelled in Provence in the wake of the past, experienced a mood which he must have believed he could only communicate in terms of some myth.[60] The result is not a new myth, as we have seen, but the recapturing, with the help of analogous circumstances, of the mood which, for Pound, must have *provoked* the original myth. Inherent in this mood is a sense of the futility of any sort of violence in love. The Ancients expressed this in the metamorphosis of those who had been cruelly abused.

The repetition of Pound's Horatian adaptation in the *Pisan Cantos* underlines the ethical significance already contained in our passage, but with this extension :

> ter flebiliter : Ityn
> to close the temple of Janus bifronte
>   the two-faced bastard   (78 : 55/508).

Apart from indicating the presence of swallows and recalling the myth, the phrase, together with what is juxtaposed, implies : if only it were possible to put an end to all violence, both in personal relationships and in affairs of state. The name of that archetypal villain, Tereus — this does not occur in our Canto until line 115 — also rings out in the Pisan sequence, and is again indicative of the swallows' presence; there it functions as a warning (V. 82 : 103/560).

Hardly has the cry of the swallows, whose function we could also compare with that of the chorus in Greek tragedy, died away, when the two-word ellipsis

> Actaeon . . .
> and a valley (ll. 33–34)

effects a rapid change of scene. What follows 'again dramatizes the importance of right relations with the gods'.[61] But in addition to the change of scene there is also a change of sphere. Here it is not Aphrodite's destructive side that is provoked, but, through a hazard of fate,[62] the destructive power of the chaste 'wood-queen' (91 : 72), Diana.

Whereas in the foregoing the classical background was drawn mainly from Horace, it is chiefly Ovid who provides it here. Starting with the transcription of an Ovidian line,[63] Pound goes on to blend in his own vision of the sacred pool. To drive home the fact that beneath the treetops there is

> Not a ray, not a slivver, not a spare disc of sunlight
> Flaking the black, soft water   (ll. 41–42)

(this is, with slight variations, repeated in lines 51 and 55), he compares the sun-drenched foliage to a roof. Its density and the glittering effect produced by the sun are suggested by the piling-up of long and short *i*-sounds respectively. Moving in stages from the organic to the inorganic, he first likens the leaves to fish-scales and then lights upon the simile :

> Like the church roof in Poictiers
> If it were gold.   (ll. 38–39)

The romanesque church of St. Hilaire in Poitiers, in the 'clean architecture of which Pound sees embodied part of the cultural values to be set against culture-destroying usury, is one of those 'medieval churches ... which are simply the Byzantine minus riches' (*Essays*, p. 151).

The superabundance of glittering gold on the foliage contrasts violently with the whiteness underneath, where the sun, even at the height of noon, the hour of Actaeon's doom, has no dominion. The comparison of the treetops to a church roof is significant : the mystery recounted in lines 43–56 demands to be 'shadow'd, o'ershadow'd' (l. 39) in order to maintain its secrecy. Only darkness like that of a medieval dome can contain air that quivers 'alight with the goddess' (l. 45).

If, as Edith Sitwell observes, the Itylus-Cabestan passage gives 'by rhythm and by the use of certain vowels, the cry of the swallows, and their swift and circling movement',[64] the Actaeon-Diana passage conveys, again by rhythm and sound, the impression not of movement but of a strange 'dimension of stillness' (49 : 39/256). It is this stillness that Actaeon unwittingly challenges. Ignorant of the ways, he trespasses, albeit innocently, in Diana's grotto. Condensing Ovid's account, Pound, with his 'body of nymphs, of nymphs, and Diana' (l. 43), voices Actaeon's shock and terror at suddenly beholding the bathing goddess and not only the more familiar nymphs. The magic stir of her light paralyses him, and his eyes remain fixed on 'the pale hair of the goddess' (l. 56); hence her divine wrath and his terrible punishment. Gyges, forced into a similar situation, has two ways open to him, either to kill himself or to kill Candaulus and marry the queen,[65] but Actaeon can never hope to be accepted by Diana.

Artemis, as Pound calls the goddess in other Cantos, thus resembles Merciless Beauty, which the beholder cannot endure :

> Your eyen two wol sleye me sodenly
> I may the beauté of hem nat susteyne. [66]

Though a myth like Actaeon's punishment must have given rise to the tradition of la belle dame sans merci, we must not forget that Artemis stood for a special kind of justice, as is well known from the Oresteia, on which Pound comments categorically : 'Agamemnon killed that stag, against hunting rites' (89 : 62). Emery considers the beginning of Canto XXX, where Artemis complains about justice-impeding pity, to be an 'editorial comment' on our passage and states : 'Offences against the verities must be judged and punished'.[67]

The man who observed proper decorum in his relations with Artemis, and who would fit in with the theme of the Ideal City, is, perhaps through an oversight of Pound's not mentioned till very late :

> He asked not
> nor wavered, seeing, nor had fear of the wood-queen, Artemis
> that is Diana
> nor had killed save by the hunting rite,
> sanctus.   (91 : 72)

This is Brute, to whom the goddess reveals the way to Britain and his descendants' destiny there. [68]

31

Whatever Actaeon's real guilt — a question which the Ancients answered variously — his experience bears some likeness to the encounter of Odysseus' companions with Circe, a recurring major theme in the *Cantos*. Like Actaeon, the crewmen stumble across the haunt of a goddess, are spellbound and, subsequently, transformed.

But whereas Diana is a manifestation of virginal beauty, which like 'the journeying and hiding ... moon is out of reach and inexorable',[69] Circe is the archetypal sorceress who, with the help of poison, ensnares men in her sensual world (V. Canto XXXIX). Odysseus alone is able to resist her witchcraft, simply because Hermes has disclosed to him the proper approach. Brute's meeting with Diana must have been consciously rendered as a partial parallel to that of Odysseus with Circe, since Brute is, to Pound's mind, an Odysseus-figure. Actaeon, however, not unlike Odysseus' companions, becomes a mere victim on whom the goddess has no compassion, a state of affairs elegiacly expressed in a passage of the *Pisan Cantos*.[70]

The intensity of the magic moment of Actaeon's metamorphosis is now suddenly interrupted. It is the same kind of interruption as :

> Lie quiet Divus. I mean Andreas Divus,
> In Officina Wecheli, 1538, out of Homer. (1 : 5/9)

Whereas in Canto I this is nothing but an ironical mention of the source from which Pound is working, the figure who pierces the vision in our Canto is actively involved in the matter presented : 'It is old Vidal speaking' (l. 53), i.e., as Pound puts it in line 65, he is 'muttering Ovid', and the fragment from the Actaeon myth, then, may be imagined to be recited by him. Moreover, we must picture him 'stumbling along in the wood' (l. 54, repeated in l. 64) in the guise of a wolf, for we know that this eccentric troubadour, Peire Vidal, subjected himself to a self-willed metamorphosis in order to be a fit mate for his lady, Loba of Penautier, whose Christian name means 'she-wolf'. Though this made him 'the fool *par excellence* of all Provence' (*Personae*, p. 44), Pound, and his young sculptor-friend, Henri Gaudier-Brzeska, who dedicated a wolf-drawing to the poet in admiration for 'Piere Vidal Old', gave this folly, caused by love of beauty, their wholehearted approval.

Contrary to the situation in the early poem, in which Old Vidal recalls his night with Loba and laments her death, although still imagining himself to be a wood-creature, we must assume that in our Canto he is recalling how he fashioned his voluntary transformation in accordance with the Greeks' tendency to identify themselves, before acting, with the hero whose experience corresponded most to their own plight.

32

When the vision of Diana in her grotto has faded and we see 'the dogs leap on Actaeon' (ll. 57 & 63), the dogs also leap on Vidal, since Vidal and Actaeon have become one, a fact which has already found an equation-like expression in what has actually first pierced the vision : 'Then Actaeon : Vidal' (l. 52). The fact that 'men hunted him with dogs' (*Personae,* p. 44) belongs as much to the Actaeon myth as to the story of Vidal's madness, and it is this feature that constitutes their obvious fundamental identity, like the eating of human flesh in the Itylus-Cabestan passage. Though one is chased in the shape of a wolf and the other in that of a stag, they are both the totems, as it were, of the lady and the goddess respectively. The stag in particular was no doubt the subject of a totemistic worship of the deity of wild life in the woods, before it was anthropomorphized. Afterwards the stag was still sacred, but not all stags remained taboo. This is exactly what makes Actaeon's death a tragedy.

Though Diana turns him into a splendid stag (otherwise her favourite animal), she does not bestow on him the sheen of silver, her characteristic attribute, but the glow of gold, thus branding him as an outlaw from her sphere. He is cast out from the protective shade of her grove, and in the 'blaze of the sun' (l. 62) his fur gleams :

> Gold, gold, a sheaf of hair,
> Thick like a wheat swath   (ll. 60–61).

We see now that in presenting the superabundance of gold on the treetops Pound has elaborately prepared the emergence of Actaeon-become-stag. If the sun produces such glittering gold on leaves, how much stronger is its effect on a golden stag. Small wonder that this dazzling sight stirs up the feverish hunting instincts of both dogs and hunters, who, in their tragic ignorance, call for their master to assist them :

> Hither, hither, Actaeon   (l. 58).

The way Pound presents the hunt, it becomes a mad gold-rush. It was this 'stag-hunt' (V. 100 : 67) that inspired Pound to write his 'war poem', 'The Coming of War : Actaeon'. As in our Canto, what incites the 'unstill, ever moving / Hosts of an ancient people' to their pursuit is 'Actaeon of golden greaves', here more the figure of a warrior than of a stag.[71] Pound must here have conceived an image of the unreality of war, because inherent in the myth is once again the idea of the utter futility of violence, as it can never win what it really wants; when gold is the cause of strife everything is ruined and falls into one common grave. Pound's usury theme is here anticipated, if only indirectly.[72]

As with Soremonda's fall from the window, time is arrested; the vision of the dogs leaping on Actaeon appears to be painted on a vase, an image also of 'the dangerous heat of the dog-days, of which probably the myth itself is but a symbol'.[73] It seems in fact that Pound recaptured intuitively not only one version, but several facets of the rich variety of versions of the Actaeon myth. Somehow the version in which Actaeon, wishing to gain the favours of the goddess, dons of his own accord the skins of a stag must lie behind the identification of Vidal with Actaeon.

When attention is again focused on Vidal 'stumbling along in the wood' (ll. 64 ff.), his yearning for lasting fulfilment of his passion is aptly objectified by his musing over pools associated with metamorphosis. Between Lake Pergusa, the scene of the rape of Proserpine, and the pool of Salmacis, where the nymph of that name and Hermaphroditus are changed into one bisexual creature, the name of the valley in which Actaeon meets his doom also occurs : Gargaphia. It is no accident that Diana's pool is placed in the centre. Judging by his discussion of pagan survivals in Provence, Pound wants us to realize that troubadours like Vidal were imbued with Greek paganism, but that at the same time they 'developed their own unofficial mysticism' (Spirit, p. 91), an example of which he finds in Vidal's 'Good Lady, I think I see God, when I gaze on your delicate body' (p. 96).

If such an attitude to woman is inherent in any of the pools brooded over, it is, of course, neither in Lake Pergusa with its rape, nor in the pool of Salmacis with its seduction, but in Gargaphia alone. Seeing the Lady of Penautier, Vidal experiences a mystery comparable to Actaeon's at the sight of 'ivory dipping in silver' (ll. 48 & 50) and 'the pale hair of the goddess' (l. 56). But whereas the change which this mystery produces in Actaeon is fatal, the change in Vidal is merely fatally quixotic. In Pound's eyes, it seems, Vidal's folly is that of the myth-maker, for he says: 'The first myths arose when a man walked sheer into "nonsense", that is to say, when some very vivid and undeniable adventure befell him' (Essays, p. 431).

The difference between Actaeon and Vidal is, to Pound, smaller than we might think. The troubadours 'have', he contends, 'in some ways, lost the names of the gods and remembered the names of lovers' (Spirit, p. 90). But how is it possible to consider Vidal's lady as an Artemis-type, since Pound, in 'Piere Vidal Old', makes him boast about her conquest? The answer is practically the same as the one given to his own, more general question : 'What is the difference between Provence and Hellas?' and furnishes a further explanation as to why Pound places Greek and Provencal matter side by side in our Canto : 'The whole break of Provence with this world [i.e. the classical world], and indeed the central theme of the troubadours, is the dogma that there is some proportion between the fine thing held in the mind, and the inferior thing ready for instant consumption' (*Essays*, p. 151). It follows, then — and we do well to note immediately that this distinction is of paramount importance in Pound's own work as well — that the troubadours do not have to be ascetics to conceive a fundamentally chaste type. According to Pound, 'The Greek aesthetic would seem to consist wholly in plastic, or in plastic moving towards coitus . . .', i.e. 'Plastic plus immediate consumption'. Hence, after he had seen her nakedness, a relationship between Actaeon and Artemis could no longer be imagined by the Greeks and Romans. The dissociation of 'the fine thing held in the mind' from 'the inferior thing' (*Essays*, pp. 150 & 151) is, as Pound sees it, brought to perfection by Cavalcanti. A glimpse of this will be gained at the end of the Canto (ll. 123–125). That Vidal, who 'was confessedly erratic', experienced the 'exalted moment, the vision unsought' (*Spirit*, pp. 96 & 97), we may assume from the utterance already quoted. We can hardly say, however, that underlying Vidal's worship of Loba of Penautier was 'a belief in affection; in a sort, intimate sympathy which is not sexual';[74] and whether his 'vision [was] gained without machination' (*Spirit*, p. 97) is another matter.

Concluding the first half of our Canto is an apparently disjunct line standing almost in the centre :

The empty armour shakes as the cygnet moves.   (l. 68)

It turns out to be based on the Ovidian verses terminating Achilles' combat with Cygnus the Invulnerable.[75]

In suggesting the simultaneity of movement in the armour and the young swan Pound achieves an ingenious spotlighting of the very instant of metamorphosis. Apart from possessing high poetic quality, and proving once again Pound's ability to recreate the phenomenon of change, it functions as a 'superpository image' imposed on the whole of the first half of the Canto; it is, indeed, its 'unifying metaphor',[76] declaring eloquently the vanity of violence; and it is a bitter irony of fate that even the hero *par excellence* — with, alas, more brawn than brains — Achilles, is forced to realize this.

The remaining sixty lines of Canto IV revolve, as we shall see, round a different pole, although they contain a reprise of some of the matter of the first half. But first let us pause to review our initial reflections on the theme of the Canto. Beginning with the debris of the Trojan War, the poem goes on to evoke the name of a bride and Athene's call to Cadmus. This forms, together with the Dawn Lyric, a first unit, in which we may see implied the admonition to MAKE IT NEW.[77] Aphrodite's sinister portent, the 'black cock', then suggests a fall back into the 'dark forest'. But even the Itylus-Cabestan passage has, apart from the gruesome aspects of love's 'revenge and cannibalism',[78] its moment of spiritual nobility, indicating the upward movement continued in the Actaeon-Vidal section. However, the thrill caused by the sight of gold again marks a downward pull into war,[79] but beyond futile violence we discover the individual struggling in search of a beauty free from vanity. This second unit bears in some degree the stamp of the humility which led Pound to write the 'Pull down thy vanity' passage of the *Pisan Cantos* (81 : 98–100/556–557). Moreover, although the phenomenon of metamorphosis is presented here mainly in its narrower, mythological sphere, as a form of punishment and redemption, it is brought to our awareness in order to 'teach ... us that things do not remain always the same. They become other things by swift and unanalysable process.' (*Essays*, p. 431) The march of civilization, which is continued in the second half, can thus be understood only after the study of such changes, one of which, the change from Hellas to Provence, takes up a large number of these sixty-eight lines.

Finally, a discussion of the treatment of the Itylus and Actaeon myths in the *Cantos* and Eliot's *Waste Land* is very instructive. Although literary allusions provide the values with both poets, Eliot employs them to criticize the rootless society of the twentieth century, in which there is, because of the degradation of all religious mysteries, no source of new life. Thus, when 'the change of Philomel' appears among the decor of a drawing-room, and the nightingale is pictured as that which remained 'inviolable' despite the rape, it comes 'to dirty ears', since in modern free love to be 'so rudely forced' is no longer a disgrace. And when the meeting of Actaeon with Diana is contrasted with that of Sweeney and Mrs. Porter we are made to realize how love and affection are in every respect profaned.[80]

On the other hand, Pound, otherwise an equally severe critic of contemporary life, demonstrates how these myths can recur under changed conditions, and yet still preserve something of their original mystery. Whereas Eliot uses them to expose the hopelessness of modern materialistic life, Pound somehow derives new hope for our times, since he continues to believe in the possibility of their recurrence.

THE NOON LYRIC

The second half of Canto IV opens with the second of the three pieces of nature lyric showing the light-process :

Thus the light rains, thus pours, *e lo soleils plovil*
The liquid and rushing crystal
      beneath the knees of the gods.
Ply over ply, thin glitter of water;
Brook film bearing white petals.
The pines at Takasago
      grow with the pines of Isé!
The water whirls up the bright pale sand in the spring's mouth
'Behold the Tree of the Visages!'
Forked branch-tips, flaming as if with lotus.
      Ply over ply
The shallow eddying fluid,
      beneath the knees of the gods.   (ll. 69—81)

As in the Dawn Lyric, it is Pound's enthusiasm for the Neoplatonists' conception of light that permeates this passage, but whereas the pattern which emerges from the Dawn Lyric is that of a Greek ritual, the centre of the Noon Lyric is intensified by a vision of the civic virtues of the East.

The introductory 'thus' seems to imply that the lyric has to be taken, primarily, as an expository comment on the sun over Diana's grotto, but its structure really hinges on the metaphor quoted from Arnaut Daniel's poem, 'Lancan son passat li giure' : 'e lo soleils plovil'.

'Daniel's diction and metaphor', Pound remarks in *The Spirit of Romance*, 'are occasionally so vivid as to seem harsh in literal translation.' (p. 25) Although he avoids this harshness in translating the line from which the metaphor is taken, 'tro lai on lo soleils plovil', by making it : 'To where the rain falls from the sun' (*Essays*, p. 122), Pound wants the reader to appreciate its full vividness in our Noon Lyric. Hence the original quotation, preceded by 'the light rains', which, apart from the substitution of 'light' for 'suns', translates it literally, and Pound's own, even more vigorous 'pours'.

Daniel's metaphor of the raining sun is still with Pound, as an undercurrent, in the *Rock-Drill* sequence, where we find :

      let the light pour   (94 : 95),

and in *Thrones* :

      To see the light pour   (99 : 46).

We may therefore assume that he had seen in it from the start a trace of Daniel's own Platonistic heritage.

Pound, at any rate, bases on it his first vision in the *Cantos* of the Platonists' 'sea crystalline and enduring, of the bright as it were molten glass that envelops us, full of light' (*Guide*, p. 44). The descriptive lines 'The liquid and rushing crystal' and 'The shallow eddying fluid', and with them the repeated phrase 'ply over ply', symmetrically frame, as it were, in this 'molten glass',[81] the series of equally clear-cut images in the middle of our thirteen-line Noon Lyric. It is only in the later Cantos, where Pound depicts a Dantescan ascent to Paradise, that the crystalline sphere is fully presented. Canto 91 especially, which can be called the Crystal Canto, furnishes the amplification needed here :

> that the body of light come forth
> > from the body of fire   (91 : 70)
>
>   . . .
>
> & from fire to crystal
> > via the body of light   (91 : 75).

It is clear from this that Pound's mind has come to operate in terms of Dante's ten heavens. The fire is the Empyrean, the immaterial tenth heaven. From it is created, 'via the body of light' (91:75), the primum mobile or crystalline heaven, the first of the material spheres.

In adhering to the concept of the tensile, 'undivided light',[82] Pound has no respect for 'Fat-headed Aquinas' (*Spirit*, p. 100), whom Dante, to Pound's annoyance, readily accepted. On the contrary, Pound's enthusiasm stems from those whose 'mental voltage is high enough' (*Guide*, p. 77), so that 'the *forma*, the immortal *concetto* . . . rises from death . . . like the rose pattern driven into the dead iron-filings by the magnet . . .' (p. 152). Thus Robert Grosseteste (1175–1253), who, especially in *De luce seu de inchoatione formarum*, 'gives us a structure' (p. 77) for which he is repeatedly quoted in the *Cantos*, is even adduced by Pound to elucidate Guido Cavalcanti's difficult 'Canzone : Donna mi priegha'.[83]

Grosseteste came to inspire the prayer-like :

> Lux in diafana,
> > Creatrix,
> > > oro,[84]

and Cavalcanti's 'Canzone' is incorporated as a whole (Canto XXXVI), for Pound appears to discover in it, ultimately, an ecstatic discussion of the 'region above the heavens',[85] that of Light and Love. Grosseteste's theory of light as the primary corporeal form, out of which all matter is generated, only restates what we already find in Scotus Erigena (fl. 850) and before him in Ocellus Lucanus and even in Confucian China :

Y Yin, Ocellus, Erigena :
>   'All things are lights'   (87 : 31).

Hence, what is really Erigena's formulation[86] holds good for all three. They are all aware of the νοῦς, the mind as the active principle of the universe.

Pound speaks of 'flowing crystal' in Canto 91 too, and 'the knees of the gods' appear again. But whereas in our Canto we see nothing but the rushing down of the 'river of crystal' (91 : 73), with the gods keeping the same height, in Canto 91 a figure has accomplished its way upwards :

>   The Princess Ra-Set has climbed
>   to the great knees of stone,
>   She enters protection. [87]

This shows that in our Canto 'The GREAT CRYSTAL' is simply visible and the ascent to that high level remains as yet unachieved; the mind has to travel still further to see the 'Crystal waves weaving together toward the gt/ healing' (91 : 71).

But the poet is at least granted a vision of the delicacy of things crystalline. The 'white petals' on the 'brook film' afford a similar pleasure to the 'petals light on the air' (91 : 75), and to see how :

>   The water whirls up the bright pale sand in the spring's mouth

is, on a microcosmic scale, the same as seeing 'Love moving the stars . . .' (91 : 72), for in both is inherent 'the rhythm of the process',[88] since Love is 'as light into water compenetrans' (100 : 74). 'The shallow eddying fluid', then, is still a form of creative light, still demonstrating that :

>   . . . the Divine Mind is abundant
>   unceasing
>   *improvisatore*
>   Omniformis
>   unstill   (92 : 80).

As in Canto 90, where 'Paradise is regained',[89] the crystalline air in our Noon Lyric contains :

>   Beatific spirits welding together
>   as in one ash-tree . . .   (90 : 65).

At Takasago in Japan stand two famous pine trees inhabited by the spirits of a married couple whose love endures for ever. This Eastern legend of conjugal loyalty corresponds to the Greek story of :

> . . . that god-feasting couple old
> That grew elm-oak amid the wold. [90]

At Isé, another Japanese sanctuary, there are two shrines sacred to the worship of the Japanese emperors and the sun-goddess, their progenetrix. [91] These shrines are apparently in a pine grove. Thus the statement :

> The pines at Takasago
>> grow with the pines of Isé!

has to be taken literally, because, probably according to a Japanese tradition, these two groups of sacred pines are believed to be mysteriously connected with each other. This, at least, we may gather from a passage where line 75 of our Canto recurs :

> 'Grow with the Pines of Ise;
> 'As the Nile swells with Inopos.
> 'As the Nile falls with Inopos.'   (21 : 99/103)

This can only mean that in Pound's eyes the connection between the pines is of the kind which the classical world assumed to exist between the Nile and the river Inopos in Delos. The mystery of the common growth of the pines of Takasago and Isé appears to afford Pound a first and intuitive glimpse of the Confucian ideal as expressed in the *Ta Hio*. There are roots common to the family unit and the ruler; and the '*semina motuum*, the inner impulses of the tree', (*Confucius*, p. 59) are the same. Hence the root is, 'From the Emperor, Son of Heaven, down to the common man . . . self-discipline . . .' (p. 33), which means to rectify one's heart (p. 31). Then one can 'contemplate . . . the luminous decree of heaven' (p. 35 f.), and when it is carried out, family and ruler are in harmony with 'the total light process' (p. 20), the ming

The 'Tree of the Visages', though again a reference to Japanese civilization, has likewise a Confucian significance. The vision of this tree originates primarily in Pound's study of Noh plays. In describing the traditional Noh stage, he explains the pine painted on the back of the stage as a 'congratulatory symbol of unchanging green and strength' and continues : 'The three real little pine trees along the bridge leading on to the stage are quite fixed; they symbolize heaven, earth, and man. The one for heaven is nearest the stage, then comes the one which symbolizes man ... Sometimes when a pine is mentioned the actors look toward it.'[92]

This knowledge of pine trees symbolizing man between heaven and earth must, however, be related to Pound's preoccupation with metamorphosis into trees, especially in :

> I stood still and was a tree amid the wood,
> Knowing the truth of things unseen before.   (*Personae*, p. 17)

From such empathetic transformation arises an awareness that 'Things have roots and branches, affairs have scopes and beginnings. To know what precedes and what follows ...' (*Confucius*, p. 27) 'will assist yr/ comprehension of process' (77 : 43/494). Thus the exhortation :

> Behold the Tree of the Visages!

may imply the Confucian : 'watching with affection the way people grow' (*Confucius*, p. 27). Moreover, this tree seems to be surrounded by something like a 'nimbus of gold flame' : 'forked branch-tips, flaming as with lotus'. This flare may remind us of the sun blazing outside Diana's pool (ll. 36—39) and of the 'blaze of gold'[93] radiating from Actaeon-become-stag. In all three passages there is a brightness which mortals cannot bear unless they are properly initiated into relations with the Divine.

On the other hand the trees, inhabited by 'beatific spirits', be they nymphs or exemplary ancestors immortalized by metamorphosis into trees, merge in the course of the *Cantos* with the 'Tree of the Visages' into the one tree which man must touch :

> That you lean 'gainst the tree of heaven,
> and know Ygdrasail   (85 : 5).

EPITHALAMIUM

Immediately after the Noon Lyric we find the mood of Catullus' 'Collis o Heliconii' (*Carmen* LXI) recreated. As was pointed out in connection with line 3, this epithalamium belongs to the tradition of classical serenity, and it is therefore no wonder that Aurunculeia's nuptial night is in juxtaposition with the evocation of the equally sane and serene spirit of Confucian China and the Japan of Noh, in which, within the framework of the civic virtues, conjugal loyalty is so highly valued.

As with the Noon Lyric, it is light that receives most of the attention in these lines, and this time the vision is enveloped in :

Blue agate casing the sky ... (l. 84).

But, whereas the 'sea crystalline' is presented as an onrushing river which gradually widens, the night sky appears to be solidified into precious stone. In a parenthesis, which was only added to the later versions of Canto IV, Pound, having recourse to his own memory, states, of course only for his private satisfaction, that this agate-cased sky imagined here is 'as at Gourdon that time'.[94]

It was conjectural to say that the emotions attached to the cry of the swallows had first beset Pound on a journey in Provence, but this parenthesis only confirms what we learn from the history of 'In a Station of the Metro' — that Pound, even where he seems to depend entirely on literary material, very often blends it with personally-experienced natural phenomena, a fact which is most apparent in the *Pisan Cantos*. It is in keeping with Pound's reverence for the mysteries that the sky should form a canopy, as it were, to ensure that the marriage-ritual is not intruded upon, just as the mystery of Diana's chastity requires a church-like roof for protection.

The torches carried by the boys on their procession to the nuptial chamber provide the main source of light here. Like the lanterns fixed to the gondolas during the traditional marriage of Venice to the sea[95] and the lights set afloat in the sea by the Greeks and Chinese,[96] these torches symbolize procreation. After all, the marriage-ritual of the Ancients is essentially a fertility rite, resembling the celebration of the Eleusinian mysteries. Light, in Pound's mythopoetic world, that 'shallow eddying fluid', is the procreative power itself. The purpose of both the marriage-ritual and the fertility rites is to make sure that this supreme moment is reached :

<blockquote>
The light has entered the cave. Io! Io!
The light has gone down into the cave,
Splendour on splendour!
</blockquote>

so that :

<blockquote>
Fruit cometh after ... (47 : 32/248).
</blockquote>

That such a wedding is a community festival is indicated by 'the corner cook-stall' (l. 83), probably linked in Pound's mind with a festival which he himself once saw.[97] It is very probably the occasion on which he perceived the pattern formed by a 'set flame' (l. 83) and the moving torches which melt in their own glare (l. 82).

Bringing the scene physically near by mentioning 'the sputter of resin' (1. 83), Pound now focuses on the centre of the procession. As with the dancing nymphs and fawns in the Dawn Lyric, only the foot is visible :

> Saffron sandal so petals the narrow foot   (1. 86).

This renders Catullus'

> huc veni niveo gerens
> luteum pede soccum,

which is, literally translated : 'Hither ... come, wearing on thy snow-white foot the yellow shoe'.[98]

It is obvious that Pound used in his version the technique he acquired in translating and adapting from Japanese and Chinese poetry. The vision of this sandal still occupies Pound in Canto V :

> Gold-yellow, saffron ... The roman shoe, Aurunculeia's.   (17/21)

Here we find him reconsidering his translation of 'luteus', and judging by the addition of 'gold-yellow', he seems to think that 'saffron' does not fully convey the light-effect he had perceived.[99]

Whereas Catullus clearly refers to Hymen's foot, Pound applies to the bride the Eastern metaphor of a foot petalled by the shoe. This we can gather from Canto V. He thus endows her with a glory similar to the gold blaze surrounding Actaeon-become-stag. When 'Hymenaeus "brings the girl to her man" ' (5 : 17/21), she is led to sacrifice like a victim. And it is the 'sacrificial concept', inherent, as Pound points out (Spirit, p. 96), in Catullus' poem, to which the concluding 'superpository image' (Miner) gives expression :

> The scarlet flower is cast on the blanch-white stone.   (1. 88)

This emotionally rich line, an echo perhaps of Sappho's 'On the earth lies fading its purple pride',[100] again presents, as with Philomela, Itys, Cabestan and Actaeon, a violation, but one 'sanctioned by the gods in the light of the processional torches and with the religious and marital undertones of Takasagó'.[101]

In the Faber edition of 1954 the traditional epithalamic refrain appears for the first time in Greek letters. Pound probably felt that since the Latin is merely a transliteration of the Greek he had just as well return it to its original form. In writing his epithalamium Pound implies that Catullus treated a Roman matter in the manner and spirit of the Greeks, especially in that of his great model : Sappho.

Lines 88–99 must be taken as a transitional interlude, the impact of which reveals itself only gradually. Their composition is linked with a Chinese 'fu', or prose poem, by Sung Yü, which has been translated by Arthur Waley as 'The Man-Wind and the Woman-Wind'.[102] This poem records a conversation between Hsiang, king of Ch'u, and the poet Sung Yü himself during a feast in the Orchid-Tower palace. That Pound composed his adaptation from a version which was first put into Japanese (perhaps contained in the Fenollosa papers, like the raw material for *Cathay*) is apparent from the use of Sung Yü's Japanese name, So-Gioku; and that he relied too much on his memory, as in other passages of the *Cantos*, is evident from his confusion of Ran-ti, which is the Japanese for 'Orchid Terrace', with the king's name, Hsiang.[103]

The meaning of Sung Yü's poem, moreover, has little to do with Pound's wind interlude. It is only in So-Gioku's insistence that the wind about the Orchid-Tower is royal, in Hsiang's (i.e. Ran-ti with Pound) baring his breast and opposing So-Gioku, and in the delicate echo, 'This wind is held in gauze curtains . . .' (l. 98), that the original lives on; but there is little trace in Pound of the indirect lesson about the people's misery which Sung Yü seeks to convey to his king. He merely recalls conversational fragments which, through their rhythm, seem to float along on the very wind discussed.

In describing the wind here Pound merely shows its contrasting aspects, its gentleness as a palace-wind and its roaring coarseness 'in the earth's bag' (l. 94), and we hear the king ridiculing its royal paternity in the ironical :

> Let every cow keep her calf.   (l. 97)

Yet this commonsense attitude towards the wind does not take into account the supernatural properties it sometimes acquires. We have seen that, in Pound's imagination, 'the wind out of Rhodez' (l. 29) intervenes, as it were, on behalf of some pitying god, to veil and redeem the falling Soremonda. And there is one legendary Greek person who could not be more aware of the wind's royal and divine nature; hence Pound's apostrophe :

> 'Danaë! Danaë!
> What wind is the king's?'   (ll. 102–103)

The wind which Pound, in our Canto and in Canto V, makes her actively expect is indeed to be the king's, i. e. the wind of Zeus.

The mystery of Danaë's motherhood will be seen to be intimately connected, in the poet's vision, with Ecbatana. One-time capital of Media Magna, this city, founded by the Median Deioces, is described by Herodotus as 'a place of great size and strength fortified by concentric walls, these so planned that each successive circle was higher than the one below it by the height of the battlements ... The circles are seven in number, and the innermost contains the royal palace and treasury ... The battlements of the five outer rings are painted in different colours, the first white, the second black, the third crimson, the fourth blue, the fifth orange; the battlements of the two inner rings are plated with silver and gold respectively'.[104]

As we observed in connection with Cadmus, Ecbatana is to Pound one of the archetypal cities which are to be built up again. 'No nation can be considered historically as such', Pound wrote in *Patria Mia*, 'until it has achieved within itself a city to which all roads lead, and from which there goes out an authority'. (p. 9) Deioces, distinguishing himself by his great sense of equity, and for this reason appointed to rule over the Medes, achieved this very thing by building the city 'of plotted streets',[105] which, we may assume, radiated in all directions.

In having us first glimpse Ecbatana through the eyes of resting camel drivers (l. 100) Pound seems to imply that the city's pattern makes even nomads want to climb up to a higher stage of civilization. To indicate the upward movement Pound employs, for the spiritual ascent, the traditional symbolism of the stairs, as Eliot does in *Ash Wednesday*.[106]

After Canto V Ecbatana does not appear again until the beginning of the *Pisan Cantos*. By this time the vision of it has become part of Pound's paradisal imagery of light :

> To build the city of Dioce whose terraces are the
> colour of stars. (74 : 3/451)

Here the seven walls of Ecbatana are seen to reproduce on earth the seven planetary heavens of the Ptolomeic system of the universe. The whole people may confidently look to such a city for 'authority [which] comes from right reason',[107] and this is 'reason from heaven' (55 : 44/311).

THE EVENING LYRIC

After this first vision of the Ideal City, and after the question put to Danaë concerning the king's wind (ll. 102—103), we come to the last of the three nature lyrics dominated by the theme of light : the Evening Lyric (ll. 104—110).

Here, too, the play of light on water constitutes the first stimulus. But whereas the water is made translucent by the first light of morning, and transparent by the downpour of light at noon, at dusk it becomes opaque and black because of the absence of light. Implied in the line :

> The peach-trees shed bright leaves in the water   (l. 105)

is the thought : like leaves in autumn, the light falls and dies. As the light is spent, only

> Smoke hangs on the stream   (l. 104),

yet we hear how 'the barge scrapes at the ford' (l. 107) and comes in sight :

> Gilt rafters above black water   (l. 108).

It is not light, e.g. dawn itself, but 'sound [that] drifts in the evening haze' (l. 106). This haze is, however, unlike the 'dew-haze' (l. 7) at dawn, no veil through which mythical visions can be perceived.

Somehow the apparition of this golden barge drifting through the evening is connected with the poet's experience in Venice, for it is in one of the Venice Cantos that we read :

> 'In the gloom the gold
> Gathers the light about it.' . . . (17 : 78/82).

'The gold', says Hugh Kenner, 'needs the gloom. It is a lordly and sinister symbol.'[108] In our Evening Lyric the floating gold suggests the feeling of an imminent departure into darkness, into death. Set against this drifting and floating, and leading beyond the visions of evening, we find :

> Three steps in an open field,
> Gray stone-posts leading . . .   (ll. 109—110).

The same vision, inverted and extended, recurs in Canto XVI :

> The grey stone posts,
>   and the stair of gray stone,
> the passage clean-squared in granite :
>   descending,
> and I through this, and into the earth.   (69/73)

Here the passage to the region beyond is accomplished, since the fear present in our Canto 'of the life after death' (29 : 145/150) has vanished. What opens in 'the light as after sun-set' (16 : 69/73) is the Elysian fields, which cannot be attained by men drifting like the lotus-eaters (V. Canto XX), but must be *earned*.[109] Here we find the figures who struggled towards the Ideal City :

> and founders, gazing at the mounts of their cities.   (16 : 69/73)

THE SPIRITS OF THE AIR

The two lines opening the remaining eighteen lines of Canto IV formed only one line in the 1921 version :

> Père Henri Jacques still seeks the sennin on Rokku.

In that illuminating letter to Felix E. Schelling of July 8 & 9, 1922, Pound gives this commentary : 'Sennin are the Chinese spirits of nature or of the air. I don't see that they are any worse than Celtic Sidhe. Rokku is a mountain. I can perhaps emend the line and make that clearer, though "on" limits to it to either a mountain or an island (an ambiguity which don't much matter at that point).'[110] In the later versions Pound did provide such a clarification, by means of an additional line :

> Mount Rokku between the rock and the cedars   (l. 112).

As for Père Henri Jacques, Pound continues in the same letter : 'The name and title indicate a French priest (as a matter of fact he is a Jesuit).' (*Letters*, p. 247) The fact that this Jesuit, whom he either read about or met, showed veneration for these spirits of the air must have impressed Pound deeply and lingered in his mind, for it appears again eighty-four Cantos later :

> Père Henri Jacques still
> > speaks with the sennin on Rokku   (88 : 42).

As in the later versions of Canto IV, the French priest not only seeks these spirits, but speaks, has communion with them. This observance of the mysteries of the air prepares the way for much of what follows.

First we are, however, plunged back into the dark forest of passion, and lines 113—114 even add to the catalogue of the evils of love. Polhonac, Viscount Héracle III of Polignac to give him his full title, did not object to a love-affair between his wife and the troubadour Guillaume de St.-Didier; he even encouraged it by singing to his wife the song that Guillaume had composed on the subject of their adulterous love.

In the story of Gyges we have one more example of a husband improperly exposing his wife to another man's eyes. We have already hinted at the similarity of Gyges' situation with that of Actaeon. Yet whereas Actaeon merely drifts into Diana's realm, Gyges penetrates the private sphere of the queen by order of King Candaulus himself, who wants Gyges, his favourite body-guard, to share his own publicly-declared admiration for his wife. But when she discovers Gyges hidden in her bedroom, the queen assumes superhuman stature and delivers her terrible ultimatum. Be it cowardice or suddenly-roused ambition, Gyges passes over the morally better way out, that of killing himself, and chooses to heap evil upon himself and the queen : he marries her, after murdering his sovereign, and usurps the throne. [111]

On one plane the names of Polhonac and Gyges stand for unseemliness on the part of the husband, on another they seem to remind us, especially as far as Gyges is concerned, that unseemliness and atrocities in love very often have political implications. In any case we may find in this one of the many variations in the *Cantos* on the themes of the Trojan War, and particularly that of the Atreides.

The name Gyges stands at the beginning of the line which appears to be a synthesis of many of the cruel feasts staged by perverse passion :

As Gyges on Thracian platter set the feast   (l. 114).

In using the adjective 'Thracian' Pound seems to point out a loose analogy between the Gyges story and the Itylus myth as well. On the other hand, 'Thracian' acquires, by way of this analogy, some of the connotations which the region of Thrace had in the poetry of the Ancients; there it figured as the land where all kinds of savagery originated. The following lines again link the legend of Cabestan and the myth of Itys. A new feature is the naming of the villain instead of his victim :

Cabestan, Terreus,
            It is Cabestan's heart in the dish   (ll. 115—116).

Pound's use of the variant spelling 'Terreus' for 'Tereus' may be a pun on 'Terreus - terror'. By implication the cry of the swallows also recurs, although no onomatopoeia in 'Terreus' seems to be intended. At any rate, Pound does not employ the form 'Tereu', which is clearly onomatopoeic in the hands of poets like Richard Barnefield and T. S. Eliot. [112]

THE BRIDE

Bearing in mind that Pound considers Vidal a forerunner of the spiritualization of love in Tuscany, we may perceive in the juxtaposition 'Vidal, or Ecbatan' (l. 117) a gradual ascent from the carnal horrors of passion towards the mysteries of divine love. Ecbatana, whose innermost battlement is of gold, replaces in Pound's thought the Argos of Greek mythology as the sole worthy place for the conception of Danaë's son. Here, in the centre of the Ideal City, 'the god's bride' awaits the miracle, the wind that *is* the king's :

> . . . upon the gilded tower of Ecbatan
> Lay the god's bride, lay ever, waiting the golden rain. (ll. 117—118)

It is not until Canto 91, in what we have called the Crystal Canto, that this theme recurs. Yet there it is not Perseus' mother to whom such a miracle happens, but the mother of Merlin, the prophet in the Arthurian story :

> Merlin's fader may no man know
> Merlin's moder is made a nun.
> Lord, thaet scop the dayes lihte,
>   all that she knew was a spirit bright,
> A movement that moved in cloth of gold
>   into her chamber. (91 : 73)

In the context of the Crystal Canto Merlin's birth forms part of the 'Crystal waves weaving toward the gt/ healing' (91 : 71). One Canto later an even closer parallel to the Danaë myth is revealed :

> To another the rain fell as of silver.
>   La Luna Regina.
> Not gold as in Ecbatan (92 : 79).

In Canto IV, however, Danaë is juxtaposed with the Virgin Mary, as is seen from the rest of the Canto. Whether it is the golden rain of Zeus or 'a spirit in cloth of gold', what descends is in both cases nothing less than the Mind of the universe itself (the νοῦς) in the form of gold, a substance which is, in the highest sense, akin to its primary emanations, fire and light. Danaë and Merlin's mother, Pound wants us to see, are on a par with the Virgin Mary, as vessels for the 'light tensile immaculata' (74 : 7/455); the phenomenon of immaculate conception is no Christian monopoly, but is capable of recurrence. From time to time the Mind of Heaven chooses the womb of a mortal to give birth to that which frees mankind from the perpetual cycle of 'birth, and copulation and death' (Eliot) and which rules :

> Over harm
> Over hate
>   overflooding, light over light   (91 : 73).

Thus the paraclete, or the comforter [113] in the shape of a prophet (Christ, Mani, Merlin, etc.) or hero (Perseus etc.), comes down to earth to spread enlightenment beyond the perpetual cycle, to banish terror (Cf. Perseus' slaying of the Medusa) and to re-build or uphold the Ideal City.

Pound demonstrates how there are two kinds of worship of the Bride of God, one impure and the other pure and liberating, by contrasting two instances from the cult of Our Lady in the Church of Rome. As with the three nature lyrics it is again the quality of light on water that demands our attention :

> The Garonne is thick like paint   (l. 120)

forms a heavy contrast to :

> Adige, thin film of images   (l. 123).

The Garonne, we may take it, has exactly the same qualities as the procession along its bank. Like the river, which meanders through the countryside without bestowing on it any brightening reflections, the procession 'Moves like a worm, in the crowd' (l. 122), or, according to the early version (1921) :

> The worm of the procession bores in the soup of the crowd.

Apart from the traditional greeting, '— "Et sa'ave, sa'ave, sa'ave Regina!" —' (l. 120), which seems to have been purposely vulgarized in the later versions, as against the proper 'Salve regina' of the early version, Pound reproduces nothing that would stamp the event as a religious ceremony.

50

'The worm of the procession', to elaborate the image, may do its fertilizing work in the crowd, but it appears to be incapable of lifting the worshippers beyond their animal natures.

It is significant that Pound deleted 'The blue thin voices against the crash of the crowd',[114] which is in the 1921 version. This minor contrast would only obscure the major contrast with the spirit of the river Adige. The use of the simile 'thick like paint' may indicate a further difference. In his Cavalcanti essay Pound quotes a crucial statement by Springer, the German art-historian : 'Durch Rafael ist das Madonnenideal Fleisch geworden.' Part of his comment on this quotation pertains directly to our passage in Canto IV : '... it is no longer the body of air clothed in the body of fire; it no longer radiates, light no longer moves from the eye, there is a great deal of meat, shock absorbing, perhaps — at any rate absorbent.' (Essays, p. 153)

It seems, then, that Pound somehow combined the memory of the real procession seen on the Garonne with the fleshiness which became fashionable in painting 'somewhere about 1527', finding in both the same kind of 'loss of values'.[115]

Unlike the Garonne, the upper Italian Adige, with its wealth of reflections, is alive with the mysteries of the air; it provides the atmosphere for a pure and sublime vision of the Bride of God, pre-Raphaelite in the strictest sense of the word.[116] The 'thin film of images' (l. 123) on the river is endowed, like the 'brook film' (l. 73) in the Noon Lyric, with the splendour and delicacy of the 'sea crystalline and enduring, of the bright as it were molten glass ..., full of light', It is on the banks of such a river that man can become aware of love's highest meaning :

> Across the Adige, by Stefano, Madonna in hortulo,
> As Cavalcanti had seen her.   (ll. 124—125)

> My Lady's face is it they worship there,
> At San Michele in Orto ...,

writes Guido Cavalcanti in one of his sonnets, and 'explains the miracles of this madonna' (Translations, p. 95). She has the power to heal and comfort and is at the same time an image of the Lady who enables men like Cavalcanti to perceive the essential identity of Love with the Light and Mind of Heaven.[117]

When Stefano da Verona painted her about two centuries later he portrayed her, Pound has it, 'as Cavalcanti had seen her', preserving, in a manner not yet affected by Raphael, an insight into the

Age of unbodied gods, the vitreous fragile images
Thin as the locust's wing
Haunting the mind . . . as of Guido . . .[118]

The subtlety of the vowel-sounds in the phrase 'Madonna in hortulo' (Latin, for Italian 'in orto') is Pound's own melopoeic attempt to bring the vision alive. (The phrase is not in the early version.)

Here, after many glimpses at human cruelty under the influence of passion, after several highlights of human and divine love, having gone through the whole of the light-process, and carrying with us the vision of the Ideal City, we reach the sphere of the contemplation of spiritual beauty. The progression of values has attained that serene height which allows man to view the great harmony of this world.

The three lines at the end of Canto IV add two ideas which have no connection with the theme of this Canto, but have to do with the method of presentation in the whole of the *Cantos*. Judging by a passage in 'The Serious Artist', the first image must refer to the double nature of poetry :

The Centaur's heel plants in the earth loam.   (l. 126)

'Poetry is a centaur', Pound says. 'The thinking, word-arranging, clarifying faculty must move and leap with the energizing, sentient, musical faculties. It is precisely the difficulty of this amphibious existence that keeps down the census record of good poets . . . Or leaving metaphor, I suppose that what, in the long run, makes the poet is a sort of persistence of the emotional nature, and, joined with this, a peculiar sort of control.' (*Essays*, p. 52) Bearing in mind, then, that Pound considers poetry, or the poet, to be partly intellectual and partly emotional, the image [119] in our Canto implies that the poet's emotions, to a certain extent intimately connected with his physical nature, are, in the last analysis, deeply rooted in the soil. If this is the correct interpretation, the image of the centaur goes beyond the question of procedure; and there are significant parallels in the *Cantos* which touch the very bedrock of the Poundian universe. This we have already seen in discussing the pines of Isé and Takasago.

The last two lines were not added to Canto IV until after 1921, probably some time after Pound had written Canto XII, which opens with the original conception :

And we sit here
    under the wall,
Arena romana, Diocletian's, les gradins
        quarante-trois rangées en calcaire.   (12 : 53/57)

There appears to be a connection between the memory of this particular arena, that in the Baths of Diocletian, the Roman Emperor, and Pound's experience of a special kind of decadence; at least, this is what we gather from the context in which it occurs and in which it is later echoed. [120] In our Canto, however, the fragmentary

> and we sit here . . .
>   there in the arena . . .   (ll. 127—128)

shows above all another dimension of this recurring motif. E. M. Glenn comments : 'Lines 127 and 128 seem to indicate the presence of the artist as presenter (instead of narrator), the almost obliterated showman before the booth mentioned in the early version of Canto I (in *Poetry*). Or perhaps Pound's intention is to indicate that the author is a companion or guide to the reader.' [121]

The two explanations are equally tenable, since Pound is out to provide his reader with both scenic presentation and, often obliquely, dramatic moments in the Virgilian manner. The pronoun 'we' in these lines, like the 'our' in the Morning Lyric, is somehow intended to make the reader share the poet's real and imaginary experiences; after all, one of the functions of the artist is that of the

> Eternal watcher of things,
> Of things, of men, of passions.   (7 : 27/31)

Part Two

IN THE WAKE OF ODYSSEUS

Yet must thou sail after knowledge   (47 : 30/246). [122]

In order 'to superimpose upon it enough of form to make it seem, at least on one level, intelligible', it is certainly very helpful to say that 'the *Cantos* can best be read as a modern *Odyssey*'.[123] It cannot be denied that there are in Pound's *Cantos* a great many parallels to Homer's *Odyssey*, but it is going too far to try to find the whole of it incorporated in the *Cantos*, as it demonstrably is in Joyce's *Ulysses*. On the contrary, care must be taken to stress only those Homeric features of Odysseus which can be proved to serve Pound's purpose. To define the characteristically Poundian Odysseus, then, is the main object of Part Two of this study. Whereas both Part One and Part Three are based on the interpretation of one particular Canto, Part Two is concerned with individual passages from a variety of Cantos, as no single Canto in itself displays the full range of the significance of the Odysseus theme for Pound.

THE NEKUIA

The most sustained passage taken over from Homer's *Odyssey* is now at the very beginning of the *Cantos*.[124] This is an adaptation of the first 104 lines of the Eleventh Book, known as the Nekuia, the Evocation of the Dead. When, in the late 1920's, Pound started to tell his intimates that he intended to produce in the *Cantos* something 'rather like, or unlike subject and response and counter subject in fugue', he listed as

A. A. Live man goes down into world of Dead.[125]

In a letter written in April 1937 he admitted that the source-hunters were right in pointing out that 'there *is* at start, descent to the shades . . .', but added mischievously that he would like to 'pull it off as reading matter, singing matter, shouting matter, the tale of the tribe' (*Letters*, p. 386).

Among the many reasons which led Pound to open his long poem with this Homeric passage is his conviction that 'The Nekuia shouts aloud that it is *older* than the rest, all that island, Cretan, etc., hinter-time, that is *not* Praxiteles, not Athens of Pericles, but Odysseus.' (*Letters*, p. 363)

Pound believes, then, that the Nekuia contains survivals of the most ancient Mediterranean civilizations, taking us back to the very cradle of them. It is significant that he refers to Odysseus' voyage to Hades as a descent, and from Cantos XXXIX and XLVII, where the hero is exhorted to 'prepare to go on a journey', we become aware that Pound is turning it into a chthonic ritual. Hence we find in Canto XXXIX fragments of ritual poetry celebrating Spring,[126] and in Canto XLVII an evocation of the Adonis myth, with tags from Bion's *Lament of Adonis,* and an allusion to Hesiod's advice on ploughing. For Pound, Odysseus' descent is, in the last analysis, nothing less than the performance of the mysteries of the earth, as is clearly apparent from the beginning of the Lynx Song in the *Pisan Cantos,* where the exhortative words just quoted occur twice (79 : 66/520). Beyond the wisdom granted him by Tiresias, he receives the enlightenment given to those initiated into mysteries like those of Eleusis. This wisdom of the earth, as we have already seen in connection with Cadmus in Part One, has come to signify for Pound the very core of existence. It is, to him, the basis of all further knowledge.

CIRCE

The fact that Odysseus sails down to Hades from Circe's island is greatly emphasized in Pound. Of all the women and goddesses the Homeric Odysseus meets Circe is the only one whose character is presented at any length in the *Cantos.* One obvious reason for her prominence in the poem is her connection with the theme of metamorphosis, the second element — after the descent to Hades — in its 'fugal structure'. Sister Bernetta Quinn writes : 'Hugh Kenner calls her [Circe] the most clearly defined character in the first half of the poem,' and then quotes Allen Tate's rather extreme opinion : 'Mr. Pound's world is the scene of a great Odyssey, and everywhere he lands it is the shore of Circe, where men "lose all companions" and are turned into swine . . . And ironically, being modern and a hater of modernity, he sees all history as deformed by the trim-coifed goddess'.

While Sister Bernetta calls 'Tate's comment . . . hardly valid as a description of the *Cantos',* she nevertheless sees in Circe little more than a symbol of usury, so that she only reformulates and modulates Tate's view of Pound's obsessive battle against usury-gripped modernity.[127] Forrest Read's elaborate analogies with Homer's *Odyssey* are admittedly rather disputable, but he certainly comes nearer the essential reason behind Pound's view of Circe when he explains : 'Odysseus underwent at Circe's house the experience which altered him, ... which opened his heart to the words of Tiresias.' [128]

Pound chose Circe to demonstrate this particular kind of experience because she represents, as an archetypal image, many of the characteristics of woman as the sensual prison of man. Odysseus' crewmen, as we have observed in connection with the Actaeon myth, cannot withstand her spell because they enter her domain unprepared, and Odysseus himself, although warned by Hermes, is unable to escape her domination completely. Hermes' instructions save him from Circe's drugs, but not from becoming ensnared by her desire for physical love, or from sinking into luxurious lethargy.

What Pound makes his Odysseus realize is that :

> ... the female
> Is an element, the female
> Is a chaos
> An octopus
> A biological process   (29 : 144/149).

She is, however, the

> wilderness of renewals, confusion
> Basis of renewals ...   (20 : 92/96).

Only after such a realization can a man establish proper relations with woman. In Canto XLVII Pound implies an analogy between 'a man's way with a woman ... [and] a ploughman's way with the land', [129] an analogy which is often found with Greek poets. The aim, then, is not that 'we seek to fulfill .../..., our desire' (29 : 144/149), but that a man unite with a woman conscious of his creative strength. To call attention to a further analogy which Pound employs, woman is like the stone to which the sculptor imparts form. [130] The act of carving has the same end as the act of begetting or ploughing : 'the creation of order (τὸ Καλὸν for Pound) out of the formless, the male organ informing the female chaos'. [131]

Of equal importance, however, is the fact that sexual union may grant a man a vision of the order of things, of what is to come : 'in coitu inluminatio' (74 : 13/462). We see, then, that Pound makes his Odysseus share the metaphysician's experience, the experience of a Cavalcanti or a Donne, only, of course, at a cruder level. In fact, what the Poundian Odysseus experiences is rather like the ritual of initiation into some earth mystery at a time when symbols had not yet replaced the real act.

Thus initiated, having thus overcome those aspects of woman which, given free play, condemn a man to slavish inactivity, Odysseus is ready for his voyage, ready for the mysteries themselves.

PERIPLUM

Following upon Odysseus' liberating initiation in Canto XXXIX, we do not find in Canto XL his voyage to the underworld, or any echo of it, but instead the sailing expedition of the Carthaginian commander Hanno. What we are given here belongs to the third element in the loosely 'fugal structure' of the *Cantos* : 'the "repeat in history"' or 'parallel' (*Letters*, pp. 285 & 386), or, to use Blackmur's term once again, 'anthropological identification'.

On a primary level, an identification of Hanno's voyage with that of Odysseus comes quite naturally to those who believe with Victor Bérard that, in telling Odysseus' adventures at sea, Homer must have worked from some περίπλους of the Mediterranean. [132] As has been noted in considering Cadmus in Part One, Pound's thought seems in fact to move along such lines, and in the *ABC of Reading* we find indirect approval of Bérard's theories :

> Another French scholar has more or less shown that the geography of the Odyssey is correct geography; not as you would find it if you had a geography book and a map, but as it would be in a 'periplum', that is, as a coasting sailor would find it.
> (pp. 43 f.) [133]

This prose comment led straight to the definition contained in the China Cantos :

> periplum, not as land looks on a map
> but as sea bord seen by men sailing.   (59 : 70/339)

The main importance attached to a voyage like Odysseus' and Hanno's is apparent from passages like :

> No trustee of the Salem Museum, who had not doubled
> both Good Hope and The Horn.
>
>   . . .
>   . . . No man theign
> said Athelstan who has not made three voyages
> going hence off this land into other lands . . .   (48 : 35 f. / 252).

A man can obtain a comprehensive outlook only after extensive travelling, that is, he 'must sail after knowledge' (47 : 30/246). It is thus that he acquires 'Savoir Faire', which Pound chooses to label with the Homeric tag 'POLLON D'ANTHROPON IDEN' (*Guide*, p. 149). This is an allusion to what is said at the beginning of the *Odyssey* : 'and of many men he saw (the cities, and knew their minds)'. The same thought is expressed in the polyglot statement : 'many men's mannirs   videt et urbes . . .' [134]

It must have been his desire to furnish a monumental demonstration of this sailing after knowledge that prompted Pound to make an adaptation of Hanno's *Periplus*. In the whole of the *Cantos*, this adaptation is one of the very few passages sustained over more than one page. In comparison with the other long and homogeneous passages, the Nekuia of Canto I, the Confucius Canto (XIII), the Cavalcanti adaptation of Canto XXXVI and the Usura Cantos (XLV & LI), it has so far received surprisingly little attention from students of Pound. The Hanno adaptation is, nevertheless, equally typical of Pound's manner and subject-matter.

The only extant text of this *Periplus* is a Greek translation of unknown date [135]; the Phoenician-Punic original is lost. It is quite possible that Pound first learned about Hanno's voyage through *Delle Navigazione et Viaggi* by J. B. Ramusio, who prefaced his collection of maritime knowledge for sailors of the Renaissance with the manual *Hanone Capitano Cartaginesi*. [136] Pliny, who himself made an adaptation of Hanno's *Periplus*, and 'who can tell us what the Greeks and Romans got out of [it]', [137] can hardly have contributed to Pound's version. Sooner or later, however, Pound must have had access to the Greek text, from which we find two transliterations in Canto XL (ll. 9 & 72). [138]

In his hands the manual becomes a chant imbued with the flavour of the Anglo-Saxon *Seafarer*, and thus continues rhythmically what the Nekuia passage starts in Canto I, where he first applied the heroic, vaguely alliterative verse developed in his translation of that Nordic sea poem. It is this formal continuity, then, that Pound put before the continuity of subject-matter, and which keeps up the sequence of the poem from Canto XXXIX to Canto XL.

Hennig speaks of the monumental shortness of Hanno's sailing report; Pound excels even the Greek, let alone the English prose translations, in this respect. The most economic of the three English translations consulted [139] employs roughly twice the number of words used by Pound (874 as against 466). This, we may take it, brings Pound's version nearer the lost Punic original than either the Greek or any other scholarly translation, since, mainly through his stylistic economy, he succeeds in restoring it to something like the form in which

Karxèdoniōn Basileos [140]
    hung this with his map in their temple.   (ll. 72—73)

It has been said that 'the Phoencians had copied this Egyptian habit of displaying their *periploi,* whether drawn or written, in temples', [141] and, wanting his reader to realize that he is face to face with an inscription, Pound had the beginning printed all in capitals :

PLEASING TO CARTHAGENIANS : HANNO.

To enhance the illusion he follows it up with a subjunctive in the classical manner : 'that he ply beyond pillars of Herakles'. At the same time it is in this line that the important feature of Hanno's expedition is mentioned; it goes *beyond* the legendary pillars set up by Heracles at the Straits of Gibraltar.

    Mr Joyce also preoccupied with Gibraltar
        and the pillars of Hercules   (74 : 25/475),

we read among Pound's personal reminiscences in the *Pisan Cantos.* [142] Near the beginning of that sequence we even find what appears to be an apostrophe to Hanno, which hints at the emotional intensity of Pound's own preoccupation :

    You who have passed the pillars and outward from Herakles
        (74 : 3/451),

Although the primary purpose of Hanno's expedition is a political and economic — one he is 'to lay out Phoenecian cities' (l. 3), i.e. to colonize the coast of West Africa with the help of no fewer than thirty thousand people — the Odyssean sailing after knowledge is equally prominent. In fact, the further south he sails, the more Odyssean Hanno's adventures become. It is only as far as Cerne ('Cyrne' in Pound) that Hanno can proceed as a city-founder, and it is only down to this point that his navigational reckonings and observations afford fairly accurate mapping (V. ll. 21—26). South of Cerne he twice encounters the kind of hostility to which Odysseus was exposed at the hands of the blinded Cyclops and the Laestrygones : [143]

    Their folk wear the hides of wild beasts
    and threw rocks to stone us,
        so preventing our landing.   (ll. 30—32),

and

the island of folk hairy and savage
whom our Lixtae said were Gorillas.

. . .

Rained stone . . .   (ll. 59–60 & 63).

The services of the Lixtae ('Lixitae' with other translators), whom Hanno takes with him as interpreters, are of no avail; both land and people are inaccessible.

The main difference between Hanno's adventures and those of Odysseus is a matter of time. Whereas Homer's Odysseus, belonging to an age of myths, expresses his experiences in terms of mythical images familiar to his audience, Hanno, the child of a more realistic age, tries to reproduce exactly what his senses register. What first impresses itself on him in the increasingly unfamiliar region to the south of Cerne is the sensation of a

. . . woody mountain
with great soft smell from the trees
all perfumes many-mingling.   (ll. 38–40)

This wealth of scents is followed by the vision of land 'busy by night with fires' (l. 42). Further on, where nothing but the forest can be seen by day (l. 45), the night becomes alive

with sound of pipe against pipe
the sound ply over ply; cymbal beat against cymbal   (ll. 47–48).

As in the Noon Lyric of Canto IV, and in the periplus-like description of Venice in Canto XVII (78/82), the phrase 'ply over ply' appears. In all three passages it lends itself to the creation of a pattern indicating an infinitely graduated phenomenon, the parts of which are complementary; in the Hanno passage, however, they are above all contrapuntal.

If, Pound wants us to realize, Hanno's sober mind is quite capable of distinguishing the instruments at the bottom of these nocturnal sounds, he is not immune to the muffled beat of drums. Though his analytical mind does not fail him, as we can see from Pound's onomatopoeic rendering :

The drum, wood, leather, beat . . .,

Hanno is finally made to admit that they 'beat noise to make terror' (l. 49). Under such circumstances even so fearless and practical a man as Hanno does well to listen to those who have premonitions :

The diviners told us to clear.   (l. 50)

Yet on he sails, even further into unpenetrated waters, even though fear
grips the ships' companies incessantly. Indeed, fires continue to haunt
them everywhere. In Pound's text the spell-binding effect is brought out
by an alliterative string of words all starting with f :

> Went *f*rom that *f*ire *f*ragrance,
> *f*lames *f*lowed into sea,
> *F*earing and swiftly, the land by night decked with *f*lame.
> (ll. 51—53)

During the three days' voyage to the South Horn, where they once again,
in the manner of Odysseus, try to inform themselves about the
inhabitants,[144] the fires no longer leave them, even by day. It is in the
middle of his account of this fiery region that Hanno, for the only time
during the whole voyage, is moved beyond reporting facts, and mentions
a myth :

> One pillar of light above others
> Scorched at the sky and stars
> By day this stood an high mountain
> That they call the gods' carroch.   (ll. 54—57)

In Falconer's prose the same passage reads :

> In the middle was a lofty fire, larger than the rest, which
> seemed to touch the stars. When day came, we discovered it to
> be a large hill, called the Chariot of the Gods.

Needless to say, Pound's version is far more powerful; it shows a poetic
intensity entirely lacking in Hanno's own down-to-earth report.[145] Even
more than in the passage on the nocturnal sounds Pound is carried away
by his poet's vision. The common feature of these two passages is the way
in which Pound's mind conceives of a pattern of gradation. Here it is a
pattern of pillars appearing on top of each other, as if forming an
acropolis, with temples in ascending order rising from bottom to summit,
and the height of this structure is such that the uppermost and most
intensely burning pillar does not only 'seem to touch the stars', but, as
the unusual phrase 'to scorch at' implies, it almost burns 'the sky and
stars' (l. 55).

The myth Hanno hears about is not the decisive reason for Pound's
elaborate treatment of this passage, although the idea of a triumphal car

seems to have had a hold on his imagination in other connections as well. In other places, too, he anglicizes the Italian for 'chariot', 'carrocchio', and makes it 'carroch', especially in depicting the festivities to celebrate the founding of the Monte Dei Paschi (V. 43 : 10, 11/225, 226), that 'true base of credit, that is / the abundance of nature' (52 : 3/267). What indicates his ultimate intention in the passage under discussion is the appearance of the word 'light' (l. 54) in place of 'fires'.

This land of fires, then, conjures up in Pound's mind, once more, the light which 'rains down upon the Universe'.[146] How much he wishes to impress on the reader that the vision of this light constitutes Hanno's most fundamental experience on his circumnavigation of West Africa emerges from Pound's comment following the end of the periplus :

> Out of which things seeking an exit
> To the high air, to the stratosphere, to the imperial
> calm, to the empyrean, to the baily of the four towers
> the νόος, the ineffable crystal   (ll. 68—71).

After sailing to the chariot of the gods[147] Hanno must, Pound implies, have brought back to Carthage a certain presage of 'the reality of the *nous*, of mind, apart from any man's individual mind, of the sea crystalline and enduring' (*Guide*, p. 44). And, as is to be expected from what we have found in Part One, this is coupled with an awareness of the civic virtues.

Like its parallel, Odysseus' voyage down to the world of the Dead, Hanno's exploration is viewed here as an act of liberation. He goes down to the sea to brave the darkness of the unknown. In Pound's eyes Hanno's *Periplus* is thus the record of an ascent out of the darkness of ignorance towards the 'light of light', in which 'is the virtù' (74 : 7/455). The line

> Out of which things seeking an exit

frames, significantly, Pound's Hanno adaptation. Before we reach it we are given, in the first half of Canto XL, a 'further statement of the perverted values of the late 19th century'. It is a voyage after knowledge like Hanno's that may offer 'an ascent out of its muddle',[148] 'to the imperial / calm' (ll. 69—70). Up there man may behold, embedded in the Empyrean and the sphere of 'the ineffable crystal',

> ... the baily of the four towers,

the walls of the four-square celestial city, the model of the city which, as we have seen in Part One, is to be achieved on earth to weld peoples together into one Ideal Nation.[149]

In both Homer's Nekuia and Hanno's *Periplus* as adapted by Pound there
is a revelation of the future. The gist of what Tiresias reveals to Odysseus
is, in Pound's phrasing :

> 'Shalt return through spiteful Neptune, over dark seas,
> Lose all companions.' (1 : 5/9)

When Pound makes Circe say to the hero :

> Always with your mind on the past . . . (39 : 45/203),

he is referring, on one level at least, to Odysseus' longing for Ithaca and
Penelope, to his being essentially homeward bound. Pound's Hanno, on
the other hand, is 'seeking an exit'. The Ancients had in general accepted
the view of Heracles, their most popular hero, that there was no passage
from the pillars to the west. In venturing beyond the confines of the
classical world Hanno becomes one of the archetypes of the outward
bound Odysseus, a figure whose incarnation keeps in step, as it were, with
man's awakening interest in science; in European consciousness this
figure is better known under the name of Faustus.

It is obvious that Pound regards Homer's Odysseus and his own Hanno
more as parallels than as contrasts, and we hardly find an indication that
he views the two as complementary, except perhaps in the *Pisan Cantos*,
where Pound himself can be seen somehow identifying himself with the
home-seeking Odysseus, as for example in the veiled message to his wife :

> O white-chested martin, God damn it,
>   as no one else will carry a message,
> say to La Cara : amo. (76 : 37/488)

Otherwise Pound's Odysseus-figures and Pound himself, who dons them
as his masks, are far more home-deserters, outward bound on their quest
for knowledge. In fact the pattern of the Poundian Odysseus-figure shows
a curious mixture of the type of the explorer-scientist and that of the
Dantescan traveller :

> between NEKUIA where are Alcmene and Tyro
>   and the Charybdis of action
>   to the solitude of Mt. Taishan (74 : 9/457).

It is from a passage like this that we see how Pound is intent on
assimilating the pattern of Homer's *Odyssey* to that of Dante's *Divine*

Comedy. One reason for this assimilation is structural, as Pound has specifically remarked : 'For forty years I have schooled myself ... to write an epic poem which begins "In the Dark Forest", crosses the Purgatory of human wrong, and ends up in the light, "fra i maestri di color che sanno".' [150]

'Thus', says Emery, 'we make our descent with Odysseus but our Odyssey with Dante ...' We must hasten to add, however, again with Emery, that 'the original nekuia in Canto I is not a descent into hell but a descent into the historical past'. [151]

THE CHARYBDIS OF ACTION

As early as Canto XX Pound gives, as he explained to his father, a 'résumé of *Odyssey*, or rather of the main part of Ulysses' voyage up to death of all his crew' (*Letters*, p. 285). What strikes the reader most is a strong note of protest in Pound's résumé :

> And beneath : the clear bones, far down,
> Thousand on thousand.
>   'What gain with Odysseus,
> 'They that died in the whirlpool
> 'And after many vain labours,
> 'Living by stolen meat, chained to the rowingbench,
> 'That he should have a great fame
>   'And lie by night with the goddess?
> 'Their names are not written in bronze
>   'Nor their rowing sticks set with Elpenor's;
> 'Nor have they mound by sea-bord.
>   'That saw never the olives under Spartha
> 'With the leaves green and then not green,
>   'The click of light in their branches;
> 'That saw not the bronze hall nor the ingle
> 'Nor lay there with the queen's waiting-maids,
> 'Nor had they Circe to couch-mate, Circe Titania,
> 'Nor had they meats of Kalüpso
> 'Or her silk skirts brushing their thighs.
> 'Give! What were they given?
>   Ear-wax.
> 'Poison and ear-wax,
>   and a salt grave by the bull-field,

'neson amumona, their heads like sea crows in the foam,
'Black splotches, sea-weed under lightning;
'Canned beef of Apollo, ten cans for a boat load.'
Ligur' aoide.   (20 : 93—94/97—98)

This passage is certainly not what one normally expects a résumé to be.
On the contrary, it brings into focus a dimension of Odysseus' voyage
which Homer does not particularly emphasize. Though Odysseus does show
concern for the fate of his companions in his narrative at the court of
Alcinous, his compassion does not extend beyond what must have been
thought the measure befitting one of his social status. Hence we find him
repeating the same stock-phrases to express his grief over the loss of his
men. [152]

Pound, however, felt the need to break with the conventions of the
heroic world, and thus gives more prominence than did Homer [153] to the
spokesman for the other side, the anonymous crews. This spokesman's
very first words raise the most pertinent question :

'What gain with Odysseus'?

This opening sets the tone for an increasingly powerful chorus-like chant.
With every line the feeling of futility and envy assumes a more bitter
tone. These mariners have been denied everything save hardship and
death. What is left to them in their death is impotent jealousy of Odysseus,
for whom they performed all those 'vain labours'.

'That he should have a great fame
'And lie by night with the goddess?'

They were not to share any of his pleasures, neither the delight of
natural and intellectual beauty ('the olives under Spartha'), nor the sight
of rich palace-interiors ('the bronze hall ... the ingle'), nor any love of
woman — not even 'with the queen's waiting maids' — let alone the love
and splendour of a goddess. But their envy also includes Elpenor, the
youngest of Odysseus' companions, 'not much of a fighting man nor very
strong in the head'. [154] He was granted full funeral honours on Circe's
island after his shade had appeared to Odysseus in Hades. His drowned
shipmates, however, were refused any such honours :

'Their names are not written in bronze
'nor their rowing sticks set with Elpenor's'.

The bitterness of the mariners' chant reaches its climax in the answer
to the initial 'What gain with Odysseus' :

'Give! What were they given?

                              Ear-wax.
'Poison and ear-wax,

                    and a salt grave by the bull-field'.

Theirs was nothing but deepest degradation and deprivation. Circe's poison turned them into swine, and although the ear-wax protected them from the Sirens' destructive allurement, it also prevented them from receiving a share of their omniscience. Neither their bodies nor their minds were awarded any prize for their toil and suffering. The biting irony implied in the mention of the first two gifts is even further enhanced by the naming of the third and final one : 'and a salt-grave by the bull-field'.

What follows in the next three lines presents a gruesome picture of how the crew of Odysseus' own and last boat perished off Thrinacia. It is only in these lines of the sailor chorus that we discover direct allusions to Homer's poem. The transliterated Greek, *'neson amumona'*, is the descriptive phrase employed by Odysseus when they make their landfall on the island of the sun-god. [155] It means 'noble island', and not what Pound told his father it meant : 'Neson amumona, literally the narrow island' (*Letters*, p. 285). The continuation of this line is directly borrowed from Homer's account of Zeus' vengeance for the slaughter of Apollo's cattle : '... their heads like sea crows'. [156] To this Homeric image, which must have impressed him greatly, Pound adds his own vision :

    'Black splotches, sea-weed under lightning'.

Struck by Zeus' lightning, the mariners' heads appear to Pound to be even more reduced in size; they are burned black and thus likened to mere sea-weed. To conclude his vision, Pound once again employs a super-pository image :

    'Canned beef of Apollo, ten cans for a boat load.'

The unifying effect of this line arises from its grotesque ambiguity : Odysseus' companions, 'living by stolen meat' on Thrinacia, take the beef of Apollo's cattle down to their 'salt grave', thereby corning it, as it were, to be canned. At the same time the drowning mariners are in the brine, themselves turned into Apollo's 'beef', since their death is to avenge him. The stating of the exact quantity, 'ten cans for a boat load', adds a final touch of grotesqueness.

The transliterated Greek phrase 'Ligur' aoide' comes from *Odyssey* XII, 183. In Homer it refers to the quality of the Sirens' singing, to their 'clear-sounding song'. As the phrase is typographically joined on to the end of the sailor chorus we must try to discover its significance in relation to this. Whereas one of the other two places in which this phrase is recalled in the first eighty-four Cantos has very little to do with our passage (V. 20 : 89/93), the other may furnish a hint as to its meaning here :

> the sharp song with sun under its radiance
> λιγύρ
> one tanka entitled the shadow
> babao, or the hawk's wing
> of no fortune and with a name to come   (74 : 17/466).

Apart from realizing that Pound must obviously be impressed by the onomatopoeia of the Greek adjective, we see from these lines how the Sirens' 'sharp song' conjures up in his mind a vision of impending doom — 'babao' is the Italian for 'bugbear' — in the shape of a bird of prey :

> 'C'è il babao,' said the young mother
> and the bathers like small birds under hawk's eye
> shrank back under the cliff's edge . . .   (74 : 16/466).

Yet in addition to this wide range of connotations, which could be further extended to statements like that supposed to come from Von Tirpitz — 'beware of their charm / ΣΕΙΡΗΝΕΣ' [157] — we discover that this Greek phrase somehow functions as a device to transpose a dramatic situation of almost unbearable intensity to the medium of mere sounds, like the cry of the swallows in Canto IV. The clearest instance of this dissolving into music is found at the end of Canto LXXXII.

The most important question that arises from the chant of Odysseus' companions is, even after this detailed commentary, still unanswered : how does Pound's concern for them fit in with the fact that we usually find him interested only in Odysseus, as he alone is 'the live man among duds' (Essays, p. 212), as he alone exhibits a 'factive personality' (Guide, p. 194)?

Hugh Kenner has shown how a fairly convincing answer can be reached by calling attention to those structural principles which Pound derived from the study of music and which he placed under the heading of 'Great Bass'. The lament for the drowned represents, in the light of this theory, an integral part, necessary to make up — in Kenner's words — 'a larger rhythm of juxtaposition and recurrence'. It 'protests', he says, 'in its immediate context, against the passionate drift of the Lotophagoi, and the

Odysseus of whom they are jealous overlaps the world of receptive aesthetic passion ("Circe to couch-mate") and the factive vigours of the Malatesta...'. This 'weighing of passage against passage', then, reveals how Pound attempts to give his poem unity through the accumulation both of contrasting elements and of elements which are intrinsically parallel. Within such a structural organization some elements necessarily imply certain 'concomitants'. Moreover, such a contrapuntal vision necessitates, within the structure of the poem, parallel contrapuntal visions. As Kenner puts it : ' "The poor devils dying of cold, outside Sorano" [10 : 42/46] counterweight the Renaissance exploits as the mariners do the Homeric ones.' Sigismundo Malatesta (1417—1468), the condottiere and patron of the arts who is singled out by Pound because of his Odyssean stature, was, like Odysseus himself, made to share the experience of any man of action, that, whether he succeed or fail in the end, nothing can be achieved without sacrifice.

Kenner goes even further in his structural analysis : 'The seamen's chorus, in fact, makes contact with everything in the preceding Cantos...'.[158] Yet, even though Kenner's interpretation is quite exhaustive as far as the function of the sailors' protest in relation to Odysseus' exploits is concerned, and even though it points out all the major parallels, we still want to know what determined Pound to give the sailor chorus its particular mood. A remark in the *ABC of Reading* enables us to penetrate Pound's associations. Odysseus' companions, he says there, 'have most of them something that must have been the Greek equivalent of shell-shock' (p. 44).

The mention of this particular form of mental derangement clearly shows that Pound came to view their behaviour in the light of what he had learnt from people who had been in World War I and had witnessed what effects the strain of combat could produce. It was this sort of tension, Pound implies, that caused the crewmen to slaughter Apollo's cattle. It is more than a mere coincidence that we find among the war reminiscences of Canto XVI a situation which somewhat resembles that on the island of the sun-god; the troops are also near to starving, like Odysseus' companions :

> Mais ces pauvres types
> A la fin y s'attaquaient pour manger,
>> Sans ordres, les bêtes sauvages, on y fait
> Prisonniers; ceux qui parlaient français disaient :
>> 'Poo quah? Ma foi on attaquait pour manger.
>>>> (16 : 73/77)

How the waste and wreckage of the Great War filled Pound with bitter anger is most easily seen in sections V and VI of *Hugh Selwyn Mauberley*. It is the mood first evoked there that is struck again in the sailor chorus. The 'Thousand upon thousand' of its opening corresponds to :

There died a myriad   (*Personae*, p. 200).

There is, however, one important difference : the outcry against the waste of human life in *Mauberley* is not counterbalanced by any reference to positive achievements, because Pound could see in World War I nothing but such waste; thus in *Guide to Kulchur* he quotes — characteristically — one Lady L. as saying : 'All they can do is to stand up and be killed.' (p. 190) But the sailor chorus, as has been shown, loses at least some of its sting of accusation in the contrapuntal setting of the *Cantos*. Further-more, we shall discover in the *Pisan Cantos* how the note of acrid suffering changes under the influence of Pound's own suffering to one of compassion, sometimes even mixed with tearfulness.

CRIME AND PUNISHMENT

A comment on the XXVIth Canto of Dante's *Inferno* shows that we have to take into account a further dimension in Pound's treatment of the fate of Odysseus and his companions :

> Re punishment of Ulysses, no one seems to note the perfectly useless, trifling, unprovoked sack of the Cicones in the *Odyssey*. ... there was no excuse handy, it is pure devilment, and Ulysses and Co. deserved all they got thereafter ... It gives a crime and punishment motif to the *Odyssey*, which is frequently over-looked ... Dante definitely accents the theft of the Palladium, whereon one could turn out a volume of comment. It binds through from Homer to Virgil to Dante. [159]

This is certainly an unusual view, but it is a fact that most *Odyssey* commentators find nothing wrong with Odysseus' action at Ismarus. Though they tend to regard it as a proper piece of buccaneering, and, because the Cicones put Odysseus to flight, an inglorious one at that, they refrain from moralizing. [160] But then moralizing is just as un-Homeric as too great a concern for the fate of Odysseus' companions. Yet Pound seems to have chosen to look upon Odysseus' fate as essentially inseparable from that of his companions. Hence, the anger of Poseidon, to which Homer repeatedly refers as the reason for Odysseus' prolonged personal suffering, does not figure prominently in the *Cantos*. There is, however, in Odysseus' account of the Ismarus incident, one comment that could be adduced to back up Pound's view. In Rieu's translation this reads : '... and it certainly looked as though Zeus meant the very worst for my unhappy following and we were in for a very bad time.'[161]

The interpretation underlying this rendering hardly illustrates Pound's point, however, as 'Zeus meant the worst' and 'a very bad time' convey nothing very definite. The way A. Weiher handled the two lines in question provides a far better illustration :

> ... Jetzt überkam uns wirklich von Zeus das Verhängnis :
> Leiden in Fülle sollten wir ernten in grausigem Schicksal.[162]

Although Pound's view is too sober for them to be really adequate, the formidable German notions for doom and fate,[163] and the anticipation in 'sollten' ('were to'), do much to strengthen Pound's contention that it was at Ismarus that both Odysseus and his companions first became guilty. Rieu's version reflects the commonly accepted opinion that the impact of these two lines is limited to the Cicones episode; Weiher's at least admits the possibility of their impact on the whole of the *Odyssey*.

Yet, what is even more important, the events at Ismarus were not directed by Destiny. As Pound says, they were 'perfectly useless, trifling, unprovoked'. Largely discarding the Greek belief in oracles, Pound characterizes the Homeric world as 'a world of irresponsible gods, a very high society without recognizable morals, the individual responsible to himself' (Guide, p. 38). Hence, in a case like the sack of Ismarus and its aftermath, the gods cannot be blamed; 'there was no excuse handy, it is pure devilment', i.e. irresponsibility, it is

> the folly of attacking that island
> and of the force ὑπὲρ μόρον   (80 : 90/547).

If Homer can be called a moralist in any respect, it is above all in connection with his reiterated depiction of human folly and its disastrous consequences. Whenever the baser appetites gain control over them, men are particularly liable to lapse into folly. Though Homer does not preach, the truth of *radix malorum est cupiditas* speaks out of most of the deeds of the companions of Odysseus. Even Odysseus himself is not invulnerable, although he possesses in far greater measure than most men that quality which alone can protect one from folly : prudence. The essential lack of this wrought his companions' undoing.

When Pound refers to 'the force ὑπὲρ μόρον', he is still considering the phenomenon of man's foolishness. The Greek phrase occurs in Zeus' speech in the council of the gods in Book I and means 'beyond what is destined'. In Rieu it reads :

> ... it was with Aegisthus in his mind that Zeus now addressed the immortals :
>
> 'What a lamentable thing it is that men should blame the gods and regard us as the source of their troubles, when it is their own wickedness that brings them sufferings worse than any which Destiny allots them. Consider Aegisthus, who flouted Destiny by stealing Agamemnon's wife and murdering her husband when he came home, though he knew the ruin this would entail, since we ourselves had sent Hermes, the keen-eyed Giant-slayer, to warn him neither to kill the man nor to make love to his wife. ... And now Aegisthus has paid the final price for all his sins.' [164]

Aegisthus fell victim to 'the force beyond what is destined', then, because he did not heed the warning. Hence the gods decline all responsibility. Through his stupidity, in the truest sense, he outlawed himself from the sphere of destiny, and so the price he had to pay for his crime had no connection with destiny either, but was blindly set by external forces, especially vengeance. As Pound says about 'Ulysses and Co.', men who stray into such unforgivable folly deserve all they get thereafter.

That Pound discovered in Confucianism an alternative to a world corrupted by an endless succession of crime and punishment is evident from the 'Terminology' section of his *Confucius : The Great Digest*. There he explains one of the key phrases as meaning 'nourishing, supporting the destiny — should be compared with the *Odyssey*, I, 34' (p. 23). 'As for ethics', Pound says in 'A Visiting Card', 'I refer the reader to the *Great Digest* of Confucius' (*Impact*, p. 60). Identifying this Confucian wisdom with the spirit of the Japanese Noh, he finally produced this ideogram in the *Pisan Cantos* :

> Greek rascality against Hagoromo
> Kumasaka vs/ vulgarity
> no sooner out of Troas
> than the damn fools attacked Ismarus of the Cicones
>
> (79 : 63/518).

Although Pound states repeatedly that the *Iliad* and the *Odyssey* are the 'shored relics of a very human and high state of culture' (*Guide*, p. 24), and finds the reason for 'the decline of the Hellenic paideuma' at the time of Aristotle in the fact that 'the Homeric vigour was gone, with its sympathetic rascality, its irascible goguenard pantheon' (p. 331), he has come to emphasize more and more the lack of 'communal responsibilities' in the whole of Greek culture, as well as in certain periods of the Christian era. This is where, according to Pound, the thinking of the East leaves most of the Occident behind :

> The same sense of responsibility, the need for coordination of individuals expressed in Kung's teaching differs radically both from early Christian absolutism and from the maritime adventure morals of Odysseus or the loose talk of argumentative greeks. (p. 38)

It is in this light that the in itself 'sympathetic rascality', exemplified by the sack of Ismarus, becomes symptomatic of the kind of foolish irresponsibility which has proved to be calamitous time and time again, and the example of Ismarus demonstrates in addition that certain people are incapable of learning a lesson in responsibility, even from events of the magnitude of the Trojan experience.

How, in utter contrast to such 'Greek rascality', the timely awakening of a merciful sense of responsibility towards the helpless can benefit a whole people is the lesson which Pound's allusion to Hagoromo wants to teach. One of the Noh plays which Pound adapted poetically from the Fenollosa manuscripts bears this title; the Hagoromo is 'the magical feather-mantle of a Tennin, an aerial spirit or celestial dancer' (*Translations*, p. 308). Such a mantle is found in the play by the priest. Though he initially intends to take this treasure home, the Tennin's insistence that she is lost without it gradually makes him willing to return it, but only if she first pays him with the dance of the Tennin, as she might not keep her promise afterwards. Yet, as we read in the *Pisan Cantos* :

> 'With us there is no deceit'
> > said the moon nymph immacolata
> > Give back my cloak, hagoromo.   (80 : 78/534)

And indeed, she instructs the people of the country in the mystery of her dance and lets them experience a new relationship with the divine; this gives them the comfort which we find Pound himself receiving as a prisoner near Pisa :

> and the nymph of the hagoromo came to me
> > > as a corona of angels
> > > > (74 : 8/456).

Now the particular 'Greek rascality' which we should bear in mind as marking a really striking contrast to this is not Ismarus, but Odysseus' 'theft of the Palladium'; however, this deed can only serve as such a contrast after a number of important dissociations. The stealing of this sacred image from the citadel of Troy belongs, like the ruse of the Wooden Horse, to the post-Homeric tradition, and moral judgment of it is equally un-Homeric, especially as its main purpose was the denigration of Homer's favourite hero. Those who consider it an unforgivable crime forget, Stanford argues, that 'Ulysses simply did his duty as a Greek leader when he conquered the Trojan ancestors of the Romans by stratagem and deceit', and that the 'motive for denouncing Ulysses was based less on righteous indignation than on angry chauvinism'. He calls Dante's 'inexorable verdict . . . propagandist, not moralistic or judicial'. [165]

Pound's implied judgment on the theft of the Palladium is, on one level, equally propagandistic, since he evidently maintains that the Greeks lacked the civic virtues operative in the Confucian East and, at times, also in the Roman Empire (*Guide*, p. 40), and that they 'never could set up a NATION!' (46 : 26/242). At the same time the fact that 'Dante definitely accents the theft of the Palladium' seems to Pound significant for the very reasons which Stanford denies. Dante's verdict *is* 'moralistic' and 'judicial', because in Pound's eyes Odysseus' deed is, irrespective of the circumstances, sheer sacrilege. It interferes with a people's relationship with the divine, and hence demands dreadful punishment.

Seen in this light, the theft of the Trojans' tutelary image may no longer appear 'un-Homeric', and we may now agree with Pound that an awareness of the consequences of infringing upon what is divine 'binds through from Homer to Virgil to Dante'. Thus the contrast implied in the line 'Greek rascality against Hagoromo' can be described as being between the violation of a mystery through irreverence and the initiation into a mystery through reverence, between two forces which manifest themselves again and again in history, 'one that divides, shatters, and kills, and one that contemplates the unity of the mystery. "The arrow hath not two points." ' (*Impact*, p. 44).

Rascality is not, however, the only sign of the Greeks' lack of communal responsibility. Pound recognizes a further symptom of it in the absence of a certain nobility of behaviour, as can be induced from the juxtaposition :

Kumasaka vs/ vulgarity.

Kumasaka is, like *Hagoromo*, the title of a Noh play. In it the spirit of the warrior hero of that name reveals himself to a wandering priest. 'The final passage is', says Pound, in his introduction to the play, 'the Homeric presentation of combat between him and the young boy Ushiwaka' (Translations, p. 248). Yet it was not the Homeric qualities that made Pound recall the play in Guide to Kulchur, but the final attitude of the hero : 'The ghost of Kumasaka returns not from a grudge and not to gain anything; but to state clearly that the very young man who had killed him had not done so by a fluke or slip, but that he had outfenced him.' (p. 81) This is restated elliptically in the Pisan Cantos, in the course of Pound's musing over the presence of a Japanese sentry at the detention-camp, and at the same time he recollects another Noh play imbued with the same attitude : Kagekiyo.

Here it is a noble irony that stops the hero from further pursuing his victim, who is able to escape because his helmet comes apart in Kagekiyo's hands. Having realized each other's strength, 'they both laughed out over the battle, and went off each his own way' (Translations, p. 321). In the Cantos we read :

> remembering Kagekiyo : 'how stiff the shaft of your neck is.'
> and they went off each his own way.   (74 : 20/470)

In a letter to John Quinn Pound says : '. . . or fine things, like the end of Kagekiyo, which is, I think, "Homeric" '.[166] Indeed, there is in this play a certain parallel to the Ismarus incident. Pound has, however, not elaborated it in the Cantos.

> 'A better fencer than I was,' said Kumasaka, a shade.
>
> (74 : 20/470)

Though it is not specifically stated anywhere in the Cantos, such an attitude is an obvious contrast to that of Ajax in the eleventh book of the Odyssey. Odysseus says about him : 'The only soul that stood aloof was that of Aias son of Telamon, still embittered by the defeat I had inflicted upon him . . .' He goes on to address him : ' "So not even death itself, Aias, could make you forget your anger with me on account of those cursed arms! . . . Curb your resentment and conquer your pride." ' But Odysseus' placating words are of no avail : 'But Aias gave me not a word in answer and went off into Erebus . . .'[167]

As far as angry resentment is concerned, Achilles could also be mentioned here; indeed, he does appear in the Cantos :

> and as for sulking
> I knew but one Achilles in my time
> and he ended up in the Vatican   (80 : 80/536).

Pound is referring to Achilles Ambrogio Damiano Ratti, Pius XI, pope during the Fascist Era.

This kind of unwillingness to admit defeat, then, must be implied in Pound's use of the word 'vulgarity'. The connecting 'vs/' (versus) makes it apparent that he definitely invites the reader to judge and reflect upon this contrast in the way we have done here. We may even go a step further. It is no doubt easier for Kumasaka to declare himself beaten than it would be for Ajax. Whereas in the case of the Japanese warrior no 'fluke or slip' is involved, Ajax, as has often been emphasized in the post-Homeric tradition, has reason to suspect some Odyssean wile at the root of the decision against him. It seems that the fact that the Greek world was, like the rest of the Occident, very often one of deceit lends itself to Pound's desire to show the superiority of the virtues of the East.

'WITH A MIND LIKE THAT'

The second part of Dante's judgment on Odysseus has, unlike the first part, never moved Pound to direct comment. Dante's vision of an Odysseus whose unquenchable thirst for further knowledge stifles the three strongest natural affections, love for his son, his wife and his father,[168] nowhere colours Pound's notion of Odysseus as the incorporation of 'the greek honour of human intelligence' (*Guide*, p. 146). Though his Odysseus-figures are, as has been remarked, primarily outward bound, a possible conflict between their explorations and their fundamental human ties is outwith Pound's immediate sphere of interest. It would be wrong to say, however, that he disregards these ties, since they are among the most essential tenets of Confucianism, which we now know to be the ethical basis of the Poundian universe. This can be seen from a passage like :

> filial, fraternal affection is the root of humaneness
> the root of the process   (74 : 15/465).

The difference is that Pound does not associate the act of extending one's 'knowledge to the utmost' (*Confucius*, p. 31) with the dualism of a Faustus, as recognized by Dante, and many European minds after him.

If there is in Pound a reflection of Dante's 'revolutionary version of the final voyage of Ulysses',[169] it is in connection with his sailing beyond the pillars of Hercules. In discussing Hanno's circumnavigation of West Africa we noted an intense emotional undertone in the *Pisan Cantos*, where Pound re-echoes the Carthaginian's boldness. Dante makes the condemned Ulysses say :

> ... venimmo a quella foce stretta
> dov' Ercule segnò li suori riguardi
> acciò che l'uom più oltre non si metta. [170]

'Lest any man drive any further', Hercules set up his pillars, which came to be 'prescribed by classical writers as the limit to legitimate exploration. There', Stanford declares, '[Ulysses] took his fatal decision.' It is *the* decision of man on the brink of the tempting unknown. Dante definitely condemns Ulysses' decision as an instance of man's disobedience and his consequent fall, but Pound, in making a model for liberating action out of the sailing account of Hanno, the man who had in reality performed what Dante's imagination invented not only for Ulysses' condemnation but also to 'convey a terrible warning to the medieval world in general' as to the 'ambivalence of the pursuit of knowledge for its own sake', [171] obviously does not consider it an act of disobedience. Admittedly, Dante's warning came before the advent of the Renaissance and the Age of Discovery, when humanity began to realize that experimentation and exploration could, despite all its dangers, be put to good use. Unlike the theft of the Palladium, then, the breaking of the taboo established by Hercules is no sacrilege.

Yet how are we to explain Pound's lasting preoccupation with Gibraltar and the Pillars of Hercules? Part of the answer is to be found in the context of the indirect apostrophe to Hanno at the beginning of the *Pisan Cantos* :

> What you depart from is not the way
>   . . .
> 'the great periplum brings in the stars to our shore.'
> You who have passed the pillars and outward from Herakles
> when Lucifer fell in N. Carolina.
>   . . .
>   ... Odysseus
>   the name of my family.   (74 : 3/451)

It is not for nothing that the voice in juxtaposition with the apostrophe to the successful explorer is that of Odysseus on the island of the Cyclops. Like Pound in Pisa, he was a prisoner in the monster's cave, reduced to 'noman' (Oytis), [172] and, once his identity was re-established, exposed to avenging hatred for daring to do what the less strong-hearted would have

79

shied away from. 'Odysseus' is the name of his spiritual family in that it was given to the king of Ithaca by Autolycus, his grandfather, and means 'the victim of enmity'.

Even though there may be a curse on Odysseus and those who act in like manner, they are carried by the assurance that 'What you depart from is not the way'. They have the natural world to guide them, as it, too, undertakes a periplum :

'the great periplum brings in the stars to our shore'. [173]

If they fall from grace and become, like Odysseus' companion Elpenor, men 'on whom the sun has gone down', [174] who, before, lay 'in Circe's swine-sty' (74 : 14/463), they experience only a temporary lapse; though they are 'men of no fortune', they are men 'with a name to come'. [175]

What they undergo is a 'dark night of the soul', which is not final, but merely the darkness preceding revelation. [176] Thus the lines

> You who have passed the pillars and outward from Herakles
> when Lucifer fell in N. Carolina

express the desire of the Odyssean traveller to venture the voyage beyond, in spite of his awareness of the fall. Although his deed verges dangerously on the hubris that wrought Lucifer's downfall, [177] the primary motive is not greed for power, but first 'to build light' and then to achieve, in all its splendour, the City, the true Ithaca (V. 98 : 36).

It is in view of this end that Pound justifies exploration beyond time-honoured limits and implicitly rejects Dante's condemnation of the outward bound Ulysses. With regard to his refusal to recognize any limits in his own literary explorations Pound declares in *Thrones* :

> *If we never write anything save what is already understood, the field of understanding will never be extended.* (96 : 11)

The end of the 'Pull down thy vanity' passage of the *Pisan Cantos*, finally, provides a most explicit justification of Odyssean ventures :

> But to have done instead of not doing
>   this not vanity
>   . . .
>   To have gathered from the air a live tradition
>   . . .
> This is not vanity.
>   Here error is all in the not done,
> all in the diffidence that faltered.   (81 : 99 f. / 557)

What really, in Pound's eyes, acquits a man like Odysseus of any major guilt — as distinct from the charges of rascality and irresponsibility — he shows us, however, in his interpretation of a passage from the council of the gods in *Odyssey* I. It is the beginning of Zeus' reply to Athene's complaint about Odysseus' plight. Rieu makes it : 'How could I ever forget the admirable Odysseus? He is not only the wisest man alive but has been most generous in his offerings to the immortals who live in heaven.' Pound's preoccupation with this utterance of Zeus', excluding, however, the comment about Odysseus' offerings, is first evident from his correspondence with W. H. D. Rouse concerning the latter's translation of the *Odyssey*. [178] Upon seeing Rouse's version of *Odyssey* I, 65 f., Pound was constrained to say :

> The *theioio* : not sure you don't shock *me* for a change. What about Zeus saying : 'How can I forget Odysseus, the fellow is one of us,' or 'How can I forget Odysseus, who is one of us, one of our own kind,' or 'almost one of us.'
> 'A man with a mind like that comes near to godhead'; 'when a man's got a mind like that even the gods respect him' ('can respect'). (*Letters*, p. 358)

θείοιο, nom. θεῖος, 'more than human' (of heroes), 'godlike, super-human, extraordinary, excellent', [179] is the first epithet applied to Odysseus. In the course of Homer's poem it becomes, like its more frequent synonym δῖος, a stock epithet. Yet Pound, as can be seen from his endeavour to render its full implications in English, considers it, be it by one of his ingenious insights or through his deficient knowledge of Greek, to reveal the nature of Odysseus' relationship with the gods. In another letter to Rouse he says : 'But, the THEOIO [sic] is strong magic.' (p. 362) His interpretative version of this Homeric passage is the culmination of his characterization of Odysseus in *Guide to Kulchur*, which unites most of the aphoristic statements about the hero in his correspondence; and his emphasis through the use of capitals leaves no doubt as to his discovery in the epithet θεῖος : 'And as Zeus said : "A chap with a mind like THAT! the fellow is one of us. One of US." ' (*Guide*, p. 146)

It was not until Pound's imprisonment in Pisa that the passage assumed a function in the *Cantos*, occurring as :

with a mind like that he is one of us (80 : 90/547).

It balances the indictment contained in the previous two lines, which we have already discussed :

the folly of attacking that island
and of the force ὑπὲρ μόρον.

In his 'Sextant', the list of books which is a condensed version of most of his previous lists, Pound calls Homer's *Odyssey* the account of 'intelligence set above brute force' (*Guide*, p. 352). Therefore, he implies, the *Odyssey* is, didactically, Homer's superior epic, and if the *Iliad* at least shows traces of the ascendancy of intellectual power over muscular strength, it is precisely because of the presence of Odysseus in that poem. It was during the Trojan campaign, as Pound put it only recently, that Odysseus was

> Getting the feel of it, of his soul,
> while they were making a fuss about Helen   (98 : 36).

The man 'equal to Zeus in counsel' becomes aware, on the fields of Troy, of the principle of 'Know thyself'. This made him not only the shrewd character — 'ce rusé personnage'[180] — who outwitted the whole conventional heroic world, who, even 'among monsters, magicians, and usurpers',[181] was 'never at a loss' (*Guide*, p. 146), but it also awakened in him a far stronger intellectual curiosity than in any other Homeric hero.

ATHENE

The fact that Odysseus is the 'special protégé' of Athene in the *Iliad* and enjoys her 'personal sympathy and affection'[182] in the *Odyssey* is not greatly stressed by Pound. The only direct apostrophe to the goddess is an invocation of justice made by the despairing Odysseus-Pound at Pisa :

> Pallas Δίκη sustain me   (78 : 57/510).

This is, however, more specifically the Athene of the *Oresteia*, the goddess whose intervention at Orestes' trial Pound repeatedly alludes to both in *Section : Rock-Drill* and in *Thrones*.

In the Cantos prior to these latest two sequences only one quality of Athene's is pinpointed in the many references to her : the 'glint' of her eyes. Pound seems to owe his awareness of this to Allen Upward (1863–1926), of whom he wrote that he 'had a lot to say about Athene's eyes, connecting them with her owl and with olive trees. The property of the glaux, and olive leaf, to shine and then not to shine, 'glint' rather than shine. Certainly a more living word if one lives among olive yards.' (*Letters*, p. 357).

When Pound refers to the 'goddess of the flashing eyes' (Rieu), then, he is primarily musing over the implications of Homer's stock epithet γλαυκῶπις. It is in this connection also that Pound, for the only time, comes near to depicting the Homeric Odysseus' relations with Athene. As can be seen from the Sailor Chorus, Odysseus had, contrary to his companions, experienced the pleasure and comfort of :

>   . . .   the olives under Spartha
>   'With the leaves green and then not green,
>   'The click of light in their branches'   (20 : 94/98),

and was thus 'getting the feel' of Athene's divine influence. Pound, as a prisoner, derives similar pleasure from the thought of being

>   under the olives
>   saeculorum Athenae
>   γλαύξ, γλαυκῶπις,
>   olivi
>   that which gleams and then does not gleam
>   as the leaf turns in the air   (74 : 16/466).

Altohugh the gods are 'now desuete' (74 : 16/465), i.e. no longer worshipped, their permanent essence remains with us.[183] So the olives are still 'immemorial of Athene' ('saeculorum Athenae'); they and the little owl (γλαύξ) still reveal the miracle of her eyes, as they once revealed it to Odysseus.

Beyond this revelation Pound is silent about the goddess. He never alludes to her as Odysseus' guide, even though, in the case of Cadmus, he does show her in the capacity of 'Mentor' (V. 4 : 13/17). But even Homer more frequently leaves Odysseus' actions to the hero's own discretion; divine advice is more needed by those who come into contact with him : Nausicaa, the Phaeacians, and in particular the adolescent Telemachus, for whose sake Athene specially created the role of Mentor. Yet Pound appears to have further reasons for excluding Athene's assistance from his picture of Odysseus in the *Cantos*. They may be deduced from at least two innuendoes. The first is in :

>   Arachne che mi porta fortuna;
>   Athene, who wrongs thee?
>   τίς ἀδικεῖ   (76 : 39/490).

Already in the opening Canto of the Pisan sequence Pound interpreted the spider he discovered on his tent as a bringer of good luck : 'Arachne mi porta fortuna' (74 : 24/474). Having employed the name 'Arachne' and encouraged the spider to display its art — 'go spin on that tent rope' (76 : 39/490) — he now uses the words uttered by Aphrodite, in Sappho's Hymn to her, to address Athene (τίς ἀδικεῖ), and thus conjures up the legend of the ill-starred weaving-contest to which Athene had been challenged by the girl Arachne. Pound's question to Athene touches a sore spot indeed.

Exactly who or what hurt the goddess? If, as it seems, the hubris in Arachne's challenge is slurred over, Athene's tearing up of the girl's web does become an act of mean jealousy. Not even after Arachne has hanged herself, since she could not bear the humiliation, does the goddess show any pity which could reconcile her with the girl. Having changed her into a spider, she leaves her hanging, and continues to hate her.[184] Pound, who otherwise can readily bring himself to respect divine punishment, appears to regard Athene's action as sheer spiteful retaliation, since he obviously fails to see how a goddess can be so offended by artistic skill, and he seems to regret her intolerance.

The second innuendo is superficially a very irreverent and coarse remark about the goddess, although it is coupled with an apology :

> Athene cd/ have done with more sex appeal
> caesia ocula
> 'Pardon me, γλαύξ'
>> ('Leave it, I'm not a fool.')   (79 : 64/519).

On a deeper level, however, it is very similar to the first, as it too seems to give vent to a certain dislike of the goddess on Pound's part. Although Athene's emblems, the owl and the olive, united in the epithet γλαυκῶπις, are very dear to his heart, he finds the goddess far less congenial a patron of his type of voyaging Odyssean hero than Aphrodite or even Artemis-Diana. It is Aphrodite, Pound implies, who guides men in quest of the 'immortal *concetto*' (*Guide*, p. 152), 'the rose in the steel dust' of experience. She, more than any other goddess, engenders that vision of 'form in the air' (25 : 119/124), the vision granted to Anchises, who, Pound says, 'saw the waves taking form as crystal'.[185] He had, as Pound puts it,

> . . . laid hold of her flanks of air
> drawing her to him   (76 : 34/485).

The offspring of such a union was destined, as no other, to realize part of that aerial vision :

and belt the citye quahr of nobil fame
    the lateyn peopil taken has their name
bringing his gods into Latium
        saving the bricabrac
'Ere he his goddis brocht in Latio'. [186]

It is highly significant that the only mention of Aeneas himself occurs in a passage devoted to various epiphanies of Aphrodite :

and from her manner of walking

    . . .

a great goddess, Aeneas knew her forthwith   (74 : 13/462).

This is an adaptation of Gavin Douglas' version of the *Aeneid* I, 405 f. :

et vera incessu patuit dea. ille ube matrem
adgnovit . . .

Douglas makes it :

And in hir passage, ane verray god did her kyith
And fra that he knew, his moder alswith.   (V. *Essays*, p. 246)

The palindrome   R O M A
                       O   M
                       M   O
                       A M O R,

which Pound employs twice in the course of his most revealing essay, 'A Visiting Card' (V. *Impact*, pp. 66 & 74), and which we are surprised not to find in the *Cantos* — or at least not yet — might very well be taken to imply that if the Odyssean traveller is to attain what Pound implicitly considers his supreme goal, the foundation on earth of the foursquare celestial city, surrounded by what Pound calls 'the baily of the four towers', he must receive his guiding vision from all-prevailing love. It is only consistent, then, that Pound should keep demanding that the statue of Aphrodite be set up again over Terracina, [187] since Aphrodite is, for Pound, the tutelary goddess of all who sail the seas of human experience in quest of the Ideal City.

Apart from being godlike (θεῖος) as far as his intellectual grasp of most situations was concerned, Odysseus needed yet another quality in order to survive. This second quality seems, at first, to be less stressed by Pound than the first. To be *polumetis*, 'of many counsels or expedients, ever-ready',[188] may make a man a mere opportunist. Pound has said, however : 'There is opportunism and opportunism. The word has a bad meaning because in a world of Metternichs, and Talleyrands it means doing the other guy the minute you get the chance.' Opportunism at its best is, however, 'the capacity to pick out the element of immediate and major importance in any tangle'. This, Pound believed, was at the same time 'the secret of the Duce' (*Jefferson and / or Mussolini*, pp. 15 & 66).

It is interesting to note that Pound has chosen, from the many available stock Homeric epithets for Odysseus, the one which is most likely to be looked upon as ambivalent. When he calls Jefferson, like Odysseus, *polumetis*, he can safely add that he had, on top of this, a 'feeling of responsibility',[189] something which we know Pound denies Odysseus. Sigismondo Malatesta, on the other hand, who also lacked a stronger sense of responsibility, is observed to carry this Odyssean quality somewhat too far :

> And it was his messianic year, Poliorcetes,
>   but he was being a bit too POLUMETIS. [190]

The same can be said of Homer's Odysseus, when he reveals himself to the Cyclops, for example, and, especially if we look at it as Pound does, during the Ismarus episode. But whereas Malatesta eventually became the victim of his exploits, Odysseus lived to see Ithaca his own again, and this was not due to divine protection alone.

When Odysseus awoke from the first of his two fateful sleeps to find that his companions had released the winds out of Aeolus' bag, he was driven to the very brink : should he drown himself and end it all, or should he go on living and quietly endure suffering? This was his narrow choice. No god or goddess was there to help him. Yet he chose to live and suffer.[191] Only after enduring a multitude of hardships did he reach his native shores.

In Pisa, at 'the gates of death', Odysseus addresses Pound thus :

> hast'ou swum in a sea of air strip
>   through an aeon of nothingness,
> when the raft broke and the waters went over me   (80 : 91/547).

Like Odysseus, Pound was not a born sufferer; he too had to learn to endure. Immersed in the sea of suffering he gradually became aware of a final purification. Hence, throughout the two latest sequels of the *Cantos*, *Rock-Drill* and *Thrones*, we keep encountering the swimmer, be it Odysseus or even Swinburne (see Part Three), on whom, finally, Leucothea takes pity. The sea in which he is swimming gradually changes into :

> the sphere moving crystal, fluid,
> > none therein carrying rancour
> Death, insanity / suicide degeneration
> that is, just getting stupider as they get older
> πολλά παθεῖν   (76 : 35/485).

Those who do not bear gracefully the many adverse things which necessarily befall a man [192] lapse, Pound says here by means of one of his juxtapositions, into darkness and mental dullness as they grow older, instead of ascending, freed and having overcome all suffering, to the brightness of the crystalline. We note here, once again, how in Pound's hands Odysseus is turned, on his way to his final destination, into the heavenly traveller, Dante.

Although the languorous atmosphere of Circe holds him in thrall for more than a year, so that his companions have to remind him to think of his and their homeward voyage, [193] and although his eagerness to know tends, at times, to become independent of his main purpose, Odysseus never actually departs from his way. He has resisted the even deeper languor of the lotus and that of Calypso; now, conscious of his aim, of the

> directio voluntatis, as lord over the heart, [194]

he drags his shipmates away from the forgetfulness of the lotus, and on the shore of Calypso's island, although he is bathed in tears, his unbending will to return cannot even be shaken by the nymph's warning of the further misery he is to encounter in the merciless sea. [195]

Such single-mindedness, such devotion to one cause, is also the strong driving force in Ezra Pound's personal Odyssey. He shares this with not a few outstanding Americans. In fact the American to whom he continually refers, and whom he credits with that singleness of purpose, is his own grandfather, Thaddeus Coleman Pound (1832–1914). The particular exploit chosen by his grandson to illustrate this is his achievement in building the first railway from Eau Claire to Chippewa Falls. Pound tells us that he did this in the face of tremendous odds :

And that man sweat blood to put through that railway,
And what he ever got out of it? [196]

He goes on to relate the struggle involved in obtaining the right of way,
and how

> ... they thought they had him flummox'd,
> Nobody'd sell any rails ...

These efforts may remind the reader of Pound of the practices adopted by
Sigismondo Maltesta to procure the marble for his Tempio (V. 9 : 36/40),
another single-minded 'Odyssean' exploit which greatly impressed Pound.
Very much the same sort of feat is, in Pound's eyes, Mussolini's draining
of the Pontine Marshes (V. 41 : 52/210), only one instance of the Duce's
'passion for construction'. [197]

We know that Pound professes to treat everything under the sun by the
ideogrammic method and is convinced of the 'applicability of scientific
method to literary criticism', the first proof of which was given to him by
Ernest Fenollosa, [198] whose life 'was the romance [read 'Odyssey'] par
excellence of modern scholarship' (Translations, p. 213). It does not
surprise us, therefore, that he should find Odyssean perseverance and
single-mindedness in scientists too, especially since the ideogrammic
method is the method of science (V. ABC of Reading, p. 26). In Canto
XXIII, after quoting in French the statement, as he says in the ABC
of Reading (p. 18), of 'a French commentator on Einstein' that ' "Science
does not consist in inventing a number of more or less abstract entities
corresponding to the number of things you wish to find out" ', he goes on :

> ... 'J'ai
> 'Obtenu une brulure' M. Curie, or some other scientist
> 'Qui m'a coûté six mois de guérison.'
>   and continued his experiments.
> Tropismes! 'We believe the attraction is chemical.'
>
> (23 : 107/111)

The same idea is echoed in Canto XXVII, but is there intended to furnish
a contrast to the 'black darkness' which results from lack of curiosity in
matters of the intellect and, of course, economics, in countries like
England and Russia. It is prefixed with :

> Ten million germs in his face
> 'That is part of the risk and happens
> 'About twice a year in tubercular research ...'   (27 : 129/134).

Like Odysseus leaving the island of Calypso, such scientists are fully aware of the dangers that lie ahead. They have met them before and have suffered in various degrees, but this does not lead them to abandon their experiments, as they are attracted to their research by what Pound refers to as tropisms, a force stronger than any desire for personal safety. As Pound says, 'they are interested in the WORK being done and the work TO DO, and not in personal considerations, personal petty vanities and so on.' That Pound himself has shown such an attitude all his life can be seen from almost any of his activities. Indeed, Mussolini's Italy would never have had such an alluring attraction for him had he not discovered in it the working of his own principal attitude. 'Such impersonality', he continues in the passage quoted above, 'seems to me implicit in fascism, in the *idea statale*' (*Jefferson and/or Mussolini*, p. 107).

It is, however, precisely because the Odyssean-type heroes whom Pound believed in and admired in Fascist Italy carried this impersonality too far that they justly deserve the very condemnation Dante pronounced on his home-deserting Ulysses. The most obvious case, apart from Mussolini himself, is probably Gabriele d'Annunzio (1863–1938), who was undoubtedly Fascism's most eloquent precursor, if not its prophet. As the subject of some of his poems is Odysseus, it is especially appropriate to mention him here. In his conception of the superman, which was influenced by Nietzsche, Odysseus became a kind of 'proto-Fascist'. From the two passages in the *Cantos* where d'Annunzio appears, we can gather that Pound shared the Italians' fondness for d'Annunzio the poet and soldier, as manifest in d'Annunzio caricatures (V. 76 : 34/485), and it is probable that he even sought his personal acquaintance (V. 76 : 39/490).

In Pound's prose we find two confirmations of his admiration for the Italian : 'Gabe (D'Annunzio) at any rate had the "sperit ova man in him", (and incidentally some of his later writings are dam good *as* writings . . .)' (*Letters*, p. 333). In *Jefferson and/or Mussolini* we are given an indirect reference to what must be d'Annunzio's rhetorical diction. This is, however, condoned by Pound, since he finds it balanced by heroic action, and the comparison with Hemingway's 'tough guy' is not without significance :

> I do not believe I am any more impressed by rhetoric than is Mr. Hemingway, I may have a greater capacity, or sympathy with, general ideas (provided they have a bearing on what I consider good action) but Gabriele [d'Annunzio] as aviator has shown just as much nerve as any of dear Hem's pet bull-bashers.
>
> (p. 107)

Yet Pound, who has said — in the same book and on numerous other occasions — that he 'can "cure" the whole trouble simply by criticism of style' (p. 17), obviously fails to see what Stanford has come to realize in his survey of the Odyssean tradition : 'D'Annunzio sounds the loudest and brassiest note in the whole tradition in solemn conviction that this is the true essence of heroism.' What Stanford goes on to say not only applies to d'Annunzio, but partly hits at Pound as well :

> If this had been merely a literary solecism, one could pass it by without further regret. But it became something far more harmful . . . As is well-known, d'Annunzio's gospel of aggressive heroism both predicted and helped to create the Fascist régime, with its screaming rodomontade, its colossal railway-stations, and the glorious conquest of Abyssinia. The Italian disasters of 1944 confirmed Dante's judgment that the end of this road is destruction. [199]

Heinrich Straumann writes much the same thing about Pound's Fascist associations during World War II :

> Pound drew the practical inferences of his own criticism of the Western World, acted upon them, and associated himself with the political enemies of that civilization, strangely unaware that the camp in which he found himself would have created much greater evils than those he was fighting against. [200]

This strange unawareness casts serious doubts indeed on Pound's powers of judgment. Recently he himself said of this fatal error :

> My method of opposing tyranny was wrong over a thirty year period . . . Oh, it was paranoia to think one could argue against the usurpations, against the folks who got the war started to get America into it. [201]

It cannot be said, however, that confessions like these show that Pound has, since the war, fully rid himself of that unawareness. It is more likely that, in spite of adopting the 'Dantesquan scale of values', and in spite of professing Confucianism, Pound is actually incapable of harmonizing the impersonality or single-mindedness of the artist, scientist and statesman with a genuine concern for the well-being of humanity. Although we have observed that the Odysseus emerging from the *Cantos* is not really guilty of neglecting the fundamental human ties, and although Pound believed that Mussolini was 'driven by a vast and deep "concern" or will for the welfare of Italy' (*Jefferson and/or Mussolini*, p. 34), we must now stress that Pound himself proved to be too much of an impassioned revolutionary to realize where and when the course taken by his declared hero began to lack any humaneness and display nothing but megalo-mania. [202]

Nothing can be achieved without sacrifice, we remarked in connection with the Sailor Chorus. Admittedly, if everyone driven into 'a Hamlet's impasse bulking the cost too large to justify any action'[203] gave up the struggle, the hopes of a better world — and these exist, undeniably, in the hearts of men — would be doomed to disappointment. But human conditions cannot be changed by brute force. In Part One we have amply demonstrated how fully Pound is otherwise aware of this fact, and the following passage from that most revealing letter to Felix E. Schelling of 1922 only serves to confirm this, but at the same time it grants us a further insight : 'Being intemperate, at moments, I shd. prefer dynamite, but in measured moments I know that all violence is useless (even the violence of language ...).' (*Letters*, p. 249) Unfortunately for Pound, what few 'measured moments' he had after Italy's entry into the war were never spent in judging Mussolini's increasing association with the barbaric violence of Hitler.

THE POUNDIAN ODYSSEUS

We shall meet the figure of Odysseus again in Part Three, in our study of Canto LXXXII and its manifold implications. Yet it is now, at the end of Part Two, time to emphasize once again the main pattern of Odysseus as we meet him in the *Cantos* and the rest of Pound's writings. It ought by now to be clear that Odysseus, in Pound's works, is not one man but many. He is, in fact, *the* recurring type in the *Cantos*. The feature common to almost all who, in Pound's eyes, belong to this type, is :

Men go on voyages.

This is number eight in 'a list of facts which I and 9,000,000 other poets have spieled endlessly'. It was sent to William Carlos Williams in 1908 (*Letters*, p. 38). Already at that early stage, then, the figure of the voyager Odysseus had a firm grip on Pound's imagination, and it had come to stay.

'And he in his young youth, in the wake of Odysseus ...', he says of Niccolò d'Este in the introductory line of his own adaptation of Luchino del Campo's account of Este's journey to Jerusalem (24 : 111 f. / 116 f.).

Part Three

THE POINT OF CRISIS

As a lone ant from a broken ant-hill
from the wreckage of Europe, ego scriptor.   (76 : 36/487).

Canto LXXXII contains in its 132 lines (counting each typographical line) no less than thirty-one separable topics. A plan shall again facilitate our interpretation. [206]

In discussing the *Pisan Cantos* every Poundian critic is bound to stress their more personal nature, as this is contrary to what Pound had been trying to achieve in the *Cantos* before his Pisan experience. If Pound's endeavour in the first seventy-one Cantos was to propagate a 'New Learning', a versified 'Guide to Kulchur', with the complete disavowal of his own person, he appears in the *Pisan Cantos* as the avowed author, whose personal misery we from time to time witness directly. Let it, however, be said immediately that Pound is neither asking the reader's pity nor overtly rousing his revolutionary passions. The outspoken protests of his broadcasts become, in the *Pisan Cantos,* one fairly subdued aspect of that vast mass of images, observations and reminiscences of every kind.

The most obvious additions in the Pisan sequence are the more frequent mentions of Pound's own past and the inclusion of one particular place, the prison-camp itself — both as a subject for direct observation and as a point of departure for the contemplation of what Pound here calls the 'process' — together with reminiscences of all time and all places.

THE CLOUDS

The device most frequently employed in the *Pisan Cantos* is the ellipsis, which not seldom consists of only a name. These extremely compressed elements are deliberately echoed, sometimes within their own Canto, but just as often in one of the later Cantos. Such echoes have always been part of the 'fugal' structure of Pound's poem, but in the *Pisan Cantos* the true dimension of Pound's thought and vision can be grasped only after a careful study of these echo-patterns. The opening image of our Canto happens to belong to one of the most elaborate successions of echoes :

When with his hunting dog I see a cloud.

The clouds over Pisa (Shelley commented on them also) have a prominent place throughout the eleven Cantos of this sequence. The first direct comment reads :

and the cloud near to Pisa
                    are as good as any in Italy   (76 : 34/485).

This is echoed, with a significant addition, three pages later :

and the clouds over the Pisan meadows
                    are indubitably as fine as any to be seen
from the peninsula
                    οἱ βάρβαροι have not destroyed them   (76 : 37/488).

In the next Canto, seven pages later, the splendour of the Pisan clouds is compared with the clouds over an American waterfall (77 : 44/495). Here Pound recalls a man contemplating ('just watchin' ') the water. Three pages further on Pound introduces the element of fertility into the echo :

the clouds over Pisa, over the two teats of Tellus, γέα
                                                  (77 : 46/498).

Not until two pages from the end of the Pisan sequence (seventy-six pages from the previous echo) do we read the final echo of the series. In fact, the mention of the clouds comes side by side with the most hopeful note of the whole of the *Pisan Cantos* :

Under the white clouds, cielo di Pisa
out of all this beauty something must come   (84 : 117/574).

In listing these five basic echoes, to which, by the very nature of the *Pisan Cantos,* every other mention of clouds is related, we have gained a fundamental insight into the development of Pound's emotions during his confinement in the Disciplinary Training Camp at Coltano near Pisa; to be more precise, it is an insight into his personal concern for the future of defeated Italy, for in Canto LXXX he asks anxiously : 'Nenni, Nenni, who will have the succession?' (73/529).

We may summarize the five stages thus : (1) even in this Pisan concentration camp Pound is still in his beloved and naturally beautiful Italy, whose splendour the barbarians (i.e. the American liberators!) could not destroy (2), and which is still (3) the place for the contemplation of the culturally good life; the land is as fertile as ever (4), so that (5) a new and even more ideal Italy should arise again.

It is only fair to say, however, that Italy is not, and never has been, inseparable from Pound's vision of the Ideal State. Fascist Italy has never been any more to him than a model commendable for its similarity to Jeffersonian America. [207] How his vision goes far beyond any particular national policy is seen in the *Pisan Cantos* from his use of two archetypal city-images, the already mentioned image of the city of Deioces and the image of the '4 times ... rebuilded' (74 : 8/457) city derived from tne Wagadu legend.[208] Moreover, the building of the Ideal City has, in the *Pisan Cantos*, become intimately linked with the ascent of Mount Taishan, a sacred mountain in China. In Pound's mind this is an image of the spiritual regeneration which must be achieved before any political reconstruction can be effective. 'From the death cells in sight of Mt Taishan @ Pisa' (74 : 5/453), out of the 'nox animae magna from the tent under Taishan' (74 : 15/464), the poet and city-builder has to ascend the shrine-studded road leading to the temples on the summit. 'The solitude of Mt Taishan' (74 : 9/457) will give rest to a mind worn by action, will bestow on it the strength for new action, and the 'clouds banked on Taishan' (74 : 8/456), which 'have made a pseudo-Vesuvius / this side of Taishan'(80 : 73/528), seem to effect part of this very process of spiritual rebirth.

In addition to those we have just discussed, there is another series of cloud images spread over the whole of the *Pisan Cantos*. This group contemplates light-effects on clouds, e.g. :

> pale the dawn cloud, la luna
> > thin as Demeter's hair   (74 : 8 f. / 457).

Apart from our Canto there are, significantly, two others in the Pisan sequence that open with a cloud image, Canto LXXVI and Canto LXXIX. These both belong to the series of cloud-light images, and the beginning of Canto LXXVI makes it clear that such delight in clouds and light provides the sensual basis for that worship of Neo-Platonic love expressed in Cavalcanti's 'Donna Mi Prega', since 'dove sta memora' (76 : 30/480) is a direct borrowing from this poem, and appears in translation in Canto XXXVI as 'where memory liveth' (27/182).

The image at the beginning of our Canto belongs to yet another group of cloud images. In this group animal forms are perceived in the clouds, as, for example, in : 'as it were a mouse, out of cloud's mountain' (76 : 34/484), or, in the same Canto : 'under the two-winged cloud' (38/489). The image in our line, 'When with his hunting dog I see a cloud', is primarily similar to one in Canto LXXX :

> man and dog
> > on the S. E. horizon,

where the two objects seen remind Pound of the Chinese character for 'dog' :

and we note that dog precedes man in the occident
as of course in the orient if the bloke in the
is proceeding to rightwards. [209]

(ch' üan³)

Although the character for 'dog' is a radical (No. 94), Pound thinks of it as being composed of the radical meaning 'man' (No. 37) [210] and a dot which, according to his analysis, stands for 'dog', the whole character thus illustrating the truth of the English saying that the dog is man's best friend (Cf. *Confucius*, pp. 149 f.).

Yet in our Canto the vision of a cloud, in which Pound seems to recognize a hunter 'with his hunting dog', is not merely food for thought on the Chinese character. It is late summer, as we may see from line 75 ('8th day of September'), and the approach of the hunting season, as it were, gives rise to the thought that

Death's seeds move in the year   (80 : 78/534),

and that Adonis is due to fall again (V. 47 : 32/248).

THE 'GOOD NIGGER'

What first strikes us about line 2 is its sheer grotesqueness :

'Guten Morgen, mein Herr' yells the black boy from the jo-cart.

That a Negro soldier driving past on a sewage-tanker (jo-cart) should use this polite German greeting-formula is certainly unusual. However, 'the sight of a good nigger is cheering', says Pound (79 : 63/517), and the heads of the negroes in the camp remind him of the ethnological collections at the Frobenius Institute for Cultural Morphology, 'of the Baluba mask' (74 : 12/461). The head of Mr. (Benin) Edwards, the negro who made Pound a table 'ex packing box' (81 : 96/554), is deemed 'a mask as fine as any in Frankfurt' (81 : 97/554). On the other hand, the 'niggers scaling the obstacle fence' (74 : 12/461) make Pound think of the frescoes by Cosimo Tura and Francesco del Cossa at the Palazzo Schifanoia in Ferrara :

and those negroes by the clothes-line are extraordinarily like the figures del Cossa. [211]

Another aspect of the superior elegance in the physique of the negro impresses him too :

> a black delicate hand
> a white's hand like a ham   (74 : 18/468).

Now the black boy in our line speaks German, or has at least picked up this one phrase. The fact that the language is German is not unduly significant, although the reader not accustomed to Pound's highly unrealistic political views might take it to be a reference to Nazi Germany. No, the fact that the negro speaks German is almost certainly an illustration of Pound's pronouncement :

> What counts is the cultural level   (81 : 96/554).

Pound's sympathy with the black soldiers in the camp is of course in keeping with his unfailing sympathy for every kind of underdog. Yeats's story about Pound feeding the cats at Rapallo will probably, if it has not already done so, become the *locus classicus* on this side of Pound's character :

> Cats are oppressed, dogs terrify them, landladies starve them, boys stone them, everybody speaks of them with contempt. If they were human beings we could talk of their oppressors with a studied violence, add our strength to theirs, even organize the oppressed and like good politicians sell our charity for power. [212]

In Pound's eyes, then, the incongruity results from the black boy's presence on the 'jo-cart', whereas the German politeness is a sign of the 'intellectual interests' (74 : 17/466) of the 'good niggers'. The boy would deserve a better mission in life than serving in a 'swine-sty' (74 : 14/463).

'COMES MISERIAE'

The two opening lines, which show us how the poet's mind usually takes its primary stimulus from what lends itself to direct observation, are followed by a parenthesis containing, in symmetrical arrangement, the names of seven fellow-prisoners. This is only one of many such lists given in the *Pisan Cantos*. Pound disclosed part of their purpose in his recently published 'Note to Base Censor' :

> The proper names given are mostly those of men on sick call seen passing my tent. A very brief allusion to further study in names, that is, I am interested to note the prevalence of early

american names, either of whites of the old tradition (most of the early presidents for example) or of descendants of slaves who took the names of their masters. Interesting in contrast to the relative scarcity of melting-pot names. [213]

Another of Pound's aims in recording American proper names is brought out in the following passage :

> the wards like a slave ship,
> > Mr Edwards, Hudson, Henry   *comes miseriae*
> > Comites Kernes, Green and Tom Wilson
> > > . . .
> of the slaver as seen between decks   (74 : 14/463 f.).

It is not for nothing that he sees his fellow-prisoners and himself, 'amid the slaves learning slavery' (74 : 9/458), on board a slave-ship. This eventually links them with Odysseus' crewmen, whom Pound has described as being 'chained to the rowingbench' (20 : 93/98) like mere galley-slaves. But his fellow-prisoners, unlike Odysseus' mariners in Canto XX, have not only his sympathy, but also his assurance that they will all be granted the funeral honours which, in the *Odyssey*, Elpenor alone received. He sees them all as :

> men of no fortune and with a name to come   (80 : 92/548).

The plural 'men' in Canto LXXX, as against the singular 'man' still employed in Canto LXXIV [214] besides the impersonal 'of no fortune and with a name to come' (74 : 17/466), is one of the signs of Pound's increasing pity for his fellow-sufferers. Especially since 'the guard's opinion is lower than that of the / prisoners' (80 : 92/549), he does not look upon the other prisoners as 'brawlers, killers, rapists, malingerers, and other species of recalcitrant soldiery', [215] but sees in them merely men drugged by Circe's poison, i.e. usury, which is 'in all the veins of the commonweal' (74 : 15/464). Their crimes appear to him to be far less detrimental to humanity than the crimes of those 'who live by debt and war profiteering', as they live

> For nowt so much as a just peace
> That wd/ obstruct future wars   (77 : 52/505 & 504).

In fact, he comments sarcastically :

> not of course that we advocate —
> and yet petty larceny

100

in a regime based on grand larceny
might rank as conformity nient' altro. [216]

If Pound formerly hardly showed enough pity for others, and then, as he himself says in one of those rare passages of self-analysis, only 'at moments that suited my own convenience' (76 : 38/489), he is now, through what can truly be called genuine empathy, the brother of those who lie under the gallows. He prays with them for forgiveness (V. 74 : 5/454) and peaceful rest (V. 80 : 91/548), and at the same time, as the borrowings in the respective passages imply, the soul of one who, to a greater dregree than most men, possessed this very sense of pity passes through him : François Villon. [217]

It is also here, among the dregs of the U. S. Army, that the truth of St. Paul's great epistle on love is brought home to Pound. When he first arrived at the prison compound at the beginning of May 1945, he was put in a specially reinforced 'cage made of airstrip, and in solitary confinement'. There were no other civilian prisoners. He was heavily guarded — '4 giants at the 4 corners' (74 : 7/455) — and 'all DTC personnel were ordered to stay away from him and not to speak to him', because there 'was the fear that the Fascists might attempt to rescue him', [218] but when he was removed to a medical tent after three weeks, having collapsed due to exposure, and not least perhaps because of 'the excess electric illumination' (77 : 43/494) trained on him at night, some of the others started coming secretly to do him a good turn.

There was above all the 'jacent benignity' of Mr Edwards, the negro 'in ward No 4' (74 : 12/461), to whom he was grateful for providing him with that makeshift writing table. Another visitor was the negro turnkey, 'God's messenger Whiteside' (74 : 14/463), who probably brought Pound more than only his food and whose kindness Pound sees reflected in his care for dogs :

> or Whiteside :
> > 'ah certainly dew lak dawgs'
> > ah goin' tuh wash you'
> (no, not to the author, to the canine unwilling in question). [219]

Apart from these people there is, as we see from line 4 of our Canto,

> also Mr Walls who has lent me a razor.

They all move him to quote that famous biblical passage, but he makes a characteristic addition :

and the greatest is charity
to be found among those who have not observed
regulations. [220]

The more we penetrate into the *Pisan Cantos*, the more we realize that it is wrong to speak of a stock sympathy with the underdog. There may be some justification for considering the sentiment as such in some of his early poems, [221] but it seems that Yeats, in his interpretation of Pound's love for cats, failed to recognize his friend's capacity for genuine sympathy with all creatures, despite the deceptive exterior. D. S. Carne-Ross's comment is not altogether appropriate either. He says :

> ... it does not say much for Pound's spiritual development that he had to be put in the death cells to discover what other poets have known all along : that human affairs cannot be profoundly contemplated without a great sense of pity and that life cannot be profoundly conceived except in terms of tragedy. [222]

But we should not forget that most poets who were truly alive to the outright inflation of all human values as a result of the Great War were unable to strike a tragic mode of expression, or that if they did it was only after their natural pity for their fellows had been thoroughly purged in the strong acid of their desire for complete honesty. The capacity was there with most of them, but the temper of the times was anything but conducive to it. Sentimentality for the sake of sentimentality would no longer suffice as it had done in the nineteenth century :

> The young Dumas weeps because the young Dumas
> has tears   (80 : 78/534).

First the really fundamental and permanent values had to be rediscovered, and this was only possible after the poets had found what they considered, in their various ways and to a varying degree, to be the cause of the evil. Only then could they accept such basic values as might inspire in man a presage that 'there is something decent in the universe' (95 : 107) after all. Only then can a man truly view human suffering 'in terms of tragedy' again, for he has become conscious of the fall from 'Heaven's process' (85 : 12). Thus he feels strong compassion once more (V. 93 : 88), for he now knows that :

> filial, fraternal affection is the root of humaneness
> the root of the process   (74 : 15/465).

As one of those 'who have passed over Lethe',[223] Pound now asserts that :

>nothing counts save the quality of the affection,[224]

and that :

>What thou lovest well remains   (81 : 98/556).

Hence he observes life in the prison compound with growing affection. There may be a superficial coarseness in his comments on the 'close-order punishment drills'[225] to which his fellow-prisoners are subjected, in, for instance :

>   'Hot   hole   hep   cat'
>or words of similar volume
>   to be recognized by the god-damned
>   or man-damned trainee   (80 : 76/531)

and

>   'Hell! don't they get a break for the whistle?'   (79 : 65/519);

but we recognize in them a strong undertone of affection, as in practically everything he says about the other trainees and records as being said by them. He himself, Norman has it, 'as in happier times and places ... became a camp character' and was seen by the others

>serving small stones from a lath racquet   (74 : 21/470)

and taking other daily exercise.[226] He was 'an old man (or oldish)', but 'still active' (74 : 20/470), even though the moments of despair, when he saw the obstacle fence round the camps as

>... 10,000 gibbet-iform posts supporting
>barbed wire   (77 : 51/503),

and felt the 'claustrophobia of the mist' (80 : 79/535), were still all too frequent.

THE CRIME

We may feel pity for Pound at Pisa and admire his newly-found all-embracing compassion, but we must not forget the crime which caused him to be imprisoned there in the first place. He was detained on a charge of high treason, as a result of his short-wave broadcasts over the Italian

Broadcasting System from 1941 to 1943. [227] What he said there differs from his views stated before and after only in that it took the form of extremely violent and sweeping protests, tactlessly worded and often garrulous (judging by the transcripts he spoke 'off the cuff'). *The* topic was, of course, usury : 'Yes, I knew that this was what the war was about. I knew the war was about gold, usury and monopoly' (Jan. 29, 1942). Along with this he raved about the lies and falsifications in the American press : 'You have been stirred up against the Germany that did not exist. For two decades your press has conducted a campaign of defamation against Italy' (May 23, 1943). In *The Six Money Pamphlets* we find a passage which sums up perfectly Pound's view of World War II; the broadcasts were mere rambling annotations to it :

> This war was no whim of Mussolini's, nor of Hitler's. This war is a chapter in the long and bloody tragedy which began with the foundation of the Bank of England in far-away 1694, with the openly declared intention of Paterson's now famous prospectus, which contains the words already quoted : 'the bank hath benefit of interest on all moneys which it creates out of nothing'. [228]

There is one more point to be made : Pound felt that he had reached the level of a 'Confucian' sage. The title of his talk on July 2, 1942, was 'Disbursement of Wisdom', and he quoted there the Chinese saying : 'In evil time the sage can enjoy his own wisdom. When the land is well governed the people benefit from his instruction', only to say later on : 'Now you are in a bloody mess ... Who got you there?' Again it is the sage who says : 'I wonder if any of you realize or could by an effort arrive at the realization of the degree of detachment that I feel at moments. If you on your own ever do, try to see the present historic moment from the outside. The thing in my case goes beyond an effort of will. I find myself simply outside observing' (July 25, 1943). Russell voices what everyone must feel on reading the transcripts of these broadcasts : '... his attitude to the war itself and the very pertinent question of who should win [was] unrealistic'. [229]

SWINBURNE

We are now sufficiently familiar with the external circumstances reflected in the *Pisan Cantos* to turn our attention to Pound's memories of London and what is evoked along with them.

Swinburne my only miss (l. 6).

There is disappointment, but also justified pride, in this remark, as we shall see. The death of Swinburne occurred on April 10, 1909. By that time Pound, who had arrived from Italy in the late summer of 1908, was 'by way of falling into the crowd that does things here'. [230] He had found the man who was to publish most of his books of the London period, C. Elkin Mathews, one-time partner of John Lane and co-founder of the Bodley Head Press : thus began Pound's contact with the writers of the 'Beardsley Period'. When the 'song-bringer of a glad new minstrelsy' [231] died, Pound's first *Personae* volume, which was to earn him first the praise and soon afterwards the friendship of William Butler Yeats, [232] was in the process of appearing. All the newspapers and journals were full of tributes to the 'wonderful Mr. Swinburne', [233] and literary London was in mourning.[234]

Pound had every reason to share this mourning; in his *A Lume Spento* (Venice, 1908) he had published a 104-line tribute to Swinburne, in the form of an ode entitled 'Salve O Pontifex', which clearly shows that he was under the spell of the older poet. [235] This ode, which speaks of Swinburne as the 'High Priest of Iacchus', may even lead one to assume that Pound's mythological and paganistic preoccupations were inspired, to a high degree, by his enthusiastic admiration for Swinburne's poetry. Most Poundian critics have so far not even suspected this connection, because, on a stylistic level, the Imagist Movement revolted against all kinds of Swinburnia.

It may have been then, amidst the talk about Swinburne's death, that Pound learned that Swinburne had 'been to see Landor' (l. 7). This made him regret all the more not having met him. As he was to say in the late 1920's : 'The decline of England began on the day when Landor packed his trunks and departed to Tuscany' (*Essays*, p. 32). Now Swinburne, who, already at Eton (1852), 'had fallen under the spell of Landor, and in particular of the "Hellenics" ', [236] paid the culturally significant visit to Landor in Florence in 1864, six months before the latter's death, and brought the Greek tradition back to English verse. The publication in the following year of *Atalanta in Calydon* and the first series of *Poems and Ballads* (1866) are clear manifestations of this.

Though the encounter between Pound and Swinburne did not take place, we can be sure that Pound had Swinburne on his list of scheduled literary contacts. Swinburne's thanks to Landor for his achievements took the form of the now-famous visit and the composition of 'In Memory of Walter Savage Landor'. Pound did the same for Swinburne, particularly because of his 'taking English metrics in hand' (*Essays*, p. 36), in his own characteristic fashion : he wrote a biting defence of Swinburne's eccentric genius against Middle Class attempts to tone it down. In fact, 'Swinburne versus his Biographers'[237] seems to have won Pound a permanent place in Swinburne criticism. A recent statement by Dame Edith Sitwell supports this : 'Mr. Ezra Pound . . . has written more finely than any other poet, any other critic, of Swinburne.'[238]

Canto LXXXII shows Pound still on the defensive :

> *and* they told me this that an'tother   (l. 8).

The italicized 'and', plus what we can gather from Pound's utterances elsewhere, leaves no doubt that this line alludes to the anecdotes Pound heard about Swinburne's disorderliness before 1879. One of them, already mentioned in 'Swinburne versus his Biographers' (V. *Essays*, p. 290), is incorporated elliptically into Canto LXXX, which also contains the only other direct reference to Swinburne in the whole poem :

> 'Tyke 'im up ter the bawth' (meaning Swinburne)   (80 : 86/543).

This is a reference to what Ford Madox Ford told Pound and recorded in *Portraits from Life*[239] about Swinburne's arriving drunk at the house of his uncle, Ford Madox Brown, the Pre-Raphaelite painter.

Pound wanted such facts to be known — not simply slurred over as they were in Gosse's life of Swinburne — because they proved to him that 'the more or less obstreperous real Victorians[240] . . . were all vital and human people' (*Essays*, p. 290). He states his opinion quite clearly in one of his 'Imaginary Letters' :

> . . . Gosse dribbling along about 'events at the Art Club which were *widely discussed at the time*' [italics mine] [Pound's] when he might have said simply 'Algernon got drunk and stove in all the hats in the cloakroom'.   (*Pavannes*, pp. 61 f.)

This is, of course, Pound the eccentric — who incidentally never was addicted to drink or any other common vice — making a somewhat puerile stand for his fellow-eccentric, but his characteristic view is that 'any poet might be justified in taking to drink on finding himself born into a world full of Gosses, Comstocks, and Sumners' (*Essays*, p. 292). Gosse's name became for Pound a symbol for everything he hated about the official English culture of his London years, the world of *The Times* and the Royal Academy. In *Guide to Kulchur* he says : 'It was Gosse's generation that was contemptible' (p. 227), whereas '. . . the men ten years older than Gosse were *simpatici* and had a very much larger humanity'.[241]

One reason for Pound's recording, in lines 9–10, Elkin Mathews' visit to Swinburne in Putney is his opinion that 'there is more Swinburne, and perhaps more is to be told of the tragedy, in a few vignettes than is to be found in all Gosse's fusty volume' (*Essays*, p. 291) :

> and when old Mathews went he saw the three teacups
>   two for Watts Dunton who liked to let his tea cool.

Since 1879 Swinburne had lived, 'heavily invigilated', in the 'dull little villa' (Gosse's phrase) belonging to Theodore Watts-Dunton (1832–1914), 'the retired provincial solicitor with literary interests',[242] who had removed him from the artists' milieu in London 'when he seemed actually at the doors of death'.[243] There, at The Pines, he speedily recovered. Watts saw to it that 'the sharp pangs of rebellion and revolt, the disorders of excess, the ecentricities of genius were deftly suppressed', and Hare adds :

> With what determined tact, with what soft yet unremitting persuasion Watts laboured to tame his captive poet, to reform his genius to the accepted moral standards of the Victorian middle class![244]

Seen in the light of Hare's observation, Pound's remarks on what Mathews had witnessed provide a rather revealing picture of the taming achieved, i.e. the removal from the brandy-bottle to the teacup, that vessel of middle-class Victorianism — and it is only appropriate that Watts, who was opposed to any hot-blooded excitement in Algernon, should drink his tea cool.

Whether these teacups correspond to actual fact is, however, another question, since Sir Max Beerbohm's classic account speaks of 'whiskey-toddy' as *the* drink at The Pines.[245] Are we here faced with the method which brought discredit to Ford Madox Ford, who said in the preface to *Ancient Lights* : 'This book, in short, is full of inaccuracies as to facts, but its accuracy as to impressions is absolute'?[246] Whatever the answer is, Pound was not the only one who did not appreciate Watts-Dunton's rescue work, as we can see from both Gosse and Hare.

Elkin Mathews carried

> . . .   Algernon's suit case *once*
> when he, Elkin, first came to London (ll. 12–13).

This was in 1887. Pound sees this as his 'one glory' (l. 11), and the lines are probably intended to recall, for his own gratification — the reader, as in so many instances in the *Cantos*, is not sufficiently initiated — the veneration with which Mathews spoke of Swinburne. J. Lewis May, who sees in Mathews' partnership with John Lane, and its break-up, 'something of a tragedy', speaks of 'the shy and meditative Mathews', 'who never ought to have left the calm of Cathedral Yard, Exeter', where he had run a 'snug little bookshop'. [247] This is certainly only the view of someone blinded by the success of John Lane's Bodley Head Press, but it is an irony of fate that the young Ezra Pound, gradually turning from an exuberant aesthete into a militant rebel, should choose as his publisher such a timid little man, for whom the publishing of a book like *Lustra* was, as we shall see in discussing lines 35–38, sheer agony.

POUND'S STRUGGLE

In the next three lines we see Pound suddenly pause and reflect :

> But given what I know now I'd have
> got through it somehow . . .   Dirce's shade
>   or a blackjack.   (ll. 14—16)

The recording of moments of self-analysis is, as Emery has pointed out, [248] the entirely new element in the *Pisan Cantos*. Of the very few such passages ours is the most revealing, for neither before nor after Canto LXXXII does Pound come so close to admitting that his lifelong struggle as an artist and political economist would have been more successful if he had always based it on the kind of fundamental knowledge which he believes he now possesses; and had he done so, the context seems to imply, he might even have succeeded in the place where he began : London.

'In 1909 the poet from Hailey, Idaho had arrived to begin the siege of the imperial capital', says Henry F. May, [249] who is not the only one to employ such a martial metaphor. Ford Madox Ford, after speaking of the *Yellow Book Group*, which brought back 'times such as London had never seen since the Mermaid Tavern closed its doors', but which, according to him, 'died of the trial of Oscar Wilde and were swept off the carpet for good by the South African war', puts it thus :

> They had a short, once more Parisio-Anglo-American revival in London in the 13's and 14's under the aegis and the powerful impulsion of Mr. Ezra Pound . . . [They] held high the banners of vorticism, imagism, futurism . . . So that for the instant it looked as if the conquest of London were, indeed, at hand. But August 1914 blew all that out of existence. [250]

Leaving aside the much-discussed question of whether Pound really was the leader of any of the movements, let us extend the metaphor in terms of the *Odyssey* and say that London was to Pound what Troy was to Odysseus. This American 'Wily One' soon met with splendid success among some of the statelier 'heroes', notably, as will be seen later, Ford and Yeats, and most of the banner-bearers of his own generation accepted him as their champion, though some of them envied or mocked him (as T. E. Hulme probably did at times). Alas, however, there were also the more conservative literary 'heroes', especially, of course, those of Gosse's generation, not forgetting the English public, a potential stumbling-block for any foreigner. So it came about that Odysseus-Pound, despite his success with his adherents, felt himself to be rejected, as indeed he was. He was unaware that, like Odysseus at Troy, he was 'among people of different heredity'. Stanford says of the Homeric Odysseus :

> In such circumstances a person of prudence — especially if, like Odysseus, he has a dubious ancestry and comes from a remote and inglorious island[251] — would be specially careful to conform to local etiquette. He is a marked man. Any individualism on his part will confirm the suspicion that he is an outsider; any ingenuity will prove he is a twister, any over-cleverness that he is a cad.[252]

So apt is this remark that it might have been written about Pound himself, or indeed any like-minded foreigner in Britain.

Pound, of course, scorned this sort of prudence, met the suspicion of the English with contempt, and allied himself with the growing number of those who, particularly in his eyes, were also oppressed. Having summed up his scorn for the English cultural scene in *Hugh Selwyn Mauberley*, which was his definitive farewell to London, he took up residence in Paris in 1921. 'Ezra a few years before', wrote Ford, 'had been called the greatest bore in Philadelphia, so ceaselessly had he raved about London and Yeats and myself to uninterested Philadelphians. Now he was an Anglophobe.'

Yet something similar happened in Paris too. After a brilliant career as an instigator of literary events, and after various musical and sculptural activities, he found himself 'discovering with startling rapidity that all Frenchmen were swine and all French art the product of scoundrels'.[253] Thus Pound, who in '1918 began investigation of causes of war, to oppose same', and who was gradually moving towards what he himself styled the 'renunciation of poetry for politics',[254] settled in Mussolini's Italy, which 'provided him with all the future he wanted'.[255] Nevertheless, his first

Troy, London, remained unconquered, a defeat from which, we may justly say, he has never quite recovered.

In Pisa, as we have seen, he blames his deficient knowledge of — shall we say — human nature for his failure. Yet the tactics employed in his struggle to convert London into a place congenial to the 'serious artist' — one important feature to be its freedom from the ills of usury — were not entirely inappropriate.

> To have gathered from the air a live tradition,

i.e., as the elliptical 'Dirce's shade' seems to imply, to have properly studied tradition, like Landor, [256] and then to have revived and advocated it,

> This is not vanity   (81 : 100/557).

Even the use of a 'blackjack', i.e. main force, is justifiable in such a struggle, if it is not the 'sabre-chop that kills', but the 'scalpel-incision that cures'. [257]

> (To break the pentameter, that was the first heave),   (81 : 96/553)

says Pound parenthetically, but purely artistic revolt, in the manner of the Rebel Art campaign of 1914—1915, with its organ, 'called — prophetically — *Blast*', [258] led Pound on to an economic revolt based on the theories of Major Douglas and voiced in A. R. Orage's magazine, called — again prophetically — the *New Age*. When, in Canto XLVI, Pound recalls his visit to the exhibition organized by the Italian Fascist party in 1932 to celebrate the tenth anniversary of Mussolini's rise to power, he makes rather a broad hint as to the effect the *New Age* might have had in England. After recording someone's surprised question to Major Douglas about the fact that in his system of Social Credit the collection of taxes would be unnecessary, Pound goes on to say :

> . . .   That office?
> Didja see the Decennio?
> ?
> Decennio exposition, reconstructed offices of Il Popolo,
> Waal, ours was like that . . .   (46 : 25/241).

The fact that the reconstruction of the office in which Mussolini started editing *Popolo D'Italia* in 1914 reminded Pound of theirs, i.e. the editorial office of the *New Age*, is very significant to him, because this superficial similarity eloquently confirmed his convictions that the ideas spread by the *Popolo* and the *New Age* were essentially the same. But as the decisive

110

'scalpel-incision', Mussolini's march on Rome, had no counterpart in England, his going to live in Fascist Italy had to make up for it. As Stella Bowen observes : 'He had become a convert to the principles of Douglas' Credit System. In Mussolini's domestic finance, he claimed to see most of these principles in operation.'[259]

It appears, however, that his residence in Italy did not altogether compensate for the refusal in all other countries to recognize Douglas' economic views, and hence his own too. England remained nevertheless his greatest challenge, paradoxically even more so than his own country, as he says outright in the first of his transcribed broadcasts : 'and I think I am perhaps still speaking a bit more to England than to the United States' (Dec. 7, 1941). Italy was merely the model to be imitated in his self-imposed mission to enlighten Anglo-Saxondom. He saw

> England off there in black darkness (27 : 129/134),

the same as Russia.

Pound probably attaches deep significance to the fact that it was the Italian Bellotti, the owner of a Soho restaurant which Pound frequented, who pointed out to him the inscription on the Shakespeare monument in Leicester Square :

> and in 40 years no one save old Bellotti
> 'There is no darkness but ignorance'
> had read the words on the pedestal.[260]

At Pisa Bellotti's discernment is recorded as, we may take it, an instance of 'the specifically ... Italian sense of civilization' (July 24, 1943), which Pound stressed in his broadcasts from Rome in contrast to the absence of such a sense in England and America. A passage from the 1942 pamphlet, *A Visiting Card*, leaves no doubt as to what Pound equates with the darkness which he sees in England and, especially, America :

> We are still in the same darkness which John Adams, Father of the Nation, described as 'downright ignorance of the nature of coin, credit, and circulation'.[261]

To pierce this darkness, above all in the minds of the English, was the primary intention behind Pound's broadcasts from Italy. He made use of Rome Radio because he considered it 'the only way of communication left open' (July 24, 1943), and because he uncritically believed the preamble read out every time before the microphone was given to him : that he was allowed to speak as a result of 'the Fascist policy of intellectual freedom

111

and free expression of opinion by those who are qualified to hold it'.
As he heard nothing of the kind from a British transmitter, he still has
it in the *Pisan Cantos* :

> ... Oh my England
> that free speech without free radio speech is as zero
> and but one point needed for Stalin. [262]

Even the passage that can be called Pound's England Lyric, at the end of
Canto LXXX, shows him still preoccupied with the question of what
would dispel the said darkness from that country. He is inspired to write
in the vein of Browning's 'Home-thoughts, from Abroad', chiefly because
Churchill, that 'arrant coward and clever scene shifter' (July 17, 1943),
who was also responsible for the return to the gold standard (V. 74 : 4/452),
has been defeated at the polls :

> Oh to be in England now that Winston's out
> Now that there is room for doubt.

He is interested in the new Labour government, not because of the
post-war problems facing it, but mainly because its coming to power
kindles in him the hope that

> the bank may be the nation's, [263]

and that

> ... money be free again,

i.e. off the gold standard. Nevertheless he cannot help doubting Labour's
honesty :

> To watch how they'll slip and slide
> watch how they'll try to hide
> the real portent   (80 : 92/549).

Gradually, however, Pound moves away from his monetary obsessions,
and we may agree with Forrest Read that there is, especially in Canto
LXXX, some kind of 'reconciliation with England'. [264] Having lyrically
roamed through the 'gothic' history of England in much-admired stanzas, [265]
he utters pure home-thoughts about the London of his early career. He
has been 'hard as youth sixty years' (80 : 91/548), but now his heart melts,
and clings to the things that have survived the war :

112

and the Serpentine will look just the same
and the gulls be as neat on the pond
and the sunken garden unchanged
and God knows what else is left of our London
                    my London, your London   (80 : 94/551).

THE SWIMMER

Lines 17—21 resume the musing over Swinburne's life. The fact that
Pound chooses the much written-about swimming-accident which he had
already given as one of the vignettes in 'Swinburne versus his Biographers'
makes it obvious that he is still fired with the spirit of his attack on Gosse.
Both in his Swinburne biography and in his *Portraits and Sketches* (1912)
Gosse took great care to establish the truth about this accident, in order
to debunk the myth which was growing up around it. [266] This was,
however, the kind of truth for which Pound did not care, as opposed
to the truth about Swinburne's disorderliness. In the already-quoted
'Imaginary Letter' he states unequivocally : 'If people would forget a bit
more, we might have a real love of poetry'. Thus he finds nothing but
distraction from such love in Gosse's 'cautioning us against De Mau-
passant's account of Swinburne, and saying that De M's unbridled fancy
gave great offence when it reached the recluse at Putney' (*Pavannes*, p. 61).

Pound would probably far more readily subscribe to the opinion of
Ford Madox Ford, who unravelled the matter thus :

> One of Maupassant's *contes* tells how Swinburne's head with
> its features and hair of a Greek god rose from the sea beside the
> French writer's boat three miles out in the Mediterranean and
> how it began gloriously to converse. And so conversing Swinburne
> had swum beside the boat to the shore. No doubt Maupassant
> had his share of a poet's imagination. But Swinburne certainly
> could swim. [267]

Though even Gosse is reminded of a myth in writing his account of
the incident, [268] Pound gives him no credit whatsoever, not least perhaps
because Gosse occasionally stressed the fact that he had been Swinburne's
friend, something that no doubt infuriated Pound.

The whole of Pound's defence is, of course, a proof of how much
Swinburne meant to him. There may even be a certain degree of
identification here : in his eyes, Swinburne was removed from London

to Putney after his riotous behaviour only because Victorian society did not wish to be shaken by anything so vital and so enthusiastically given to the idea of liberty, both religious and political. Pound, too, was forced to leave, for London, still largely 'brought up Victorian' (Impact, p. 246), still refused to have the enthusiasm of a revolutionary and vital poet injected into its blood. It was still a place where Milton received the highest praise, a state of affairs which, if we can believe Ford Madox Ford, enraged Pound so much that when yet another Milton eulogy appeared in The Times Literary Supplement he challenged the author, Lascelles Abercrombie, 'to fight a duel with him in Hyde Park'.[269] This, if true, makes Pound's departure from London an escape from justice as well.

Although Pound has never been conscious of it himself, we may also see a parallel between Swinburne's enthusiasm for Mazzini and the Italian Risorgimento — as expressed in Songs Before Sunrise (1871), and particularly in 'Hertha' — and Pound's enthusiasm for Mussolini and Fascist Italy, as demonstrated in the prose of Jefferson and/or Mussolini (1935), in some of the Cantos and elsewhere.

To return to Swinburne's swimming-accident, this is how Pound puts it at Pisa :

> When the french fishermen hauled him out he
> recited 'em
>   might have been Aeschylus
>   till they got into Le Portel, or wherever
> in the original   (ll. 17–21).

Pound is quite aware that he may be mentioning the wrong fishing port on the French Channel coast, but in adding 'or wherever in the original' he not only admits this, but appears to be making an oblique reference, coupled with a sneer, to Gosse, who so painstakingly sought to recover the 'original' story and present it to the world. According to Gosse, the French fishing vessel which picked up Swinburne, afloat on a tidal current, put in at Yport.[270] On the other hand, when Pound speaks of Le Portel it does not seem to be a mere guess; apparently he also has certain personal associations with the place of that name (V. 80 : 93/550), and if we look at one of the two passages in Thrones in which the name recurs, we discover that at least four different elements have gradually been fused in his mind :

> So that the mist was quite white on that part of the sea-coast
>   Le Portel, Phaecia
>   and he dropped the scarf in the tide-rips
>   (100 : 68).

There are (1) Pound's personal memories of Le Portel and (2) together with them, judging by the context of our Canto, his picture of Swinburne, not so much as the victim of a swimming-accident, but far more as being surrounded by 'the glory of the strong swimmer'. [271] In merging the vision of the Channel coast near Le Portel with a vision of the coast of Phaecia, Pound identifies Swinburne with (3) that other hero whose 'strong stroke in swimming' (Guide, p. 146) he has specially noted : Odysseus; and since Odysseus' struggle in the sea, 'when the raft broke and the waters went over' him (80 : 91/547), and the pity of the goddess of the sea, Ino Leucothea, the once-mortal daughter of Cadmus, [272] make up the mythical incident most frequently referred to in both Section : Rock-Drill and Thrones, [273] we recognize in it (4) an image of Pound's own struggle 'from under the rubble heap' (90 : 66) 'upward/and to Castalia' (90 : 67) and beyond, on to the tensile light of heaven.

Although Pound visualizes his own ascent mainly as a 'Dantescan rising', and, since 'Aquinas [is] not valid now' (Letters, p. 418), 'by no means an orderly [one]' (74 : 21/471), we may confidently say that it is the lasting impression of Swinburne the 'strong swimmer' that is at the bottom of his other vision of the same ascent. Had it not been for Swinburne, the Odysseus-Leucothea episode might never have been employed here, despite Pound's conspicuous fondness for sea-imagery, which also shows in his use of Dante's boat image, 'O voi che siete in piccioletta barca', [274] and of Landor's also (V. 1. 71). We must not forget, moreover, that although he has had his early enthusiastic hymn to Swinburne, 'Salve O Pontifex', withdrawn from circulation, he said as late as 1942 : 'Théophile Gautier and Swinburne are members of my church' (Impact, p. 59).

In suggesting, in our Canto, that what Swinburne recited to his rescuers on the fishing-boat 'might have been Aeschylus', and not Victor Hugo, as Pound himself wrote in 'Swinburne versus his Biographers', he may be remembering that George Moore once came upon Swinburne in his rooms, 'howling Aeschylus' (Essays, p. 292). T. Earl Welby has it that during his last days, when he was stricken with the fatal pneumonia, Swinburne's 'sweet, frail voice went on and on, repeating the choruses of Aeschylus and of Sophocles'. [275] At the same time, the naming of Aeschylus is clearly a transitional device, a link-up with the Agamemnon ellipsis.

THE AGAMEMNON ELLIPSIS

Pound admitted to W. H. D. Rouse that he was 'too god damn iggurunt of Greek', but went on :

When I do sink into the Greek, what I dig up is too con-
centrative; I don't see how to get unity of the *whole* (*Letters*,
p. 363).

In tracing the long history of the elliptical rendering of the *Agamemnon*
in ll. 22–29, we do well to bear in mind these and other, similar comments
which Pound makes about his knowledge of Greek. Why, we may ask,
does he bother to use Greek in the *Cantos*, especially since he is aware
that the 'misprints occurring every time I endeavour to quote that
language must give infinite pleasure to those students who know
(professionally) enough of it to be sure that I don't' (*Guide*, p. 300)? A
broad answer to this was given in one of his radio speeches : 'You may
remember that Doc Rouse called Greek a necessity of civilized life. It is.
So is Latin.' (July 24, 1943) Hence, these languages must necessarily appear
in a work which is to set up a new Paideuma. Perhaps we shall be prepared
to concede, after discussing the following lines, that some of Pound's
unabashed attempts at quoting Greek and Latin, however full of errors
— because he is in the habit of quoting from memory — have nevertheless
a good deal of interest.

Pound first set down his attitude to the *Agamemnon*, and Greek drama
in general, in an article which appeared in the *Egoist* in 1919, entitled
'Translation of Aeschylus' (V. *Essays*, pp. 267–275), and later in Chapter
12 of *Guide to Kulchur* under the title : 'Aeschylus and . . .'. In addition
there are stray remarks on the subject in the *ABC of Reading*[276] and in
other essays. That his attitude has recently changed slightly is evident
from his translation of Sophocles' *Women of Trachis*. Eliot also speaks of
unpublished notes (V. *Essays*, p. 27 n.).

Pound's opinion is (1) that 'the greek writers were on the down grade
AFTER Homer' (*Guide*, p. 93), and, therefore, 'taken as READING
MATTER, I do NOT believe that the Greek dramatists are up to Homer'
(*ABC of Reading*, p. 47). He feels also that (2) 'even Aeschylus is rhetorical'
(*Essays*, p. 27), and that (3) there are no translations; Gilbert Murray
— Pound agrees with Eliot and quotes him — 'erected a barrier between
Euripides and the reader more impassable than the greek language' (*Guide*,
p. 92).

Pound is not alone in holding such views, but most of those who share
them are far more moderate. Pound's strong formulations clearly reveal
that he was dissatisfied with Greek drama from the start, so that he was
never dispassionate enough to discover it as a world in itself. Instead,
however, of leaving it to more patient people, he could not resist the
challenge arising from the lack of adequate translations. In the wake of
the majority of classical scholars, he singled out Aeschylus' *Agamemnon*

116

as the best specimen and began to indulge his passion for modern versions. He tells us that Eliot was persuaded to try his hand at it too, but gave up, so that he 'took over' (Guide, p. 92). In 1936 Faber and Faber published a verse translation of the Agamemnon by Louis MacNeice, especially written for the stage. It is a pity that Pound failed to notice it, for it is *the* attempt by a modern poet to render the play in English, and all the more a pity because Eliot, as a director of Faber and Faber, probably gave it his approval. The only modern versions of Greek drama expressly approved of by Pound are those by Cocteau. What Pound himself did to the Agamemnon he describes in Guide to Kulchur :

> I twisted, turned, tried every elipsis and elimination. I made the watchman talk nigger, and by the time you had taken out the remplissage, there was no play left on one's page. (pp. 92 f.)

Lines 22–26 of our Canto are, we may confidently assume, more or less identical with what *was* left on the page :

> 'On the Atreides' roof'
> 'like a dog . . . and a good job
>   ΕΜΟΣ ΠΟΣΙΣ . . . ΧΕΡΟΣ
>   hac dextera mortuus
>   dead by this hand. [277]

Line 22 comes from the very beginning of the play. The watchman informs us that he is 'couchant upon the palace roof of the Atreidae'. Line 23 gives the watchman's simile : he says that he is lying there 'like a hound'. [278] But, as Achilles Fang has pointed out, Pound must also have had in mind the passage from the *Iliad* where Achilles mocks Agamemnon :

> You drunkard, with eyes like a bitch and heart like a fawn. [279]

This view is strengthened by the fact that in Canto V Pound had already made use of the epithet 'Dog-eye! !' in connection with Alessandro de' Medici (5 : 19/23). Moreover, we know from the essay 'Early Translators of Homer' that Achilles' speaking of Agamemnon as the ' "dog-faced" chicken-hearted' one impressed Pound as one of the best instances of Homer's writing 'in the actual swing of words spoken' (Essays, p. 250), and Fang refers to a comment of Pound's in the New English Weekly where Achilles' words are alluded to as 'a phrase frequent in the mouth of Mr. Hemingway and other large-hearted authors, which describes . . . men in terms of totemism and heritage'. [280]

117

Having thus also — indirectly — evoked the presence of Agamemnon, Pound rushes straight on to the point where the deed is acknowledged by Clytemnestra : '. . . and a good job'. The chorus of Elders sees her in the now open palace, standing, an image of vengeance, between the bodies of Agamemnon and Cassandra, saying boldly :

> . . . here is Agamemnon, my husband, done to death, the work of this right hand, a workman true. So stands the case. [281]

Pound's 'and a good job' is to render what Weir Smyth, translating literally, makes 'a workman true'. In discussing Browning's translation of the *Agamemnon* (1877) — the only one which he found worthy of consideration in 1919 — Pound had put side by side the Greek, the Latin of Thomas Stanley's 1811 Cambridge edition, Browning's version and his own 'bungling translation' of this passage (V. *Essays,* p. 269 f.). He admired the economy of words in the Latin version, which used even fewer words to say 'done to death, the work of this right hand' (Weir Smyth) than the Greek, which is exactly the reason why Pound chose 'hac dextera mortuus' for our Canto, adding underneath the literal translation of it, to repeat, as it were, his comment : 'I can conceive no improvement on the Latin' (*Essays,* p. 270). Why he had to use the Greek, merely to say 'my husband . . . hand' (ΕΜΟΣ ΠΟΣΙΣ . . . ΧΕΡΟΣ), is hard to tell, unless we accept the naive reason that because it is, after all, a Greek play, there must be a little Greek, just to make the reader pause and realize this fact. We see, of course, that the Latin fills the gap between 'my husband . . . hand' exactly; but the Greek for 'hand' is actually superfluous, since it is already contained in 'hac *dextera*'.

To sum up : the passage in our Canto is intended to prove, like the corresponding part of his 1919 essay, that 'Browning's Aeschylus, to say nothing of forty other translations of Aeschylus, is unreadable' (*Essays,* p. 270). Hence there is not one phrase that could be said to come from Browning. [282] Although Pound called Browning's *Men and Women* 'the most interesting poems in Victorian England' (*Essays,* p. 419), and although he professed to 'have read Browning off and on for seventeen years with no small pleasure and admiration', [283] he was unable 'to get through his *Agamemnon*' (*Essays,* p. 269). If, in the *Cantos,* Browning has 'his name in the record' (97 : 24), it is not for his Aeschylus translation, but above all for his *Sordello,* the form of which Pound tried to make his model for the *Cantos,* but, as evident from the cancellation of the original versions of Cantos I–III, later found inimitable. That is why he wrote :

> Hang it all, Robert Browning,
> there can be but one 'Sordello' (2 : 6/10).

Quite apart from following up Swinburne's passion for the Greek drama and recalling Pound's 'labouring'[284] the *Agamemnon*, this ellipsis forms part of a whole net of references — to this play and the rest of the *Oresteia* — which Pound has, so to speak, cast over his *Cantos* as one of his structural devices. Already in Part One we had occasion, in connection with Pound's allusions to Troy and to a time when passion and violence reigned supreme, to refer to the *Agamemnon* passage where the Chorus comments on Helen's name. The Chorus says, to give Weir Smyth's version once more :

> — who named that bride of the spear and source of strife with the name of Helen? For, true to her name, a Hell she proved to ships, Hell to men, Hell to City . . .[285]

Finding parallels to the Troy legend in medieval France, and especially since the name of Eleanor of Aquitaine vaguely rhymes with that of Helen,[286] Pound echoed this choral passage in three variations. In Canto XLVI, however, the agent of destruction is no longer a woman, but something which, to Pound, brings far greater ruin to the world :

> Aurum est commune sepulchrum. Usura commune sepulchrum.
> Helandros kai heleptolis kai helarxe.
> Hic Geryon est. Hic hyperusura.   (46 : 28 f. / 245)

The first two epithets, 'helandros' (man-slaying) and 'heleptolis' (city-destroying) are directly transliterated from *Agamemnon* 689—690. The third, 'helarxe', is, as F. Peachy says in Appendix A of the *Index*, 'coined by Pound on the same pattern, from ἐλ- plus ἀρχή (note that Pound likes to transcribe χ by x)'. Thus it means 'government-wrecking'. Geryon, the three-headed or three-bodied monster, is seen by Dante in the *Inferno* XVII.

The shift of emphasis in this, Pound's strongest single condemnation of gold and usury, is characteristic. On the human level, the real villain is not woman, but the man who usurps the right to issue money for his private gain,[287] thus turning the creation of money into the most 'jealously guarded'[288] secret, so that :

> '. . . The general public will probably not
> 'see it's against their interest.'   (46 : 27/243)

Since it is this very man, the usurer, who, true to his puritanical religion, directs 'popular attention to the minor sins, particularly that of Lust', and uses woman

>   . . .   as red herring
> to keep man's mind off the creation of money   (78 : 60/514),

Pound has, in his hell Cantos (XIV and XV), 'purposely avoided the possibility of sex's stealing the limelight from fraud'.[289]

If we look at what Pound calls, beyond the human level, the 'doom of Atreus' (77 : 49/501), we find that he may have borrowed less from Aeschylus and his 'impassioned contemplation' of 'the principle of Retribution', of which Clytemnestra is 'only an instrument',[290] than from Homer, who, when treating the Atridae, above all tells the tale of the evil wrought by the Mycenian gold.[291] When Pound says about the Este :

>   . . .   and the house
> Called also Atreides   (8 : 32/36 f.),

he must be implying that they were locked in a Blood Feud comparable to that in the House of Atreus; but he is clearly making an analogy to what happened in 'Mycenae rich in gold'[292] when he writes :

> and they say the gold her grandmother carried under her
> skirts for Jeff Davis
> drowned her when she slipped from the landing boat;
> doom of Atreus.[293]

Hence we may say that Pound feels Agamemnon's doom to be also a fall into the 'commune sepulchrum' which is gold.

Passages from *Section : Rock-Drill* and *Thrones* show, however, that Pound has come to realize the importance of the dénouement of Aeschylus' *Oresteia* :

> Was not unanimous
> > ’Aθάνα broke tie,
> That is 6 jurors against 6 jurors
> > > needed ’Aθάνα.   (87 : 31)

This is preceded by the Chinese radical No. 77, meaning 'to stop, to desist':

through which Pound seems to imply that 'Athene Pronoia' (109 : 106), i.e. Athene endowed with 'the providence of the gods', came to 'deliver us from the burden of futility, from the never-ending chain of vengeances

120

reavenged'. [294] Thus she ushered in a new era, inaugurated by an act of divine forgiveness, so that in future murder would no longer call for new murder, but would be judged by a state court standing above mere vengeance. It is in this light that we must read Pound's observation : 'Jury trial was in Athens' (85 : 19 & 109 : 126). Though he asserts that there was complete justice in the China of the Shang dynasty (BC 1766–1121), he considers the changes in the function of the Areopagus, which are reflected in Aeschylus, to have brought a true advance towards ideal equity, and so he comments :

> Right, all of it, was under Shang
> save what came in Athens.   (87 : 31)

Pound must have had mainly this in mind when he wrote in his 'Sextant', contrary to what he generally holds about the Greeks at large : 'The Greek TRAGEDIANS : rise of civic responsibility' (*Guide*, p. 352).

Finally, we may conclude from the fact that the figure of Cassandra is intoduced into the *Pisan Cantos* that Pound himself, caught in the net of America's 'rising θέμις' (80 : 71/526), feels somewhat like Agamemnon come home to the avenger. Cassandra's eyes, which are 'like tigers', [295] may inspire in him something of the all-pervading undercurrent in Aeschylus' *Agamemnon* : anxiety, [296] an anxiety created by his own impending doom.

BLUNT THE BULLFIGHTER

The three lines following upon the *Agamemnon* ellipsis are in so far the most obscure portion of Canto LXXXII as neither Packard nor 'brother Percy' have yet been identified : [297]

> believe Lytton first saw Blunt in the bull ring
> as it might have been brother Packard
> and 'our brother Percy'   (ll. 27–29).

We shall therefore restrict ourselves to a discussion of line 27, a policy which is justified, since lines 28–29 very probably contain merely another analogy.

The recently published letters of Edward Robert, First Earl of Lytton, the English diplomat and poet (1831–1891), prove Pound to be quite wrong in his belief that Lytton first met Wilfrid Scawen Blunt (1840–1922) 'in the bull ring'. They first met in Lisbon in 1865, when Blunt joined the British Legation there. Blunt, it is true, 'had won quite a reputation as a matador', when he was 'an attaché at Madrid in 1862', and Lytton wrote to his wife : 'His [Blunt's] great passion in life is — Bullfighting — and he has already killed three bulls with his own hand.'[298] The man who first saw Blunt 'in the bull ring' was Lady Gregory's husband, Sir William Gregory. 'He', wrote Lady Gregory, 'had told us how ... at a bull fight in Madrid he had been struck by the extraordinary good looks of a young matador awaiting the rush of the bull in the arena and asking who he was heard he was an attaché from the English Embassy, Wilfrid Blunt.'[299]

Pound knew Blunt personally; with Yeats he went to celebrate Blunt's seventieth birthday in 1910,[300] and he seems to have been friendly with Blunt's wife, Lady Anne, too, as a reference in Canto LXXX suggests (V. 80 : 93/550). The reason why he placed a recollection of Blunt the bullfighter in our Canto is probably to give a contrast to the old Blunt, who, after the outbreak of World War One, had 'barred his front door and put up a sign "BELLIGERENTS WILL PLEASE GO ROUND TO THE KITCHEN" ' (*Letters*, p. 87). As we can gather from the 'Pull down thy vanity' chant of the previous Canto, Pound must have tried to see Blunt, in spite of the barricaded front door :

> To have, with decency, knocked
> That a Blunt should open   (81 : 100/557).

Whatever the motive behind Pound's call, here in Pisa it seems to him by no means to have been vanity on the part of a young man.

THE PRINTING PRESS

The next four lines (30–33) combine allusions to the Italian Renaissance with references to the cultural activities of the American Founding Fathers :

> Basinio's manuscript with the
> greek moulds in the margin
> Otis, Soncino,
> the 'marble men' shall pass into nothingness.

In bringing together Basinio, Otis and Soncino, who have each been introduced separately in earlier Cantos, Pound attempts to drive home the importance of the printing press as a means of immortalizing cultural achievements. In Canto XXX he devotes no fewer than 19 lines to excerpts from what is presumably the dedication of the 1503 Petrarch edition, written by the printer, Hieronymus Soncinus. [301] Although Pound quotes it mainly for the sake of the argument it contains about the invention of italic type — it is obviously aimed at those who, he thinks, too readily assume that the famous Aldus Manutius (1450–1515) deserves all the credit for it — what we have to bear in mind for our passage is the fact that Soncino had '... printers not vile and vulgar', but

> notable and sufficient compositors
> and a die-cutter for greek fonts ...   (30 : 148/153).

Soncino and other Renaissance printers, then, were sufficiently equipped for the printing of a manuscript like that of Basinio de Basanii (1425–1457), who put

> greek moulds in the margin

of his *Isottaeus*, the poem about Sigismondo Malatesta's love for Isotta degli Atti. Basinio, whose literary 'duel' with Procellio Pandone (1405–1485) is included in the Malatesta Cantos, [302] 'left greek tags in his margin', Pound clearly states in *Thrones*, for the purpose of 'moulding his cadence' (104 : 92). This is nothing but an elliptical version of the fuller statement about this poet, whom he calls 'the most intelligent of the Quattrocento Latinists', in the *ABC of Reading* :

> In the margins of his Latin narrative you can still see the tags of
> Homer that he was using to keep his melodic sense active. [303]

Pound's contention seems to be that the America of the Founding Fathers possessed men comparable in stature to Basinio, the one singled out being James Otis (1725–1783); but, as Pound discovered on reading John Adams' correspondence, this lawyer and one-time Advocate General, as steeped in Classical Learning as the men of the Italian Renaissance, had no printer like Soncino to communicate his insights. As John Adams tells us :

> Otis wrote on greek prosody
>> I published what he wrote on the latin.

He continues, in Pound's adaptation :

> I begged Otis to print it (the greek prosody)
> He said there were no greek types in America
> and if there were, were no typesetters cd/ use 'em. [304]

As we see, this is a situation quite different from that described by Soncino in Canto XXX. The loss of this work 'for lack of a competent printer' is serious in so far as Pound considers 'the culture of Adams and Jefferson . . . a latin culture with a mixture of greek' (*Impact*, p. 26), but more serious still is, as John Adams wrote, the fact 'that the true history of the American Revolution [can]not be recovered', because 'the memorials of Mr. James Otis and Mr. Samuel Adams'[305] were destroyed before anybody had a mind to print them. Adapting Adams, Pound writes :

> Joseph Hawley, Otis, Sam Adams, Hancock
> add Jay, without knowing their actions
> you know not what made us our revolution   (71 : 166/442),

and Adams himself was moved to write :

> If ever human beings had a right to say :
>   'Hos ego versiculos feci, tulit alter honores;
>   Sic vos, non vobis mellificatis apes',
> they were James Otis and Samuel Adams; and to them ought statues to be erected.[306]

Although Pound sees the 'Jefferson-Adams Letters as a Shrine and a Monument',[307] most of the other 'Fathers of the Republic' (*Impact*, p. 19), i.e. 'the "marble men" [,]shall pass into nothingness',[308] since no printer has given permanence to their actions and motives. Without printers they have no scope, and are bound to fade out of human consciousness.

After line 34, the first mention of the presence of singing-birds on the wire fence round the prison-camp (cf. ll. 75—79 & 129—131), Pound continues the theme of the printing press by recalling the 'fine row' (*Letters*, p. 133) he had over *Lustra* :

> so requested Mr Clowes to sleep on the same
> and as to who wd/ pay for the composition
> if same were not used
>   (Elkin Mathews, my bantam)   (ll. 35—38).

What led to the situation ridiculed here in business-letter jargon can be seen from Pound's letters of the time. 'The idiot Mathews has got the whole volume set up in type', he wrote to Iris Barry in May 1916, 'and now has got a panic and marked 25 poems for deletion. Most of them have already been printed in magazines without causing any scandal whatsoever . . . It is part printer and part Mathews . . . The printers have gone quite mad since the Lawrence fuss.'[309] In the essay 'Murder by

124

Capital' (1933) Pound gives the probable reason for this 'panic' and shows his utter contempt for the situation : 'My one modern volume issued by Mathews was sent to the ineffable printer before dear old Elkin had read it ... The story of getting *Lustra* into print is beyond the scope of this study, it belongs to stage comedy, not even to memoirs.' (*Impact,* p. 84)

Our passage in the *Cantos* shows the deadlock in the negotiations, and it should not be overlooked that Pound remembers that Messrs William Clowes and Sons, printers and publishers of *Hymns Ancient and Modern,* were not only afraid of losing their good name, but were equally worried about sustaining a financial loss. Pound must think it only typical that scruples of the Victorian type must not interfere with one's business interests, and the effect their attitude had on him is shown in the following remark :

> Whatever economic passions I now have, began *ab initio* from having crimes against living art thrust under my perceptions (*Impact,* p. 88).

The brackets in line 38 contain, of course, the answer to the question, 'who wd/ pay for the composition / if same were not used'. Pound probably calls Mathews 'my bantam' in order to insinuate that his challenger, moneyed middle-class respectability, was a heavyweight and so bound to win.

Today we may agree with Pound that the poems in *Lustra* are 'innocent enough' (*Letters,* p. 132), and that he was 'edged into these tacit hypocrisies' (p. 131) by being forced into having the *Lustra* volume printed 'castrato' (p. 133). Mathews could, however, be 'persuaded into doing 200 copies unabridged for the elect' (p. 132). 'The thing the bourgeois will always hate', he wrote to Harriet Monroe in connection with the poem 'To a Friend Writing on Cabaret Dancers' (V. *Personae,* pp. 172 ff.), 'is the fact that I make people *real.* I treat the dancers as human beings, not as "symbols of sin". That is the crime and the "obscenity" ' (*Letters,* p. 131).

Pound considered the completion of *Lustra* a highly important stage in his career, because it was in this volume that he achieved, to a greater extent than ever before, his main goal : to produce poetry that is 'written at least as well as prose', 'that comes as close as prose, *pour donner une idée claire et précise*', something that brings 'contemporary verse up to the level of contemporary prose'.[310] When John Quinn wrote and told Pound that he had 'really enjoyed *Lustra*', Pound replied :

> I have always wanted to write 'poetry' that a grown man could read without groans of ennui, or without having to have it cooed into his ear by a flapper (*Letters,* p. 156).

Side by side with the flashback to 'poor Mathews' and the 'awful week' (*Letters*, p. 132) he spent trying to decide what to do with *Lustra*, which Clowes had already set up, we find a remark on the situation, apparently made by Augustine Birrell, critic and civil servant (1850–1933), whose 'passing comment(s) on life, pungent yet kindly' gave rise to the expressions 'Birrel(l)ism' and 'to birrell'[311] :

> 'After all' said Mr. Birrell, 'it is only the old story
> of Tom Moore and Rogers' (ll. 39–40).

Samuel Rogers (1763–1855), literary dictator in England over a long period, had, we may take it, disapproved of something that Thomas Moore (1779–1852) had written,[312] just like Clowes and Mathews, forced by public opinion, in the case of Pound's *Lustra*. Hence it is 'only the old story' of the puritanical suppression of art 'on grounds of indecorum' (*Letters*, p. 133).

Summing up the three different positions of the printing press at three different times, as hinted at in lines 30–40, we may say :

(1) In the Quattrocento the printers were the equals of the men of learning, and thus saw at once how to make their proper 'contribution to ushering in the Renaissance'.[313]

(2) In the America of the Founding Fathers the printers were culturally so far beneath the driving minds of the time that they were unaware of their proper function.

(3) In the early twentieth century printers and publishers were still so much enslaved by hypocritical moral standards that they either did not dare to have a hand in the spreading of the new realistic honesty or, if they did, were sure to be charged with obscenity, a state of affairs which has not greatly changed since.

DECADENCE

In the following five lines Pound presents an image, set against the revitalizing efforts of class-abnegating artists, of the decay of the aristocracy (ll. 41–45). When 'her Ladyship YX ... arose in the night / and moved all her furniture', it was a symptom of utter frustration. Equally, 'her Ladyship Z disliked dining alone' is intended to show that the nobility, after 'the belly-flop or collapse of a number of kingdoms and empires, all of them rotten' (*Guide*, p. 81), had lost all of its former splendour and was no longer the 'beau monde' that governed.[314] Their world might not, as yet, have disappeared completely, but it had lost its purpose and interest :

> and Kokka thought there might be some society (good) left in
> Spain, wd. he care to frequent it, my god, no![315]

Least of all did the artist of Pound's stature wish to spend his time with this dying caste. The biblical sounding

> The proud shall not lie by the proud   (l. 45)

seems to imply furthermore that pride, the only thing left to them, forced this aristocracy into lonely agony.

YEATS AND CONVERSATION

With line 46 the scene changes :

> amid dim green lighted with candles
> Mabel Beardsley's red head for a glory.

We find ourselves in the 'celtic twilight' of Yeats's flat at 18, Woburn Buildings (V. l. 56). This image brings back to Pound the characteristic atmosphere of the Monday evenings Yeats used to hold while in London. The radiant figure in the candlelight is the sister of the *Yellow Book* artist Aubrey Beardsley. She, the 'sweet Catholic saint whom ... everyone worshipped',[316] 'was an occasional guest at Yeats's'.[317] What Yeats and all the others saw in her appearance must have been, consciously or unconsciously, 'the red hair or the curled lips or the columnar throat of the Rossetti woman'.[318] Pound, at any rate, was most impressed by her hair :

> As Mabel's red head was a fine sight
> worthy of his minstrelsy   (80 : 85/542).

By 'his minstrelsy' Pound means Yeats's seven poems forming the series 'Upon a Dying Lady'. 'Mabel was stricken by cancer, and Yeats was but one of many friends to admire the gay manner in which she rose superior to her suffering'.[319]

Among the regulars at Yeats's Mondays was also John Masefield, who has called 18, Woburn Buildings the most interesting place in London in the pre-war years.[320] Pound, who found it 'frankly ridiculous ... that Masefield should be having a boom' (*Essays*, p. 387), nicknamed the author of 'I must go down to the seas again' Old Neptune; at least it seems so when we read :

> 'It is the sons pent up within a man'
> mumbled old Neptune   (80 : 84/541),

although the observation has not yet been traced. The mumbling must, however, somehow correspond to 'Mr Masefield murmuring' (l. 48), in which case we must imagine a full stop after 'Death', indicating the end of the direct speech. Pound probably considered Masefield's contributions to that 'discussion of Flaubert' (l. 50) irrelevant anyway, and if 'Old Neptune' is indeed a nickname, we may sense something rather disparaging in it. After all, Pound hated Masefield's popularity (V. *Letters*, pp. 47 & 88).

That Pound wants to show that the activities at Yeats's flat were not only literary is seen from the reference to one Miss Tomczyk, one of the mediums performing at the spiritual séances held by Yeats. Pound never shared Yeats's preoccupation with 'psychic evidence and automatic writing', but the fact that even the learned Society for Psychical Research[321] was baffled at times must have filled him with the malicious joy he always felt on discovering instances of incompetence in organized bodies.

The memories of Yeats's Mondays also bring to Pound's mind

> the idea that CONversation ...
> should not utterly wither   (ll. 53—54).

Those who met Pound at parties during his London years have observed how he could dominate a room and how he 'laid down the law about poetry', reducing other people 'to a glum silence'.[322] Jessie Chambers has recorded that he was 'the life of the party' and that 'he flung out observations in an abrupt way that reminded me of his poetry'.[323] Such observations do not make him a model CONversationalist himself. Nevertheless, his talk, if highly unconventional, like his appearance, must have been electrifying. Yeats especially, who professed to have been 'united by affection'[324] with 'this queer creature Ezra Pound',[325] seems to have enjoyed it and even to have invited it.

> Sd Mr Yeats (W. B.) 'Nothing affects these people
> except our conversation'   (83 : 106/563).

Whatever the occasion and the exact connection of this statement, Yeats was conscious of the high potentialities of conversation such as his with Pound. It is, as Hugh Kenner puts it, 'the heat of conversation generating public light'.[326]

When Pound goes on to record an address made to Yeats by Frederic W. Tancred, one of Hulme's 'satellites in 1909',[327] whose name makes Pound playfully recall his historic namesakes (l. 58) and whose resemblance to Dickens makes him regret the sinking into obscurity of such an original character (ll. 63—64), it is the neatness of wording and tone that impresses him. Hence the typographical arrangement :

> 'If you would read us one of your own choice
> > and
> > > perfect
> > > > lyrics' (ll. 58—62).

Otherwise Pound wants conversation above all to be charged with substance and intelligence. The British habit of making polite conversation is therefore apt to make him lose what little patience he has. If we except the circle of his fellow artists, we can safely say that the reason for including in the Cantos the following remark by Charles Francis Adams, American Ambassador to Great Britain from 1861 to 1868, was to voice his own opinion :

> there was no good conversation. At no single entertainment in London did I find any good conversation (48 : 34/250).

We must remember Pound's definition :

> THE CULTURE OF AN AGE is what you can pick up and/or get in touch with, by talk with the most intelligent men of the period. (Guide, p. 217)

People who bar serious thought from conversation, even though they do so out of good breeding, Pound implies, render poor service to their own culture, which may even atrophy because of it. Landor's Imaginary Conversations show, Pound has it, that a man is forced

> ... to write dialogue because there is
> > no one to converse with (80 : 77/533).

In 1933, looking back to his London years, Pound wrote that 'the best conversation was to be found, 1912 to 1914, in quadriviis et angiportis, under a railway arch out by Putney [i.e. Gaudier-Brzeska's studio], in cheap restaurants and not in official circles or in the offices of rich periodicals.' (*Impact*, p. 85)

For the next five lines, although the theme of conversation is carried on, we must leave the 'Celtic stronghold of W. B. Yeats',[328] as the judgment contained in them is based on what Pound experienced in the company of Ford Madox Ford (at one time Ford Madox Hueffer [1873–1939]) — either at the editorial office of the *English Review*, or at South Lodge, the home of Violet Hunt, Ford's wife — Pound had instituted tennis parties there — or down in Kent.

FORD MADOX FORD

'I went to England in 1908', Pound says, 'to "learn" from Yeats — and stayed to learn from Yeats *and* Ford. From 1910 onwards, Fordie and I growled at each other for nigh on twenty years. *Anyway* without all his *spumare* and his rising *soufflées*, how long it would have taken me to get to the present — wherever — if I hadn't plugged up Camden Hill almost daily when the fat man was in residence, Gawd alone knows.'[329] Pound has every reason to acknowledge his indebtedness to Ford, as Hugh Kenner shows in the chapter 'Digression — French Prose' of his *Poetry of Ezra Pound*. He sees in Ford's use of the 'time-shift', the technique of stringing together 'little shreds one contrasting with the other', an 'adumbration of the ideogrammic method itself'.[330]

Kenneth Young goes even further and says, rather oversimplifying the matter, that Pound's 'startlingly original method of writing poetry was identical with Ford's "juxtaposition of composed renderings"', and he holds that 'from this his "ideogram", despite Chinese parallels, really descended'.[331] A student of Pound must, however, qualify this in the way Kenner does when he argues that whereas Ford justified his method psychologically and 'passed it off lightly as verisimilitude : the mind remembering in various, unordered pictures', Pound has no need for such justification, as he is solely concerned with the 'realization of quiddities'. In this rendering — the device was taken over from Flaubert — as opposed to telling, to 'arrange not primarily words, but things; or words as *mimesis* of things' (in other words, said Ford, to find the 'language which renders its object accurately', i.e. *le mot juste*) is, of course, the dominating principle.[332] Thus, when Pound points out that, despite the enlightening effect on everyone present of conversation with Yeats, and 'despite

William's anecdotes' (1. 67), some of which Pound has recorded because of their pertinence,[333]

> ... old Ford's conversation was better (1. 65),

the reason is that the idea of the *mot juste* determined both its manner and its topics.

In his conversation Ford appears to have done much the same as in his writings, where, Kenneth Young comments, he 'aims at presenting the essential natures of the men and writers he discusses'. The poses he was in the habit of adopting — they were interpreted by men like H. G. Wells as an 'extraordinary drift towards self-dramatization'[334] — 'were really', Young continues, 'Ford trying out what it felt like to be, for instance, Cpt. Edward Ashburnham, the soldier-landowner of *The Good Soldier*, and observing the reactions of others to that particular sort of person'.[335] He was always intent on recording his impressions with absolute accuracy, in the wake of Flaubert, and, as Pound comments, 'never dented an idea for a phrase's sake' (1. 68).

Indeed, he is known to have preferred denting the facts, which Wells interprets as a 'copious carelessness of reminiscence'.[336] Like Flaubert, however, he did not primarily arrange words, but ideas and impressions. Words and facts were to him merely mimetic tools that he 'forged' according to his needs. Most other people, even Yeats, Pound implies, are much more given to being dragged away from the concept in mind by the tone and impressiveness of a phrase. The characterization :

> consisting in *res* non *verba* (1. 66)

is a compressed version of the comment found in the essay 'The Prose Tradition in Verse' :

> It is he [Ford] who has insisted, in the face of a still Victorian press, upon the importance of good writing as opposed to the opalescent word, the rhetorical tradition. (*Essays*, p. 371)

We must note, of course, that it is above all the impact of Ford's conversation that makes Pound remember it as better than Yeats's, for Pound wrote in *Polite Essays* : 'The revolution of the word began so far as it affected the men who were of my age in London in 1908, with the LONE whisper of Ford Madox Hueffer.' (p. 50) In fact, it was he who caused Pound to realize that Yeats was what he called 'a "gargoyle, a great poet but a gargoyle", meaning by gargoyle a man with peculiar or gothic opinions about writing'.[337]

Long before Pound arrived in England, Ford had been associated with another writer and had, according to H. G. Wells, 'conversed interminably with him about the precise word and about perfection in writing'.[338] That writer was Joseph Conrad, but literary history tends to ignore this association, because Ford's name became something unmentionable in most circles, due to the circumstances of his divorce from his first wife and various other things too. Pound is one of the very few who have remained faithful to him. At Pisa it is still his conviction that, compared with Yeats, Ford

. . . had more humanitas 仁 jen (l. 69).

Douglas Goldring's respect for Ford, whose assistant editor he had been in the days of the *English Review*, was equally high :

> It was Ford's mission, if a cliché may be excused, to be a Torchbearer of Civilization, an Apostle of Humanism and a transmitter to succeeding ages of a great cultural tradition. In the teeth of obloquy and at the cost of much personal discomfort and financial loss, he defined and defended, in art as in every other department of human activity, a standard of values.[339]

Stella Bowen, who was Ford's companion after the Great War,[340] speaks of Ford's 'tremendous humanity, his taste for all things living and growing and modest and un-selfconscious, and his knowledge of the aches and pains of the human heart'.[341] Since we have such testimonies, we should not be surprised to find in our text 'the juxtaposition of Latin "humanitas" and Chinese "jen" which raises the concept of the full human nature to the status of a permanent perception informing eastern and western cultures alike'.[342]

In ascribing to Ford a higher degree of humaneness,[343] Pound certainly did his share in erecting a monument to

a man of no fortune and with a name to come (1 : 4/8).

This analogy to the fate of Elpenor is particularly appropriate in the light of Graham Greene's observation that Ford's 'middle life had been made miserable by passion', but that 'he had come through it with . . . a half-belief in posterity which would care for good writing'.[344] In *Thrones* Pound has included a statement made by Ford, in connection with an interview printed in the Rapallo paper *Il Mare*,[345] as his ultimate axiom on writing :

132

And as Ford said : get a dictionary
                and learn the meaning of words.   (98 : 41; V. 100 : 71)

Concluding this discussion of Pound's recollections of Yeats and Ford in Canto LXXXII, we ought not to forget that both, in the *Pisan Cantos* and later, figure among all the other lost shipmates of Odysseus-Pound. On one occasion he quotes a line from his own version of 'The Seafarer', since he is reminded of the Old English mariner's sense of loss :

        Lordly men are to earth o'ergiven,
and he continues :

            these the companions :
        Fordie that wrote of giants
            and William who dreamed of nobility   (74 : 10 f. / 459).

Though they are dead, and though their loss, together with other losses, makes him experience a sadness unknown before,[346] their deeds and anecdotes shine on in his mind and are 'not blacked out' (78 : 57/510).

CYTHERA

Line 70 must be read as a formula :

        (Cythera   Cythera).

From the *Pisan Cantos* onwards 'Cythera' is the most frequent name used by Pound to evoke that 'great goddess' (74 : 13/462) Aphrodite. 'Cythera' is actually the name of the island (V. 24 : 111/116) on which, according to one version of the legend, the goddess landed. Otherwise the usual form is 'Cytherea', also found in Pound. Although 'Cytherea' does not occur so often as 'Cypris', it seems to be the name many poets used when their vision of the goddess was most intimate and linked with the celebration of the mysteries. Judging by his Lynx Song (79 : 66—70/ 521—525), we may indeed say that Pound himself makes it a mystic name, known, as it were, only to the initiated. The power of the 'Cytherean goddess' (*Pavannes*, p. 97), seen by Pound in its full ambiguity — 'Cythera potens' (76 : 34/485), 'Cythera egoista' (80 : 79/534), and not least 'κύθηρα δεινά',[347] i.e. 'the terrible one' — is, significantly, identified with the omnipotence of Light and Love in the passage where 'Cythera' is put twice in one line as in our Canto :

Le Paradis n'est pas artificiel

Κύθηρα,   Κύθηρα,

Moving ὑπὸ   χθονὸς enters the hall of the records
      the forms of men rose out of γέα
            Le Paradis n'est pas artificiel   (77 : 46/498).

Pound's paradise, we see here very clearly, does not lie outside natural process; on the contrary, it comes into being when the principle of fertility achieves complete fulfilment. Love must move 'under the earth' in order to bring forth new Cadmeans, new city-builders. Once again Pound's central vision emerges, the only difference being that the creative agent appears in the shape of 'Queen Cytherea' (V. 91 : 77).

When Pound goes on to quote the second line from Landor's Dirce epigram, 'With Dirce in one bark convey'd' (l. 71), we may take it that he sees the 'Stygian set' of his companions passing over Lethe, but Dirce, the beauty they lived and strove for, sails with them and still needs their care,

> Or Charon, seeing, may forget
> That he is old and she a shade. [348]

Yet where else would they be conveyed but to the 'hall of the records', and once 'Queen Cytherea' enters it they will return from oblivion and 'ascend those high places' (91 : 76) with the writer of the *Cantos*, so 'that the tone change from elegy' (91 : 77). Like the 'poor beaste' in line 72, it seems that they ought to 'be glad', because 'love follows after' them. [349] Those initiated into the mysteries of the great goddess of love and fertility are, Pound appears to imply, borne up by the assurance that, whatever happens, there will be fresh growth and novel beauty; the soil will give forth its rich crops again and Adonis will return (V. Canto XLVII).

THE CRICKET

But Pound is suddenly aroused from this vision of Love's power to heal and renew,[350] because, in the stark reality of the prison-camp, in the barren 'drill field', even the cricket refuses to be the proverbial bringer of mirth :

> Till the cricket hops
>   but does not chirrp in the drill field   (ll. 73–74).

He is suddenly aware of the 'waste land' around him,

>   . . .   where the sun beats,
> And the dead trees give no shelter, the cricket no relief. [351]

Otherwise the *Pisan Cantos* record many a moment in which Pound's spirits derived comfort and hope from the insects and other small animals that he watched from his tent.

> A lizard upheld me   (74 : 6/455),

he says about an equally dark moment, and when he is

> . . . given a new green katydid of a Sunday   (74 : 13/462)

he is reminded of Eos' lover, Tithonus (ΤΙΘΩΝΩΣ in Pound), for whom the goddess had obtained from Zeus the gift of immortality, but had forgotten to ask for eternal youth as well.

It is, however, not the Tithonus entirely shrivelled up and reduced to babbling senility that Pound receives in his tent as a companion, but a Tithonus who, as it were, has regained his youth by being changed into a chirping insect and is an 'eater of grape pulp' (74 : 13/462), a creature in which the poet sees a proof of 'the earth's continuing fertility'. [352]

The only time Pound records being cheered by the chirping of the cricket is at night, and he therefore humorously reminds the chirper that he is breaking army regulations :

> Be welcome, O cricket my grillo, but you must not
> >   sing after taps.   (78 : 58/511)

What really makes him rejoice at hearing the cricket's song is that in his mind it becomes one with Mozart's music, of which he must just have learned that it will be played again at the annual festivals :

> So Salzburg reopens
> >   Qui suona Wolfgang grillo   (78 : 58/511).

Thus, compared with such passages of merry playfulness, the absence of the cricket's song is felt as a lapse into gloom, especially if we hear in Pound's 'Till the cricket hops' an echo of Yeats's 'to where / the cricket sings', [353] here supplemented by a full negation in the but-clause.

The date that appears in the next line establishes a further link with reality :

> 8th day of September   (l. 75).

Whereas two of the altogether five recorded dates which lie within the period spent in Pisa must be related to the fact that Pound not only heard 'news by grapevine' but also read it in the 'magazines circulated by the trainees',[354] the rest of them date his experiences and moods, and, in turn, the drafting of the *Pisan Cantos*. By September 8, 1945, Pound had been in the D. T. C. Pisa for roughly four months, and there were still over two months to go before he was flown to Washington. A little later in the month the peace of mind of a sage came back to him with the first autumn rains :

> in the drenched tent there is quiet
> sered eyes are at rest   (83 : 107/564)；

and the 'September sun on the pools' (83 : 108/566) enables him to contemplate the crystal river of light again. Even so, the nearer we get to the end of our Canto, the more we become aware of the poet's 'consciousness of death as death'.[355]

THE BIRDS

The date in line 75 also appears to be the heading of the musical notation that follows (ll. 76—78).

> Three birds on the wire,

we heard Pound comment in line 34. It is in Canto LXXIX that Pound starts writing down such observations :

> with 8 birds on a wire
> or rather on 3 wires, Mr Allingham
> The new Bechstein is electric   (79 : 63/517).

He sees the birds perched on the electrically charged wires surrounding the camp and concludes humorously, in what seems to be a remark to a fellow-prisoner by the name of Allingham, that this is the latest innovation in the world of pianos. Soon after the discovery of this new game, ten lines further down, Pound reveals what makes him enjoy it and follow it through for almost three pages :

> some minds take pleasure in counterpoint
> pleasure in counterpoint,

and, hinting, as it were, that this seemingly childish game is capable of conjuring up a graver mood too, he adds :

and the later Beethoven on the new Bechstein.

Beethoven's music, we must remember, is to Pound, like his *Cantos*, 'the record of a personal struggle' (*Guide*, p. 135). At the end of our Canto we shall find, at the conclusion of Pound's superficially light-hearted musical pastime, that this takes him, like some of Beethoven's music, to the brink of the very abyss. The actual stimulus for Pound's unusual 'bird-watching' is, of course, Clement Janequin's 'Chant des Oiseaux', which is to him a perfect example of 'why the monument outlasts the bronze casting' (*ABC of Reading*, p. 54), i.e. of an 'immortal concetto', a 'masterwork [that has] the right of rebirth and recurrence'. As such he considered himself justified in including the score of the transcription in Canto LXXV made at his instigation by his friend and protégé, Gerhart Münch. As Janequin's song is 'music of representative outline' (*Guide*, p. 153), real bird-calls are imitated in it,[356] and Pound states that 'when Münch transcribed it for modern instruments the birds were still there. They ARE still there in the violin part' (*ABC of Reading*, p. 54), the part which he had printed in the *Pisan Cantos*.

It seems, moreover, that when Pound watches the birds on the Pisan wire fence, he is somehow reminded of the Janequin arrangement at which Francesco di Milano arrived 'per metamorfosi' (75 : 28/478), since he has remarked in *Guide to Kulchur* that 'Janequin's concept' gained 'its second [life] on the wires of Francesco Milano's lute' (p. 152). Hence we may say that with the birds on the prison-camp fence Janequin's song once again gains similar life. What they write 'in their treble scale' (l. 79) 'on their wire staff', Sister B. Quinn has it, is again 'a musical score, truly a "canzone degli Uccelli"'. She also points out that in a draft of the hitherto missing Canto LXXII Pound wrote :

We have heard the birds praising Janequin.[357]

NO JUST WARS

The name in line 80, given like '(Cythera   Cythera)' as an evocative formula, modulates the voices of the birds, and now, in a graver key, they leave Janequin behind and approach something like the pathos of a Beethoven :

Terreus! Terreus!

This is clearly a fusion with the cry of the swallows heard in Canto IV.
Indeed, it is likely that the birds on the wires are swallows. Though
Pound's mind visualizes with pleasure

> ... two larks in contrappunto
> at sunset   (74 : 9/457),

it is only after

> ... the lark squawk has passed out of season   (79 : 63/517) —

this apparently suggested to him, still locked up in one of the 'death cells'
(V. 74 : 4/452), a harbinger of doom — that Pound starts recording the
birds' musical score on the wire staff, and we find him saying in one
place :

> with 6 on 3, swallow-tails   (79 : 65/519).

Thus it is once again the swallows that, apart from writing an apparently
soul-oppressing cadence on the wires, cry out against all violence, as in
Canto IV and in the echo of it in Canto LXXVIII (55/508), and Pound
furnishes the appropriate text :

> there are no righteous wars in 'The Spring and Autumn'   (l. 80).

This statement is taken over from Mencius, as we can see from Pound's
1938 essay on the 'Ethics of Mencius', where he quotes it complete with
the concluding 'some are better than others' and explains : '*Spring and
Autumn* is the title of Confucius' history book.' (*Impact*, p. 127) It also
appears at the end of Canto LXXVIII, where, because of the typographical
arrangement, it is, even more than in our passage, an outright
condemnation of war :

> In 'The Spring and Autumn'
> > there
> > are
> > no
> > righteous
> > wars   (78 : 61/515).

Before, in Canto LXXVI, which also ends with a condemnation of war, he had called down curses upon all aggressors :

> woe to them that conquer with armies
> and whose only right is their power   (76 : 41/492).

In our passage, the two long explanatory lines following the Mencian comment on the absence of just wars in the annals supposedly compiled by Confucius [358] give emphasis to an attitude which may be justified as the product of post-war disillusionment, but which no government fighting a war can afford to tolerate :

> that is, perfectly right on one side or the other
> total right on either side of the battle line   (ll. 82—83).

This is, however, precisely the kind of attitude Pound was foolish enough to exhibit in his Rome broadcasts. Though he recently told Donald Hall : 'I certainly wasn't telling the troops to revolt', [359] he did say on July 20, 1943 : 'I . . . regret the modus in which the American troops obey their high commander.' Pound has a 'dislike of professional pacifists' (*Impact*, p. 252) and he considers 'the military virtues . . . a possession so precious that it is almost worth a war to preserve them' (p. 251), but when America joined the war in Europe he refused to recognize any justification for this, because he believed that the American people were led into it by nothing but lies, especially, as he thought, lies coming from Churchill (V. Broadcasts of February 3, 1942 & July 17, 1943).

This, and his insistence that 'the war was about gold, usury, and monopoly' (Jan. 29, 1942), was bound to make him a marked man. Though he had directed attention to 'usury age-old and age-thick' and the 'liars in public places' (*Personae*, p. 200) as early as the period after World War I, to repeat the same thing in far more specific terms, mixed with open attacks on particular statesmen in time of war, and that from the camp of his people's enemy, could only be regarded as treason. It may, however, give some comfort to know that the comment which triggered off this discussion (ll. 82—83) was made after the end of the war :

> Now that there's room for doubt   (80 : 92/549).

This was also true after the Great War, when probably more people were inclined to agree with Pound than after the last one. [360]

The five subsequent lines are in so far related to the foregoing as they contain an observation on the time-lag between the discovery of something that might prevent a future war and its tardy recognition :

and the news is a long time moving
a long time in arriving
                    through the impenetrable
crystalline, indestructible
                    ignorance of locality   (ll. 84—88).

'Artists are the antennae of the race', Pound maintains. 'Artists and poets undoubtedly get excited and "overexcited" about things before the general public.' (*ABC of Reading*, pp. 81 & 82) Nobody can deny that this applies to Pound himself to an unusually high degree, particularly the 'over-excited'; but Pound also shows, more than most other artists, an obstinate determination to get his discoveries recognized, so much so that he is virtually unaware of the moment when he starts blundering or even committing technical treason. The more he became what he himself styles with grim humour a 'credit-crank' (*Guide*, p. 182), the less patient he became with people who would not listen. We find many instances of this in his prose and also in his broadcasts, e.g. : 'I mean you have been such dull thundering asses that you have not, not for forty years, listened to any Englishman or alien critic who could tell you anything sensible.' (June 19, 1943).

The Englishman they should above all have listened to is, we may guess, Major C. H. Douglas, the founder of Social Credit. H. L. Mencken managed to impress Pound greatly with a remark about the refusal of a nation to accept economic changes, or indeed any changes : '. . . I believe that all schemes of monetary reform collide inevitably with the nature of man in the mass. He can't be convinced in anything less than a geological epoch.' (*Guide*, p. 182) Thus these words are variously echoed in the *Cantos*,[361] and we should be open to the charge of misinterpretation if we did not connect the 'crystalline' in our passage with Mencken's 'geological epoch', as it has nothing to do with Dante's crystalline heaven here.

What Pound wants to convey, then, is that the masses have heard about a new accounting system, but that their ignorant parochial minds are as impenetrable as a mountain of granite, and, like such a mountain of crystalline rock, their ignorance is seemingly indestructible; they give the matter no thought. However, as Pound says ironically, Mencken's 'statement does not invalidate geological process' and 'the news' must eventually 'arrive', or else they will atrophy. Referring to Clytemnestra's 'beacon telegraph' (*Guide*, p. 93), Pound says in the same vein :

The news was quicker in Troy's time   (l. 89).

It would indeed be ideal if the news of the artist or of any man of exceptional perception travelled from land to sea, from mind to mind, with the speed of light, and was immediately put into action.

GREECE

Line 90 furnishes two examples of a time and nation which showed at least some of this ideal 'news sense' (V. 41 : 55/213), not in the field of economics, but in art :

a match on Cnidos, a glow worm on Mitylene.

Together with line 89, this forms a neat little imagist epigram, line 90 being the 'superpository image', or rather images. Apart from this the two place names are, of course, 'used to recall' everything that is related to them in Pound's mind. He would probably tell us that they are 'very elliptical', as in the case of 'Eleusis' in Canto XLV. [362]

We know that the Pound of *The Spirit of Romance* (1910) was considerably influenced by J. W. Mackail (1859—1945), and especially by his *Latin Literature* (1895). Though he later started to quarrel with some of Mackail's ideas (V. *Letters,* pp. 245 f.), he still recommended his *Select Epigrams from the Greek Anthology* (1890) to his literary 'ward', Iris Barry, as containing prose translations 'worth reading' and 'O. K.' (*Letters,* p. 137), and we can be sure that Pound was using the book himself when he made his adaptations of Greek epigrams, which he grouped together under the title 'Homage to Quintus Septimus Christianus'. Among them is one by Anyte :

This place is the Cyprian's for she has ever the fancy
To be looking out across the bright sea,
Therefore the sailors are cheered, and the waves
Keep small with reverence, beholding her image.

(*Personae*, p. 175)

Mackail's version bears the title, 'The Shrine by the Sea', and he appended this note : 'According to the heading in the MS., which may be taken for what it is worth, this was the famous temple of Aphrodite in Cnidos.' [363]

There is little doubt that Pound, in writing 'Cnidos' in our Canto, has this epigram and Mackail's comment in mind. The last doubt is removed when we take account of the fact that it must have been mainly this epigram that inspired Pound to write :

> till the shrine be again white with marble
> till the stone eyes look again seaward   (74 : 13/462).

The only thing that tends to obscure the connection is that Pound has come to locate the 'shrine by the sea' not on Cnidos, the promontory in Caria, but on a mountain near Terracina in Italy, on which he appears to have inspected the remains of the temple dedicated to Venus Obsequens. [364]

Thus the 'match on Cnidos', the light of which spread and immediately penetrated the hearts of men 'in Troy's time', is the gaze of the 'continually reincarnated goddess'. [365] The important point here is not that it was Praxiteles' world-renowned first nude representation of Aphrodite which the Cnidians bought and which quickly attracted to Cnidos pilgrims from all over Greece, for Praxiteles represents to Pound, as to his sculptor friend, Gaudier-Brzeska, a decline into 'the caressable' from which is seen the 'romance of Galatea' (*Gaudier*, p. 97). Far more important is the religious power that he attributes to the goddess's seaward-gazing stone eyes. [366] 'I wd. set up the statue of Aphrodite again over Terracina. I doubt, to a reasonable extent, whether you can attain a living catholicism save after a greek pagan revival.' [367] As early as Canto XXIII he lets Georgius Gemistus, the Greek founder of the Florentine Academy, say about Christianity :

> 'Never with this religion
> 'Will you make men of the greeks'   (23 : 107/111).

What is 'brought to mind' (V. 5 : 18/22) by a 'glow worm on Mitylene' is, of course, Sappho. Her poems, the first in Occidental literature to sing of love and affection both tenderly intimate and passionately burning, indeed needed only a short time to spread from her native town of Lesbos to every shore of the Aegean and to make the Ancient World aware that a tenth muse had been born. Though time has reduced all but one of her odes to mere fragments, the news of her singing, her worshipping and pining, has stayed news, [368] and most people would still say with Pound that they 'know of no better ode than the POIKILOTHRON' (*ABC of Reading*, p. 47), i.e. Sappho's 'Hymn to Aphrodite'. Her gift to the world is really perdurable, for the 'hush of the older song' (5 : 17/21), her song, is still alive in Catullus and wherever men have a deep craving for the beauty that stems from the Cyprian goddess. So in the 1890's, when a considerable number of artists were really consumed by the love of beauty, they, like lotophagoi,

> 'Feared neither death nor pain for this beauty'   (20 : 93/97).

Sappho, together with practically everything her verses had ever inspired in English poets, whether translations or adaptations, was once and for all collected through the devoted and loving efforts of one whose life was otherwise humdrum enough : he became known as Sappho-Wharton.[369] His Sappho, published, it is well worth noting, as one of those beautifully produced Bodley Head books, with a cover design by Aubrey Beardsley, truly a jewel of the Yellow Book circle, was recommended by Pound to Iris Barry as 'the classical achievement' (*Letters*, p. 137).

If we look at what is juxtaposed with some of the Greek phrases from Sappho in the *Pisan Cantos*, we find that it is indeed Beauty as 'the cruel mistress of the artist'[370] of the nineties. In both of the places where Pound uses the Aeolic form of the adjective meaning 'rosy-fingered', reminiscent of Sappho's line, 'The moon with rosy fingers spread',[371] we meet in its proximity both Aubrey Beardsley saying to Yeats that

> 'beauty is difficult',[372]

and, among other Poundian memories pertaining to the nineties, two different quotations from Arthur Symons' 'Modern Beauty', the poem with which Pound had opened his anthology *Profile* (1932). The first is :

> and 'my fondest knight lie dead' ...[373]

and the second :

> ' I am the torch' wrote Arthur 'she saith'.[374]

When Sappho apostrophized the evening star as 'fairest of all the stars' or sang of the 'rosy-fingered moon', her soul went up to these luminaries as if to the 'many-splendoured throne' of Aphrodite. Recalling her hymn to the goddess with the two opening words, Pound seeks to identify Sappho with a butterfly which, like the moth in Symons' poem, is drawn into beauty's burning brightness, here simply the light of day :

> ΠΟΙΚΙΛΟΘΡΟΝ', 'ΑΘΑΝΑΤΑ
> that butterfly has gone out thru my smoke hole
> 'ΑΘΑΝΑΤΑ, saeva.[375]

The Latan 'saeva', 'cruel', makes it even more reminiscent of Symons. Finally, since the vision of Hesperus reminds Pound of Sappho, he must see her identified with what Keats called the 'amorous glow-worm of the sky'.[376] Hence our 'glow worm on Mitylene'.

For the second time in Canto LXXXII it is the conjunction 'till' that, for want of an antecedent, effects an abrupt change of mood (Cf. l. 73):

> Till forty years since, Reithmuller indignant :
> 'Fvy! in Tdaenmarck efen dh' beasantz gnow him',
> meaning Whitman, exotic, still suspect
> four miles from Camden   (ll. 91—93).

From his musing over a people at the time when their 'living catholicism' (V. *Guide*, p. 191) made them quick to welcome an extension of their sensibility, he is suddenly brought back to his immediate American past, to a time when original artistic perception was incapable of arousing the nation as a whole from its complacency.

Now that Pound's hitherto unknown essay entitled 'What I Feel About Walt Whitman' has been made accessible, it has become much clearer than from his scattered remarks in various other pieces of critical prose that Pound was very early conscious of his kinship with Whitman. 'Mentally', he wrote in 1909, 'I am a Walt Whitman who has learned to wear a collar and a dress shirt (although at times inimical to both). Personally I might be very glad to conceal my relationship to my spiritual father and brag about my more congenial ancestry — Dante, Shakespeare, Theocritus, Villon, but the descent is a bit difficult to establish. And, to be frank, Whitman is to my fatherland (Patriam quam odi et amo for no uncertain reasons) what Dante is to Italy and I at my best can only be a strife for a renaissance in America of all the lost or temporarily mislaid beauty, truth, valour, glory of Greece, Italy, England and all the rest of it.'[377]

Notwithstanding the humorous beginning and the note of rather juvenile enthusiasm at the end, this passage strikingly reveals that a great deal of what Pound subsequently set out to do was undertaken as a mission bequeathed to him by Whitman. Although he found Whitman's 'crudity... an exceeding great stench',[378] spoke of Whitman's egotism as 'that horrible air of rectitude with which Whitman rejoices in being Whitman' (*Spirit*, p. 168), violently attacked at least one of Whitman's crucial ideas — that 'to have great poets there must be great audiences too'[379] — and repeatedly confessed that he could not read Whitman 'without swearing at the author almost continuously' (*Letters*, p. 57), there was more seriousness in his making 'A Pact' with Walt Whitman than the humorous surface of that poem might suggest, for he did mean 'to go on from where he [Whitman] started' (*Essays*, p. 218), to carve the new wood Whitman had broken (V. *Personae*, p. 98). It is Whitman's language that needs Pound's sculptoral touch; as for 'his fundamental meaning' (*ABC of Reading*, p. 192), Pound said in 1909 : 'His message is my message. We will see that men hear it.'[380] Eliot, who, very probably for didactic reasons, for a long time refused to recognize any connection between Pound and Whitman, says in 'Isolated Superiority' : '... it is better to absorb your Whitman through Pound'.

Whitman does not appear in the *Cantos* until the Pisan sequence and vanishes again afterwards. He comes in at a moment when Pound is looking for proof that it was not he who betrayed America, but that it was the official America that betrayed the Constitution.[381] Hence he needs reassurance that the hypothesis from which he started does have roots in America :

> Hier wohnt the tradition, as per Whitman in Camden
> (80 : 86/542).

Whitman '*is* America', wrote Pound in his young days, '... I honour him for he prophesied me ...'[382] In *Patria Mia* he says : '... I find in him ... our American keynote ... It is, as nearly as I can define it, a certain generosity; a certain carelessness, or looseness, if you like; a hatred of the sordid, an ability to forget the part for the sake af the whole, a desire for largeness, a willingness to stand exposed' (p. 45), and a little later on : 'Whitman goes bail for the nation' (p. 47).

In recalling in our Canto the indignant comment made by one Richard Henri Riethmueller (1881–1942), who, instructor in German at the University of Pennsylvania (1905–1907) when Pound was there, published a study entitled *Walt Whitman and the Germans* (1906), Pound gives vent to his own indignation at the Americans' refusal to hear Whitman's message. That Whitman, as Pound was told by this young German, whose heavy accent he still remembers, should have become a household word even with Danish farmers, whereas nothing of the kind has ever happened in the country which was Whitman's first and last concern, is largely because certain minds in nineteenth-century Europe discovered in *Leaves of Grass* and *Democratic Vistas* their own dreams of liberty from what Whitman called scornfully 'feudalism'.

Hence, in order to carry this good news from democratic America to as many of their oppressed fellow-countrymen as possible, the Europeans soon published translations, the German poet Freiligrath in 1868 and the Danish socialist editor Rudolf Schmidt in the 1870's.[383] Even before that Whitman had caused a considerable wave of enthusiasm among English poets and intellectuals. starting with Swinburne, of course, affecting undergraduates and reaching even Tennyson.[384] Yet in America itself most of Whitman's literary contemporaries, 'those genteel little creatures', continued to put out their 'paste-pot work',[385] pedantically upholding standards borrowed from Victorian England, and after his death, Pound has it, Whitman remained :

> . . . exotic, still suspect
> four miles from Camden.

'Whitman was neglected by prigs', he wrote in 1938, 'and then the snobs overlooked that part of him which was quite simply exotic' (*Impact*, p. 8). Failure to dissociate the 'exotic', by which Pound probably implies the eccentricities springing from Whitman's homosexual tendencies, from Whitman's real greatness was bound to make him appear suspect to all but his disciples, and even 'four miles from Camden', i.e. at the University of Pennsylvania, this suspicion seems to have been the rule in Pound's student days.

At Pisa, Pound's recollection of Whitman also had an external cause. Although he might, in his attempt to justify his allegedly treasonable action during the war, have been driven to fall back on Whitman without this, we can at least say that we owe the quotation from Whitman in lines 95—96 to the book he happened to pick up in significantly low surroundings :

> That from the gates of death,
>   that from the gates of death : Whitman or Lovelace
>   found on the jo-house seat at that
> in a cheap edition! [and thanks to Professor Speare] (80 : 91/547).

This incredible item of lost property was Morris Edmund Speare's *Pocket Book of Verse* (1940).[386]

Now Pound once again had access to some Whitman, and what he said in *Patria Mia* about the need for Whitman proved to be completely true in his own predicament :

> One may not need him at home. It is in the air, this tonic of his. But if one is abroad; if one is ever likely to forget one's birthright, to lose faith, being surrounded by disparagers, one can find, in Whitman, the reassurance. (p. 47)

Some of the confidence Pound is in need of on this September day, at
'the gates of death', he tries to get from 'Out of the Cradle Endlessly
Rocking'. It is as if, like Whitman himself, he used the two lines from
the middle part of the poem, where the boy-poet is 'translating' the
mocking-bird's wailing over its lost mate, to express his 'elemental
desires' :[387]

> 'O troubled reflection
> 'O Throat, O throbbing heart'   (ll. 95—96).[388]

Whitman's articulation of the mocking-bird's desperate yearning must be
taken here to express Pound's own real despair. All that is left him of the
radiant world is suddenly no more than a reflection made faint by his own
delirious sensations, and what we read from here to the end of the Canto
is all knit together by that 'consciousness of death as death'.

As he lies there in his prison-camp tent, an irresistible downward pull
overpowers him. He must surrender to it, for he is forced to recognize in
it the power from which no mortal can escape, but as he is sinking he
utters with a sigh two of the many names men have given it :

> How drawn, O GEA TERRA,
>   what draws as thou drawest   (ll. 97—98).

Whatever the name, it is less dreadful for those who see in it the female
element, to which one may give oneself in the guise of a lover, although
one must be annihilated by such love. Yet if it is love at all, something
must come after. Then the final thought is not nothingness :

> till one sink into thee by an arm's width
> embracing thee. Drawest,
>   truly thou drawest.
> Wisdom lies next thee,
>   simply, past metaphor.   (ll. 99—103)

The more the individual is drawn into the Earth and ceases to be a
separate being, the more he becomes like Earth herself, who, like mortal
man, however, must, in the great cycle of the year, also die. And as she
makes man die with her, she reveals to him her wisdom, which is so
fundamental, and so incomparable to anything man can know, that there
is no metaphor to express it. But its manifestations are innumerable. Out
of her who is temporarily nothing but the grave will come forth new life :

> Where I lie let the thyme rise
>> and basilicum
>>> let the herbs rise in April abundant   (ll. 104—106).

Once the season of death is over she will bring forth, where death was, the 'sovereign' remedy, as the name 'basilicum', found in ancient herbals, implies, and as these herbs rise again their spring scents give back to man, purged by grief, a fuller confidence in Earth's 'gift of healing' (47 : 33/249). Such confidence is granted to those who have been initiated into the mysteries of the Earth, which are celebrated in rites symbolizing the great 'process', the drama of all life.

As we have seen in Part Two, Pound's Odysseus becomes, at the house of Circe, an initiate of these very mysteries. Cantos XXXIX and XLVII, and their echoes in many other Cantos, must, in fact, be taken as an assertion of Pound's own belief 'that the mysteries exist' (*Letters*, p. 425). He holds up this belief in the face of 'the power of putrefaction ... [which] ... seeks to destroy not one but every religion, by destroying the symbols, by leading off into theoretical argument' (*Impact*, p. 54). This force 'that divides, shatters and kills' in all history, the very opposite, Pound has it, of the 'one that contemplates the unity of the mystery' (*Impact*, p. 44), has, of course, as far as the modern age is concerned, largely become synonymous for Pound with his notion of usury. It is usury that has 'brought whores for Eleusis' (45 : 24/240), for 'usury is against Nature's increase' (51 : 44/261), and all the things that go together with usury provide the answer to Pound's rhetorical question : 'Who has wiped the consciousness of the greatest mystery out of the mind of Europe, to arrive at an atheism proclaimed by Bolshevism?' (*Impact*, p. 55)

What is new in the *Pisan Cantos* is the personal note in Pound's contemplation of the mysteries, and the personal comfort that can be derived from it. We find a great variety of passages where their wisdom is brought home to him by portents of rebirth. Chief among these are the aromatic herbs wished for in our Canto. The

> ... smell of mint under the tent flaps   (74 : 6/454)

is in fact one of the fragments which show that

> Le Paradis n'est pas artificiel   (V. 74 : 16/465).

Nowhere is the power of regeneration and healing vested in the great chthonic goddess brought nearer to his heart than in 'listening to the incense' (V. *Translations*, p. 213) of these herbs growing in the camp. He even calls her 'mother' once :

148

χθόνια γέα, Μάτηρ,
　　by thy herbs menthe, thyme and basilicum　(74 : 13/462).

'hus the smell and vision of these plants makes him recognize his own
rue deity which comprises, as it were, all the others :

　　... Tellus γέα feconda
　'each one in the name of its god'
　mint, thyme and basilicum　(79 : 65/519).

With the addition of the plea that no one god should have the monopoly
ver every other, for which Pound even discovered an unsuspected instance
n Micah, 4, 5 (in the famous chapter on world peace), he comes very
:lose to that union with the process sought in Pisa and ever since, and
.alled in Canto LXXVI 'atasol' (V. 36, 37/486, 487).

　As he is experiencing that irresistible downward pull he begins even
1ere, using the method so characteristic of the Cantos, to view his own
ubjective drama against the background of its eternal recurrence. He now
ees a personal parallel in the fact that Niccolò d'Este (1384—1441), whom
we have seen in Canto XXIV as one of his Renaissance Odysseus-figures,
:xpressed in his will the desire to be

　　... sepulto nudo, ...
　Without decoration ... [389]

This member of the House of Este, Pound implies, also had the intuition
:hat, in dying, man is meant to give his body to the Earth as a lover. Then
death has no sting, but is a communion, and we may take the Italian in
line 108,

　　e di qua di la del Po,

as a 'melopoeic' [390] expression of the peace that follows such yielding to
'Gea Terra', a peace bestowed on the land '... on this side and the other
side of the Po' by the softly running water. This anticipates the 'HUDOR
et pax' theme of the next Canto (V. 84 : 106/563).

　As if borne on the wind, which 'also is of the process' (74 : 3/451), some
fragmentary Greek reaches our ears :

　　wind : ἐμὸν τὸν ἄνδρα　(l. 109).

Pound thus recalls Theocritus' second idyll, where these words occur in
the ten times repeated refrain of the incantation uttered by a deserted girl.

Already in Canto LXXXI we find him trying to reproduce this refrain from memory :

Ἴυγξ . . . ἐμὸν ποτί δῶμα τὸν ἄνδρα   (81 : 96/554).

It was in 1914 that Pound selected 'Theocritus' idyll of the woman spinning with charmed wheel' as one of the 'pure colours' for the 'palette from which a literary renaissance should work (V. *Essays*, p. 215), and as such he again recommended it to Iris Barry, pointing out that 'there is a translation of Theocritus; I think Andrew Lang had something to do with it. Parts are readable and beautiful, especially the "Wheel of the Magic Spells" ' (*Letters*, p, 137). Yet in Pisa his own attempts to recall the original text of the girl's 'song which was to charm her lover home' suddenly lead him to hear in the girl's refrain,

> My magic wheel, draw home to me the man I love, [391]

the far more compelling call of her to whom he is so powerfully drawn.

While Pound thus becomes conscious of being lured by Gea Terra he remembers Kipling, for the only time in the *Cantos*, and acknowledges the fact that Kipling's vision of death has something in common with his own :

> Kipling suspected it   (l. 111).

Although one would hardly feel tempted ever to connect Kipling's name with Pound's, since Kipling upheld a great deal of what Pound hated most about the British Empire, Pound, unlike most literary critics, has always shown himself capable of dissociating Kipling the advocate of jingoistic imperialism from Kipling the artist. Mixed as his appreciation is, he says in his Henry James essay : '. . . one wonders if parts of Kipling by the sheer force of content, of tale to tell, will not outlast most of James' cobweb', and a little later : 'Kipling really does the psychic, ghosts, etc., to say nothing of his having the "sense of story" ' (*Essays*, pp. 324 & 326).

What comes back to Pound in the despair of the prison-camp seems to be that Kipling, too, in the words of a recent study, had a presentiment 'that the abyss is not empty; that it is the abode of power or Powers; that out of it come influences that affect the life of man'. He, too, knew about the 'Wisdom of the Grave', of 'love surviving death'. [392]

With what primeval, 'Cretan' intensity of emotion Pound experiences his submission to Earth we may gauge if we compare the lines which surround the mention of Kipling —

> lie into earth to the breastbone, to the left shoulder
>
> . . .
>
> to the height of ten inches or over   (ll. 110—112) —

with an astonishing parallel in the *Odyssey* of the modern Greek poet, Nikos Kazantzakis, a man powerfully imbued with the spirit of the ancient cults of his native Crete. There we find Laertes desiring to melt into the earth in very much the same way :

> and lay down without speaking, merged his back and hips
> with the warm earth . . . [393]

IDENTITY

It is under such emotional pressure that Pound arrives at a vision of the hardest basic fact, and only entrance to all facts', compressed into :

> man, earth : two halves of the tally   (l. 113).

Whitman called such recognition of Man's place in the cosmos 'the thought of identity', and he urged : 'America needs, and the world needs, a class of bards who will now and ever, so link and tally the rational physical being of man, with the ensemble of time and space, and with his vast and multiform show, Nature, surrounding him, ever tantalizing him, equally a part, and yet not a part of him, as to essentially harmonize, satisfy, and put at rest.'[394] Pound, amidst the 'death cells', has, after admonishing himself to 'Pull down thy vanity' come to say with Whitman in all humility :

> Earth, my likeness . . . [395]

Irrespective of whether Pound actually remembered Whitman's use of the verb 'tally', we must note that 'two halves of the tally' is a translation of the Chinese character fu[2]

Pound first called attention to it in his 1938 essay on Mencius, where he gives it in its Mencian context : 'When the aims of Shun and Wan were set together, though after a thousand years interval, they were as two halves of a tally stick', and having, it seems, found this imagistic translation of the character independently first, it gave him great satisfaction to add in brackets : 'Even the greatly learned translator has translated this "seal" in the text with a foot-note to say 'tally-stick''' (*Impact*, p. 124). Had it not been for the deep impression which the image of the seal or tally-stick left on him, he might not have used the Mencian comment again, first in a broadcast (Feb. 3, 1942) and then in the *Pisan Cantos*, this time significantly extended, the gist of it being :

Their aims as one
directio voluntatis, as lord over the heart
the two sages united
. . .
'halves of a seal'   (77 : 45 f. / 497).

The aims of the two sages were identical, Pound emphasizes, because
they were the result of one and the same 'direction of the will', and it i
implied in this phrase, which 'brings us ultimately both to Confucius an
Dante' (*Jefferson and/or Mussolini*, pp. 15 f.), that these two sages' idea
and actions were rooted in 'looking straight into the heart' (*Confucius*
p. 21) with absolute sincerity and fidelity, thus 'coming to rest, being a
ease in perfect equity' (p. 29). And this, like the breath from the 'brightnes
of '*udor*' perceived in Canto LXXXIII,

. . . joins with the process   (109/566).

Moreover, the identity of the two sages' wills implies 'the durability o
natural process' and provides an 'affirmation . . . of a permanent huma
process' (*Impact*, p. 125). The identity between man and Earth then, is
since Pound portrays this too by applying the image of the tally-stick, o
the same kind, but at the same time the 'fundamental basis of existence',[39]
a likeness which must be perceived before man can fully grasp his plac
in the cosmos. We find this expressed in *Thrones* as :

Heaven, man, earth, our law as written
not outside their natural colour,
water, earth and biceps   (99 : 50 f.).

THE SPOUSE

Whereas the vision of the grave inspires in Pound the calm of cosmi
consciousness, the thought of again having to face the world of mer
makes him despair :

but I will come out of this knowing no one
neither they me   (ll. 114—115).

This is the realization of a man who feels

. . . fatigue deep as the grave   (83 : 111/569),

who no longer feels himself to be part of living humanity — 'put me down
for temporis acti' (80 : 77/532) — and whose only worldly wish is :

Oh let an old man rest   (83 : 114/571).

Hence his fervent desire for immersion in 'fluid ΧΘΟΝΟΣ' (l. 118), for

connubium terrae   (l. 116),

i.e. 'marriage with the Earth'. If it was simply 'my man' in the Greek
from Theocritus, here it is, in what 'looks like an anaphora of Clytemnestra's words in *Agamemnon* 1404—1405', 'my husband', πόσις ἐμός
(l. 116). At the same time Pound seems to recall, through the use of the
Homeric ἔφατα (i.e. 'she said'),[397] Circe's invitation to Odysseus to 'make
love in bed'.[398] He himself is now, as it were, called 'to the cave'
(47 : 31/247), which here clearly holds the bridal bed of the chthonic
mysteries ('ΧΘΟΝΟΣ, mysterium', l. 117) of Eleusis. He becomes, to
pick out one of the many references to the deities connected with Eleusis,
'Zeus [who] lies in Ceres' bosom' (81 : 95/552).

In the whole of the *Cantos*, as Emery has pointed out, 'the Eleusinian
(or Dionysian) concept of natural fecundity' forms, together with its
antipode, the 'Confucian concept of human ordering', one of the poem's
main spiritual tensions.[399] These two concepts, twice given in the formula
'KUNG and ELEUSIS',[400] must indeed be regarded as the strongest
civilizing factors, since they contain the 'Taught and the not taught'
(53 : 18/283). The teaching of ideas of order like those of Confucius can
only set up a civilization if there is along with them an understanding of
the Mysteries, and these are revealed in 'no guide book' (*Letters*, p. 423),
and granted

to catechumen alone   (53 : 18/283),

only to those who are admitted to perform the ritual themselves. Having
a premonition of the 'sleep of death', Pound himself, for the only time in
the *Cantos*, comes near to a physical experience of the rites of a mystery
religion, 'whereby men should attain to closer communion with their
gods'.[401] He experiences directly, without substitution by symbols and
emblems, as it were, 'the literal act of synousia [i.e. 'holy marriage'] with
the deity'.[402]

Earth, who has become his spouse, is no longer a solid; she receives him
as a liquid would :

fluid ΧΘΟΝΟΣ o'erflowed me
lay in the fluid ΧΘΟΝΟΣ   (ll. 118—119).[403]

153

The air, on the other hand, changes into a solid, and thus he experiences a complete inversion. He has been admitted to those 'that lie / under the air's solidity' (ll. 120–121). And they are those who drink of 'the fluid that flows in the veins of the gods',[404] and,

drunk with 'ΙΧΩΡ of ΧΘΟΝΙΟΣ   (l. 122),

they may, like Tiresias, have a vision of the future.

Finally, in comparing the strength of the liquified primeval chthonic goddess with that observable in 'the undertow / of the wave receding' (ll. 123–124), Pound somehow brings us back to Whitman's vision of the Ocean as the 'fierce old mother'[405] in which he, too, desired to be immersed. With Pound we are more specifically reminded of the sea in which a Swinburne floated like Dionysos, himself a ΧΘΟΝΙΟΣ.

DESPAIR

Yet, as soon as his experience and vision of the mysteries ceases, Pound is again thrown back into utter despair :

but that a man should live in that further terror, and live (l. 125).

This comes very close to a death-wish. Whereas it was the fear of losing every contact with his fellow-men that gave rise to despair in lines 114–115, here it is the lagging behind of easeful and redeeming death. Already near the beginning of the *Pisan Cantos* there is that great desire to lie down on the bed of reunion and lasting rest :

Her bed-posts are of sapphire
for this stone giveth sleep.   (77 : 37/488)

If found, this sleep

staria senza più scosse   (74 : 13/462),

i.e. 'would rest without further tossing'.[406] Lying with Villon under the gallows, Pound has prayed for absolution (V. 74 : 5/454), and, thus prepared to enter, has prayed, again in Villon's words, to the Virgin :

repos donnez à cils . . .[407]

But, although he has now had further private revelation of the mystery, which is the bridal sleep of death, his admission to it is as yet only

154

momentary and the union with the process still essentially unachieved. Hence he is still lacking the final certainty which would prevent any 'back-swing of the emotional pendulum'. [408]

Though it is equally momentary — '(at 3 P. M., for an instant)' (l. 127) — he now experiences that which is the very opposite of the bliss of reunion, the sting of ultimate desolation :

> the loneliness of death came upon me   (l. 126).

Never before, and never again afterwards, does Pound record so directly his being on the brink of the abyss. But this blackest of all thoughts — not even in St. John of the Cross's Dark Night of the Soul, we may say in answer to Pound's question in Canto LXXIV, 'is there a blacker' (16/465) — is not simply left to call forth the most frightening dissonance in life. Pound's primary reaction to it, as indicated in the marginal Greek, is : 'weeping / thereupon'. Like Odysseus far from home on the shores of Ogygia, [409] Pound has in Pisa learnt more and more to 'drink of the bitterness' (80 : 91/548). Apart from shedding tears for his 'comes miseriae' (74 : 14/463) out of an increased sense of pity, [410] and apart from shedding nostalgic tears because he is separated from the world he loves, [411] it is above all this new, intense feeling of sadness that makes him tearful :

> Les larmes que j'ai créées m'inondent
> Tard, très tard je t'ai connue, la Tristesse,
> I have been hard as youth sixty years   (80 : 91/548).

In dropping his hardness as far as personal emotions are concerned and letting tears well forth, Pound shows, as it were, the same kind of submissiveness as in letting himself be drawn by Gea Terra. There could thus be seen a parallel between the tears that flood him and the Earth which turns liquid to receive him, and therefore we may attribute to the tears in our Canto the effect of initiating a gradual removal from the blackest thought of disharmony back to the harmony of blissful union. The birds which provide the concluding image of the Canto lead the poet's emotions even further on in that direction :

> Three solemn half notes
>   their white downy chests black-rimmed
> on the middle wire   (ll. 129–131).

In discussing the birds' musical notation and its implications we have already observed that Pound's contrapuntal pastime was capable of evoking in him emotions like those in the Beethoven of later years.

155

Whereas in all the other passages he does not — except by juxtapositional implication — attempt to qualify the birds' song, whether actually heard or forming a pattern in the mind, here he directly interprets it as 'solemn'. He hears in it something like a dirge performed for him by the birds because they, as his brothers and fellow-songsters, have pity on him. 'As they supply the requiem', says Forrest Read, 'they are simultaneously given full visual form ("white downy chests black-rimmed") and artistic form ("three solemn half notes"). Instead of art imitating nature, nature moves into art and Pound articulates it there.'[412]

From the allusion to the birds there emerges a sense of sweetness and softness which dissolves the bitterness of blackest loneliness and makes love and hope return, since the birds' song is part of heaven. We may feel here something of what Spitzer has called 'the fusion of nature and humanity into one Stimmung', and if it is true to say of Whitman's 'Out of the Cradle Endlessly Rocking' that 'out of the cradle of death, the poet will sing life',[413] we may be equally justified in saying that out of the darkness of death Pound will sing of the lifegiving 'tensile light, the Immaculata', of which it is written that 'there is no end to its action' (Confucius, p. 187).

The word 'periplum' at the end of Canto LXXXII and the comments on light in Canto LXXXIII are sufficient indication that Pound was capable of journeying on from this moment of utter despair and, in the subsequent Cantos, moving 'out from egoism and to establish some definition of an order possible or at any rate conceivable on earth'.[414] Further proof of this lies in the fact that about a month after writing Canto LXXXII, while still in Pisa, Pound put down on paper his second version of the Great Digest of Confucius (V. Confucius, p. 89), which, as Hugh Kenner states, 'registers a gain in technical and emotional maturity' over the 1928 version 'in exactly the same way' as the Pisan sequence compared with the earlier Cantos.[415] Behind it lies Pound's experience of the 'Wisdom ... past metaphor', of the fact that :

> In nature are signatures
> needing no verbal tradition   (87 : 33).

Epilogue

AMO ERGO SUM

'And if I see her not,
    no sight is worth the beauty of my thought.'[416]

As far as the whole of the poem now published is concerned, the reading of Pound's *Cantos* presented in the foregoing pages is anything but complete. A full appreciation of all the various groups of Cantos was not even attempted; indeed, sections like the 'Jefferson Nuevo Mundo' Cantos (XXXI–XLI), the China Cantos (LIII–LXI) and the Adams Cantos (LXII–LXXI) have remained virtually untouched. Although the *Pisan Cantos* has been drawn on most heavily, it cannot be claimed that it has ever been focused in its entirety. There is no doubt that a really inclusive synopsis of the *Cantos* would be a good many times longer than the poem itself, because so much would have to be added from outside to produce something more than a mere list of topics. It is well worth noting that a computor was used to arrange the material given in the *Annotated Index*. Yet this work covers only proper names, foreign language items and the traceable quotations; the more immediately poetic elements such as key images and key motifs and their scattered echoes *are* treated, but only incidentally.

Paraphrasing and indexing do not, then, appear to be the answer. The result reached by the chief method employed here, that of selecting mostly short passages which can be seen to fit together, strikes one as more satisfactory. But then the disconcerting question arises : does this not falsify the nature of the work as a whole? Anyone who goes back to a consecutive reading of the *Cantos* after looking at an examination like the present one will on many pages feel just as baffled as before. Nevertheless, as soon as one allows for the existence of a fundamental structure one may be carried over even the most obscure and exasperating blocks of text. That such a structure exists and is present not only in the *Cantos* but, as an undercurrent, in the greater part of Pound's creative and critical output, an undercurrent which at moments wells up into an unbelievably powerful rush of visions and emotions, is hard to refute after patient perusal of the evidence. To show the Poundian centre, the nucleus around which so much in Pound's work orbits, is one aim that this study has constantly pursued.

Before a restatement of this magnetic centre is attempted, some space has to given to those of Pound's critics who are not so much concerned with the poetic quintessence of his work as with his opinions as opinions. 'Every man has a right to have his ideas examined one at a time', Pound has said more than once in the past few years. 'You never get clarity as long as you have these package words, as long as a word is used by twenty-five people in twenty-five different ways.'[417] This implies, of course, that no man who really tries to communicate live thought can be pinned down to one single branch of philosophy. Now to call Pound — preferably with disparagement — a nominalist striving with positivistic science and knowing nothing but visual perception may seem a justifiable classification on the strength of certain portions of Pound's prose, notably the *ABC of Reading*,[418] but the term 'nominalism' is very open to the charge of being one of those 'package words'. Besides, if we consider that a nominalistic trend has been pointed out as a permanent, or at any rate recurrent feature of Anglo-Saxon thought and culture, the 'nominalist' label loses its relevance.

Such philosophical comments occur, of course, in connection with attacks on Pound's 'ideogrammic method', the most shattering of which has just been launched by Noel Stock,[419] in 1960 the enthusiastic editor of *Impact,* now a disillusioned disciple. Whereas no one else can claim to have had such unrestricted access to 'Poundiana', and whereas, it seems, no one else has so eagerly re-examined the fields of knowledge about which Pound has made pronouncements, we must not overlook the fact that he now writes as one who has discovered that his fundamental view of life is diametrically opposed to Pound's. Hence he has disqualified himself from unbiased criticism. However, Stock's discovery that Pound does not, like the scientist, first accumulate facts and then arrange them systematically, but, in actual fact, gropes about for facts to fit his intuition — 'the form in the air', as we could now say — lends a great deal of weight to the kind of criticism of the *Cantos* begun by Kenner. True, this invalidates to a large extent Pound's own theory as outlined in the *ABC of Reading,* but it illustrates the well-known fact that when an artist gets down to creating he almost invariably goes beyond his theoretical statements, thus asserting the necessity of freedom in creating.

Asked about how he planned a new Canto, Pound told Donald Hall : 'One is working on the life vouchsafed, I should think. I don't know about method. The *what* is so much more important than how.' Of course, when he started drafting the first Cantos more than half a century ago, 'the problem was to get a form — something elastic enough to take the necessary material'. Once the basic form was found, and it was to be 'a musical form', most of what he 'had to say fitted the general scheme'. From this point onwards the main task was 'to build up a circle of reference'. In this, technique was merely 'the test of sincerity. If a thing isn't worth getting the technique to say, it is of inferior value' and so 'it has to go out'. True to his own definition that 'artists are the antennae of the race', he then spent 'the whole energy of a lifetime' on 'the transit from the reception of stimuli to the recording, to the correlation',[420] and out of this the *Cantos* grew up into a compendium of all the things that have ever acted as proper stimuli on Pound — it became both a *Guide to Culture* and an intellectual and spiritual autobiography.

What emerges from these telescoped quotations may be called less vulnerable than Pound's exposition of the 'ideogrammic method' in the 1930's. How he has striven, often over a long period of years, to record his initial stimuli, we have often had occasion to observe. The two lines of 'In a Station of the Metro' stand out as the classic example of this phenomenon, which at the same time goes to show that such recording is a deeply emotional matter. It may even be maintained that when Pound makes a statement like the now famous one from *The Spirit of Romance*, that 'poetry is a sort of inspired mathematics, which gives us equations, not for abstract figures, triangles, spheres, and the like, but equations for human emotions' (p. 14), or when he says that 'the proper METHOD for studying poetry and good letters is the method of contemporary biologists' (*ABC of Reading*, p. 17), he is not blindly admiring mathematics and science and substituting them for the pursuit and study of poetry, but merely pointing out analogies, although these are unfortunately of a kind that seems to trap not a few critics. There is even in connection with what has been chosen as the title of this study a very distinctly negative view of modern science :

> For the modern scientist energy has no borders, it is a shapeless 'mass' of force; even his capacity to differentiate it to a degree never dreamed of by the ancients has not led him to think of its shape or even its loci. The rose that his magnet makes in the iron filings, does not lead him to think of the force in botanic terms, or wish to visualize that force as floral and extant (*ex stare*).

The lack of this kind of 'floral' and patterned vision in the modern scientific mind makes him continue :

> A medieval 'natural philosopher' would find this modern world full of enchantments, not only the light in the electric bulb, but the thought of the current hidden in air and in wire would give him a mind full of forms, '*Fuor di color*' or having their hyper-colours. The medieval philosopher would probably have been unable to think the electric world, and *not* think of it as a world of forms. (*Essays*, pp. 154 f.)

161

It is in this light that we must read Pound's comment that 'Leibniz was the last philosopher who "got hold of something", his unsquashable monad may by now have been pulverized into sub-electrons, it may have been magnified in the microscope's eye to the elaborate structure of a solar system, but it holds as a concept.' (Guide, p. 74) Having noted that Pound himself clings to such visionary concepts even after the splitting of the atom, it is now time to emphasize how much more important central luminous visions are to him than all mere opinions. Opinions are always in danger of being contradictory, and indeed, if we try to arrange Pound's opinions, we are, alas, faced with a bundle of contradictions. This is certainly a serious flaw, especially since they figure — more often implicitly than explicitly — very largely in the Cantos, mainly because of Pound's not seldom uncontrolled obsessions.

In view of the astounding intensity of Pound's visions, it still seems legitimate, however, to consider his opinions of subsidiary importance. However much one may succeed in discarding them as inconsistent and not founded on facts, his visions are 'now in the heart indestructible' (77 : 43/494), and that not in Pound's alone, but — let it be admitted — also in the hearts of all those who have not yet relinquished all belief in the harmonizing qualities of the natural and spiritual world around us. Here the poet-visionary Pound makes us all but forget Pound the propagandist and makes us aware of how poetry, in fact all art of the first intensity, soars far above all argument. It is a great pity — this, too, we must concede — that Pound has not produced more poetry of the highest intensity but has all too frequently let his struggle against perversions, both real and imaginary, run away with him.

When Noel Stock writes that 'for Pound, a Jeffersonian and offspring of the Enlightenment, human cruelty and greed could be cured by the application of knowledge. Get your facts right and everything else will fall into place', adding that this 'is a crude way of putting it, but is, nevertheless, a just summary of his philosophy', he is, of course, underlining the fact that for Pound original sin does not exist. He feels that chiefly because of this Pound's philosophy 'seems to ignore completely the depth and the glories of the human heart', and that his view of the world is mechanical — this is a point which Stock makes again and again. [421] We must first remember, however, that Stock is biased. Though it would need a more detailed discussion than that sketched in this epilogue to refute such charges — and even then one would be up against theological convictions which can neither be proved nor disproved — it is nevertheless possible to suggest some modification.

Certainly, Pound refuses to recognize the essential Christian doctrine of Divine Grace, but, from what we have seen from his preoccupation with the mysteries, we can say that he does recognize the redeeming influence of divine powers, however unorthodox they may seem to a Christian. There is also, as we shall observe again later, the idea of the fall, no less a departure from the 'luminous decree of heaven' than Adam's fall from Paradise. Admittedly the wellbeing of the individual human heart is less in the foreground than the wellbeing of humankind as a whole, but to call it nothing but a materialistic and mechanical concern is to ignore the importance which Pound attaches to the contemplation of the spiritual world in an Ideal State.

Stock is not the only one to point out Pound's roots in the Enlightenment.[422] Stripped of his eagerness to write hard, clear-cut verse Pound, with his platonistic love of beauty, his revolutionary zeal and the idea of the perfectability of man, is far more of a modern Shelley than we are inclined to believe. Such a bent of mind is, however, not necessarily outdated and need not make us belittle Pound's attempts to urge men to improve their awareness of what might come from 'right reason', from the visions which exceptional minds in the past have tried to communicate.

Pound's own endeavours to communicate such visions and insights are, it must be allowed, not always successful. He is quite aware of this himself, but he comments :

> I mean or imply that certain truth exists. Certain colours exist in nature though great painters have striven vainly, and though the colour film is not yet perfected. Truth is not untrue'd by reason of our failing to fix it on paper. Certain objects are communicable to a man or woman only 'with proper lighting', they are perceptible in our own minds only with proper 'lighting', fitfully and by instants.   (*Guide*, p. 295)

This might drag us back into a discussion of the 'ideogrammic method'. However, it is much more appropriate to quote a so far little known passage from 'A Visiting Card', headed 'C'est Toujours le Beau Monde Qui Gouverne', as it will take us to the very core of Pound's preoccupation with civilization. By 'beau monde' he means 'the best society, meaning the society that, among other things, reads the best books, possesses a certain ration of good manners and, especially, of sincerity and frankness, modulated by silence'. Now it is exactly this sort of elite that Pound presupposes the readers of his *Cantos* to belong to; he is writing his poem for people who must bring such a background with them. Yet, as is only too well known, there is in our times no such thing as a uniformly educated class left. The specialization of knowledge has gone so far that it is only the small clique that can be said to share a common background.

This is what Pound often seems to ignore, for he is wont to write about subjects like economics, as Eliot once observed, as if the general reader were bound to be on a familiar footing with it already. Many of Pound's failures to communicate his meaning are explained in this way. If there really were, as at certain times in the Middle Ages, a common culture among men, Pound would no doubt be more right than he actually is in asserting that

> Le beau monde governs because it has the most rapid means of communication. It does not need to read blocks of three columns of printed matter. It communicates by the detached phrase, variable in length, but timely. (*Impact*, p. 50)

Since the intellectuals and the people in governing positions are now, as a rule, as far apart as possible, this assumption is particularly illusory. In our kind of over-specialized society, to attempt a correlation of knowledge 'by the detached phrase', as Pound has done, is to be quixotic indeed. Pound, however, has never stopped putting this idea into practice.

Yet, unlike the orthodox scholar, he appears never to have based his researches on bibliographical bulletins and the like but to have left the finding of his material to 'the life vouchsafed'. Had he not, 'in the year of grace 1906, 1908, or 1910 . . . picked from the Paris quais a Latin version of the *Odyssey* by Andreas Divus Justinopolitanus' (*Essays*, p. 259), who knows what the beginning of the *Cantos* would now look like. Such chance finds are, of course, in keeping with the intellectual voyage on which he set out, and they often, together with chance meetings with various people, assumed a significance which only a poetical genius is capable of bestowing, but it seems that in Italy he finally developed a real passion for making excerpts from old documents, and books old and new, which had caught his imagination.[423] Pound's obsessive raking for information and enlightenment and, subsequently, his compulsive inclusion of it in the *Cantos*, has led to what Stock calls 'the final collapse of the work in *Thrones*'.[424] Be that as it may, Pound's delving into books has nevertheless often resulted in what he saw to be his task as a (self-styled) 'aphorist' : 'to establish axes of reference' (*Guide*, p. 195) for the next voyager to sail by.

If Pound's *Cantos* is rightly called an epic, we might expect to find, as in most epics, an initial declaration like Virgil's 'arma virumque cano', stating clearly what the poet is above all going to sing of. In vain do we look for this at the beginning of Pound's epic. We suddenly find it, however, in the *Rock-Drill* Cantos :

> Bellum cano perenne . . .
> . . .   between the usurer and any man who
>   wants to do a good job
>   (perenne). [425]

If war and strife are taken as *the* characteristic subject of epic, to speak of the struggle between the usurer-exploiter and the honestly striving individual as a 'perennial war' is to make this subject epic indeed, especially since Pound employs the historical method to depict it and since he holds that 'an epic is a poem containing history'. [426]

That this may very well serve as one description of the principal subject of the *Cantos*, and of Pound's own personal struggle, should have become sufficiently clear in the course of this study. Up to Canto XLV, as Pound himself said in the BBC Broadcasts, the poem was a kind of detective story where one was trying to find the crime. Yet how has investigation of usurious practices come to take up so much of Pound's energy, why has he spent so many years of his life 'on this case/ first case' to 'set down part of / The Evidence' (46 : 28/245), asking in his capacity as investigator the question :

> 'Can we take this into court?
> 'Will any jury convict on this evidence?
>   . . .
>   will any
>   JURY convict 'um?   (46 : 27/243)

(meaning the usurers). 'Whatever economic passions I now have', we know Pound to have said in 1933, 'began *ab initio* from having crimes against living art thrust under my perceptions.' (*Impact*, p. 88) If this were his only reason, we might with little hesitation call him an intellectual snob. [427]

Having struck people in 1912 as possessing 'gno bolidigal basshunts', [428] he has himself been inclined to assume that, although he could not 'say exactly where [his] study of government started', 'the *New Age* office helped [him] to see the war as a separate event but as part of a system, one war after another'. [429] Here, coming from his association with Major C. H. Douglas and A. R. Orage, is an entirely different emphasis, one on political economy, responsible, as we have shown, for his admiration for Mussolini. Here he found, at any rate, the basis which he thought his fellow-poets were singularly lacking :

> But the lot of 'em, Yeats, Possum and Wyndham
> > had no ground beneath 'em
> > > Orage had. [430]

Apart from the fact that his interest in the issue of money may have been to a certain extent hereditary, as his grandfather, T. C. Pound, 'had already in 1878 been writing about, or urging among his fellow Congressmen, the same essentials of monetary and statal economics' [431] as Pound was writing about during World War II, he has come to hold that 'monetary theory is worthy of study because it leads us to the contemplation of justice' (*Impact*, p. 69). As long as there is no 'just and honest currency', with, preferably, 'state authority behind it' (*Impact*, p. 94), 'the real aim of Law [which is] to prevent coercion, either by force or by fraud' (BBC), cannot be achieved. Hence he believes that unless man conquers his 'ignorance of coin, credit, and circulation', his real enemy (V. *Impact*, p. 109), he will never see that the usurers' 'technique is two lies at once', [432] and he will never enjoy proper justice. Economics, in this light, is not 'a cold thing'; if he refuses to be moved by it [433] he will never acquire the knowledge 'sans which a loss of freedom is consequent', this knowledge and safeguard being 'monetary literacy' (103 : 84). The struggle between the exploiter and the individual is thus part of a more comprehensive one, 'the struggle for individual rights', to which Pound refers specifically as 'an epic subject, consecutive from jury trial in Athens to Anselm versus William Rufus, to the murder of Becket and to Coke and through John Adams'. [434]

Although, as Sir Herbert Read has it, 'it is still possible to maintain, with reason and scientific proof, that usury has been the major cause of misery in the modern world, and that for wickedness one cannot suggest a rival to those financial and technological monopolies that profit from war and the propagations for war', [435] a discussion of the truth of this and its bearing on Pound's treasonable broadcasts is inappropriate here. Instead we leave this controversial subject and focus our attention on that side of Pound's preoccupation with usury which has a long literary tradition.

Since he insists that

> ... the true base of credit ... is
> > the abundance of nature [436]

and not gold, we find him truly in the company of Dante, who placed the usurers next to the sodomites in his hell, of Chaucer, and not least of Shakespeare, from whom he significantly quotes the question put to Shylock :

Or is your gold ... ewes and rams? [437]

What is even more significant is that in the comment following this Shakespearean fragment the word 'usury' — perhaps a misleading and unhappy metonymy for Pound's monetary concerns anyway — does not occur, but a far more general statement :

> No! it is not money that is the root of the evil. The root is greed, the lust for monopoly. 'Captans annonam, maledictus in plebe sit!' thundered St. Ambrose — 'Hoggers of harvest, cursed among the people!' (*Impact*, p. 113)

We need only quote two more comments from *Impact* on gold in order to realize fully that it is nature, in the way a Shakespeare understood it, that Pound has come to accept as the basis of everything :

> Gold is durable, but does not reproduce itself ... It is absurd to speak of it as bearing fruit or yielding interest. Gold does not germinate like grain. To represent gold as doing this is to represent it falsely. (p. 115)

In basing money on gold, man 'invented something against nature, a false representation in the mineral world of laws which apply only to animals and vegetables' (p. 112). This is the great error which Pound wants us to understand. Here lies the fatal departure from :

> The plan [which] is in nature (99 : 61).

Whenever men lapse into such an error, they become victims of that force in history which 'divides, shatters, and kills'.

The one man who, being in harmony with the other force in history, the 'one that contemplates the unity of the mystery' (*Impact*, p. 44), is most likely to have found the wisdom that may 'keep them from falling'[438] is Confucius, in his *Ta Hio*, for Pound says about it : 'The proponents of a world order will neglect at their peril the study of the only process that has repeatedly proved its efficiency as social coordinate.' (*Confucius*, p. 19) Here is, for Pound, the soundest ethical basis the world has yet discovered. If 'the process of looking straight into one's heart' is followed, and 'what results, i.e. the action resultant from this straight gaze into the heart', is 'spread ... thru the people' (85 : 8), a nation will come 'to rest, being at ease in perfect equity' (*Confucius*, pp. 27, 21 & 29).

Confucius, then, has provided Pound with the ethical standards by which the great variety of figures appearing in the *Cantos* are implicitly judged. Their place in Pound's hierarchy of values depends on the degree to which they have acted upon the straight gaze into the heart. In the degree that their hearts are straight (V. 99 : 54) they bestow treasure on mankind, for 'honesty is the treasure of states' (Confucius, p. 89), and upon honesty and sincerity civic order may be established and perfected.

What has to be added to Pound's Confucianism to make a description of the centre of the Cantos fuller does not actually lead away from Confucius, but merely amplifies his teaching :

> Beyond civic order :
> l'AMOR.   (94 : 94)

This takes us back not only to what we have studied in connection with Pound's Neo-Platonism, but also to the very core of Pound. In Pisa he wrote :

> Amo ergo sum, and in just that proportion   (80 : 71/526).

Even before World War II, he had used the French version of this, 'J'ayme donc je suis', printed as a letterhead on his stationery, [439] and in 1942 he had said : 'Without strong tastes one does not love, nor, therefore, exist.' (Impact, p. 68).

Pound asserts :

> That love is the 'form' of philosophy,
> is its shape (è forma di Filosofia)
> and that men are naturally friendly
> at any rate from his (Dant's) point of view   (93 : 86);

and since we philosophize, since 'we think because we do not know', [440] to think is to love, and to love is to perceive with 'strong tastes'. But this may make us 'furious from perception' (104 : 93) and engender its very opposite, hate, which utterly destroys, if not checked, because it may lead to 'a blindness that comes from inside' (104 : 93). Here is the great tension that has so largely determined Pound's life.

'Patriam quam odi et amo for no uncertain reasons', Pound wrote in 1909 in 'What I Feel About Walt Whitman'. As long as hate is not allowed to break loose from love, as long as it does not obstruct the 'straight gaze into the heart', it is morally justified, because then it is identical with just indignation at what is against nature and the honesty that comes from being in harmony with it, and helps 'to know good from evil' (89 : 50). Then it is the hate operative even in 'the true theologians [who] sought and fought against the roots and beginnings of error' (Guide,

p. 317). Otherwise hate becomes evil itself, and it must be said that here Pound himself has erred at times, misguided as he was in his reforming zeal.

Yet if man's first aim is to live a full life, he will for ever try to make his love a full love, and that is achieved by desiring to know. 'To improve [his] curiosity and not to fake',[441] that is the road to love. On this journeying, in this sailing after knowledge, 'what counts is the direction of the will' (*Impact*, p. 50), the desire for 'the lifting up', to 'raise the will' (*Impact*, p. 136). Once this 'humanitas' has been attained, men will share in the divine vision, the crux of which is that

> things have roots and branches; affairs have scopes and
> > > beginnings,[442]

that, as the motto of *Jefferson and/or Mussolini* states,

> nothing is without efficient cause.

The divine does not, however, reveal itself if there is no reverence; the mysteries must be approached humbly; it demands total piety. Kung must be joined by Eleusis, as Civic order is nothing without religion. Only when the Odes have been studied [443] and the rites performed can the vision be threefold :

ALTAR   CITY   ROSE.[444]

The City is based on the mysteries, and the order of the city must harmonize with the order above; and 'above all this' there is, Pound asserts, 'the substantiality of the soul, and the substantiality of the gods' (*Impact*, p. 66).

The less love is mixed with hate the nearer the soul is to the gods in the heaven of Light and Love, and the more it shares the divine vision, 'the *forma*, the immortal *concetto*' (*Guide*, p. 152). However :

> So slow is the rose to open.
> A match flares in the eyes' hearth,
> > then darkness   (106 : 104).

You have this vision only

> For a flash,
> > for an hour,
> Then agony,
> > then an hour,
> > > then agony   (92 : 80).

But although the vision is not continuous, the knowledge of its beauty

> . . . has carved the trace in the mind
> dove sta memoria   (76 : 35/485).

The 'steel dust' of a lifetime's experience, for which 'there is no substitute' (98 : 43), has nevertheless sprung 'into order' (*Guide*, p. 152).

Yet the question which must worry literary criticism most is whether Pound's *Cantos* is really good poetry. As far as his major poems up to and including *Hugh Selwyn Mauberley* and his merits as one of the men who made twentieth-century verse possible are concerned, there is practically a consensus of opinion; as to the *Cantos* there is none so far. Of the critics who do not dismiss the *Cantos* from the start most have their lists of 'flawless' Cantos, some of which have already established themselves as anthology pieces, [445] and despite Kenner's advocacy for the whole poem, critical opinion now tends to stress its unevenness.

It seems to me, however, that there is one kind of poetry in the *Cantos* in which Pound's mastery and intensity have, right through to the end of *Thrones* and to the fragments of the continuation already accessible, never slackened. I refer to the nature lyrics, which range from simple observation of natural phenomena to mythically heightened chants. The three lyrics of the various times of day in Canto IV, discussed in Part One, have given us fair proof of this. The most conspicuous example is, however, Canto XLIX, what Kenner calls 'the emotional still point of the *Cantos*', [446] with the most exquisite opening line :

> For the seven lakes, and by no man these verses.

That these nature lyrics impress themselves on the mind more than most of the other verses of perfect cadence and phrasing is as it should be, for they embody that great guide for Pound : the natural process; and that Pound puts his warmest affection into them we may gather from these lines written in Pisa :

> the sage
> delighteth in water
> the humane man has amity with the hills   (83 : 107/564).

To the delight in water, one of the great early stimuli having been Homer's epithet 'poluphloisboios' (V. *Personae*, p. 191 & 74 : 5/453), add his worship of the tensile light, and Pound's poetic nucleus is all there, as in this passage from Canto CXV :

ubi amor
ibi oculus
? to all men for an instant ?
beati
The sky leaded with elm boughs
A blown husk that is finished
but the light sings eternal
a pale flare over marshes
where the salt hay whispers to tide's change. [447]

Remembering the early Pound, one cannot but quote the opening line of Δώρία, because it most aptly brings out what we experience :

Be in me as the eternal moods   (*Personae*, p. 80).

As the poet of such moods, full of affectionate identification with trees, hills, lakes — anything in the 'green world' (V. 81 : 99/556) — the author of the *Cantos* has no rival.

On the whole, and notwithstanding all that now passes as failures, there certainly are in the *Cantos*, as Charles Norman says, 'passages by the score [which] make one fall in love again with the English tongue'. [448] Even now a great deal of it can be read 'just for the tone' (Tate); that charm of a Catullus which was very early felt [449] is still there to be enjoyed. On the other hand, Pound himself is aware that 'there's need of elaboration, of clarification ... There is no doubt that the writing is too obscure as it stands'. [450] He even said on the BBC that the idea would be to 'tuck in all the footnotes', and then heaved a long sigh. Pound is, however, not too worried about this himself, because it has become more important to him just to point out that there is 'something decent in the universe' (95 : 107), and that :

In short, the cosmos continues   (87 : 33),

than to write nothing but poetry acceptable by traditional literary standards. The Cosmos, he says,

... coheres all right
even if my notes do not cohere. [451]

A recent interview showed Pound to have sunk into a state of lethargy. He now confesses that a lot of what he did is wrong, and he speaks of great doubts. [452] This has led the popular press to rejoice and virtually to say : 'Ah good, the old blighter is finally recanting!' Has Pound really been wrong about everything? We leave this question for all those to ponder who care, but quote Pound once more, saying about himself :

> Many errors,
> > a little rightness,
> to excuse his hell and my paradiso,

and :

> It is difficult to write a paradiso when all the superficial indications are that you ought to write an apocalypse. [453]

APPENDIX

PLAN OF CANTO IV

1. ll. 1–2 : Troy – Ancient Blood Feud.
2. l. 3 : Lords of the Lyre – of whom shall we sing?
3. l. 3 : Answer to 2 : Of Women!
4. l. 4 : Cadmus and Athene.
5. ll. 5–12 : The Dawn Lyric.
6. ll. 13–15 : The Mourner.
   6a. ll. 16–17 : Mourning over Itys.
7. ll. 18–32 : Soremonda's suicide because of Cabestan.
   ll. 19–23 : 7 merging with 6a.
   ll. 31–32 : 6a concluding 7.
8. ll. 33–51 : Actaeon beholding Diana.
9. ll. 52–54 : Vidal in his self-willed metamorphosis.
   ll. 55–56 : Continuation of 8.
   ll. 57–63 : Actaeon after metamorphosis.
   ll. 64–65 : Vidal 'muttering Ovid'.
10. ll. 66–67 : The Pools famed for Metamorphosis.
11. l. 68 : The very instant of metamorphosis : Cygnus.
   (10 and 11 are in the very centre of Canto IV.)
12. ll. 69–81 : The Noon Lyric.
13. ll. 74–75 : The worship of conjugal and civic virtues.
   13a. l. 77 : The world of the Noh plays.
14. ll. 82–88 : Epithalamium.
15. ll. 89–99 : Who rules over the wind?
16. ll. 100–101 : The beholders of THE CITY.
17. l. 102 : Danaë : 'the god's bride'.
   l. 103 : echo of 15.
18. ll. 104–110 : The Evening Lyric.
19. ll. 111–112 : The Spirits of the Air.
20. l. 113 : Polhonac.
21. l. 114 : Gyges.
   ll. 115–116 form a general 'reprise'.
   ll. 117–118 : 17 further developed.
22. ll. 119–122 : Procession in honour of the Holy Virgin.
23. ll. 123–124 : The 'unbodied' image of the Madonna.
   23a. l. 125 : Cavalcanti.
24. l. 126 : 'Poetry is a Centaur'.
25. ll. 127–128 : 'Eternal watcher of things'.

As there is no discernible literary form grafted onto Canto LXXXII, and as the sequence of images, observations, memories, momentary moods and personal experiences is entirely dependent on the poet as experiencer, no purely structural comments are made in the course of its discussion. The form of Canto IV has, however, been shown to be less subjective. We have therefore been able to trace a certain amount of conscious construction (in the Dawn, the Noon and Evening Lyrics). Yet in both Cantos there seems to be a fundamental unity of time: it all occurs to the poet in one day. Beyond this we may feel some 'ultimate and absolute rhythm..., the most primal of all things' (*Translations*, p. 23), which will always escape analysis.

1. l. 1 : Clouds over Pisa.
2. l. 2 : The 'good nigger'.
3. ll. 3–5 : '*Comes miseriae*'.
4. ll. 6–7 : The Landor – Swinburne – Pound axis.
   l. 8 : 'Swinburne Versus His Biographers'.
   ll. 9–10 : Elkin Mathews at The Pines, Putney.
   ll. 11–13 : Elkin's 'one glory'.
5. ll. 14–16 : Momentary reflections on his own struggle.
   ll. 17–21 : 4 continued – Swinburne the swimmer.
6. ll. 22–26 : The Agamemnon Ellipsis.
7. ll. 27–29 : Blunt the bullfighter (in obscure juxtaposition).
8. ll. 30–33 : The printing press and monuments.
9. l. 34 : The Birds.
10. ll. 35–38 : The printing press and *Lustra*.
    ll. 39–40 : A Birrellism.
11. ll. 41–45 : The decadent *beau monde*.
12. ll. 46 ff. : Yeats's Mondays.
    ll. 46–47 : Mabel Beardsley, 'for a glory'.
    ll. 48–50 : 'Old Neptune Masefield'.
    ll. 51–52 : Psychical experiments.
    ll. 53–64 : CONversation and Tancred.
13. ll. 65–69 : Ford Madox Ford, his monument.
14. l. 70 : The Cytherean goddess.
15. l. 71 : To 'the hall of the records'.
16. l. 72 : 'Fear not!'
17. ll. 73–74 : 'The cricket no relief'.
    ll. 75–79 : Continuation of 9 – The Birds.
18. l. 80 : Terreus.
19. ll. 81–83 : 'No just wars'.

20. ll. 84–88 : Not 'in anything less than a geological epoch'.

21. ll. 89–90 : Happier days.

22. ll. 91 ff. : Whitman.
    ll. 91–92 : His non-recognition in America.
    ll. 93–94 : Whitman 'exotic, still suspect'.
    ll. 95–96 : 'From the gates of death' — 9 continued (The Birds).

23. ll. 97–103 : Gea Terra's downward pull — 'past metaphor'.

24. ll. 104–106 : Herbs — regeneration.

25. ll. 107–108 : Toward 'HUDOR et pax' (Niccolò d'Este).

26. l. 109 : Longing for reunion.
    ll. 110 & 112 : 23 continued.

27. l. 111 : Kipling an initiate.
    l. 113 : 23 continued — 'tally Nature', Identity.

28. ll. 114–115 : Feeling of isolation, coming despair.
    ll. 116–124 : 23 concluded : Marriage with Earth (Mystery). Immersion.
    l. 125 : 28 modified — despair.

29. ll. 126–127 : The blackest of all thoughts.

30. ll. 127–128 : The tears overflow.
    ll. 129–131 : 9 concluded — Requiem.

31. l. 132 : Arising ('Est consummatum, Ite' — cf. 74 : 10/458).

Although we have said that no literary form is apparent from Canto LXXXII — literary in the traditional and accepted sense — it may now be conceded, after studying (and trying to improve on) this plan, that there is undeniably a certain musical pattern running through it. There is theme, repetition and variation of theme, for example with the Birds (9), with Gea Terra (23) and with Despair (28), and there is contrapuntal setting of passages and lines; and, above all, the subtle rise and fall of the poet's voice cannot be missed, now swift, now slow, now conversing and observing, now chanting.

'Only a musical form would take the material', Pound had found even before properly embarking on the *Cantos*, and although he explicitly denied an exact parallel with a Bach fugue, he did point out on the BBC that there is an analogy.

The one notable attempt at such musical analysis is that made by Rainer M. Gerhardt (died 1954) in a broadcast about the *Pisan Cantos*, an illuminating part of which Emery has translated from the original German and included in *Ideas into Action* (pp. 79–81). This kind of enquiry is badly needed, because in spite of its necessary musical bias it might still provide literary criticism with criteria which could be used to distinguish really accomplished non-metrical modern verse from would-be free verse.

That Pound himself has for long enough investigated the relationship between music and poetry is common knowledge, and Noel Stock's reviewer in *The Times Literary Supplement* remarked parenthetically, but very succinctly, that 'some of his points might well be looked up again by recent correspondents on syllabic verse' (May 28, 1964). Nevertheless his observations have so far hardly been applied with profit to the study of his own verse. Stock's account of the matter in the chapter 'Words and Music' of his *Poet in Exile* (pp. 84–120) certainly comes nearest.

SELECT BIBLIOGRAPHY

Note : Where the place of publication is omitted it is always London.

THE WRITINGS OF EZRA POUND

No more is attempted here than to list the editions used for this study. Anything else would be futile after the publication of

Gallup, Donald. *A Bibliography of Ezra Pound* (Soho Bibliographies XVIII, Rupert Hart-Davis, 1963).

Gives detailed bibliographical descriptions and analyses of the contents (though not by pages) and contains an invaluable Index comprising every single poem and article and their appearance in periodicals and in book form.

Poetry

The Cantos of Ezra Pound (New York: New Directions, 1948).
    Cantos I–LXXI and LXXIV–LXXXIV.
The Cantos of Ezra Pound (Faber and Faber, 1954).
    Contents identical with the New Directions edition.
Section : Rock-Drill : 85–95 de los cantares (Faber and Faber, 1957).
    Change to Arabic numerals.
Thrones : 96–109 de los cantares (Faber and Faber, 1960).
'Two Cantos', *Paris Review*, 28 (Summer/Fall 1962), 13–16.
    From Canto 115 und Canto 116.
'Sections from New Cantos', *Agenda*, 3 (Dec.–Jan. 1963/4), 1–3.
    From Cantos 110, 112, 115 and an unassigned passage.
Poems 1918–21 (New York : Boni and Liveright, 1921).
    Contains the early version of Canto IV.
Personae : Collected Shorter Poems of Ezra Pound (Faber and Faber, 1952).
    (quoted as *Personae*).

Translations

The Classical Anthology Defined by Confucius (Cambridge, Mass. : Harvard University Press, 1954).

Confucian Analects (Peter Owen, 1956).

Confucius : The Great Digest & Unwobbling Pivot (Peter Owen, 1952).
  (quoted as *Confucius*).

The Translations of Ezra Pound, ed. H. Kenner (Faber and Faber, 1953).
  (quoted as *Translations*).

Sophocles : Women of Trachis (Neville Spearman, 1956).

Prose

ABC of Reading (Norfolk, Conn. : New Directions, [1951]).
  (quoted as *ABC of Reading*).

ABC of Economics (Peter Russell, 1953).

Gaudier-Brzeska : A Memoir (Hessle : The Marvell Press, 1960).
  (quoted as *Gaudier*).

Guide to Kulchur (Norfolk, Conn. : New Directions, [1952]).
  (quoted as *Guide*).

Impact : Essays on Ignorance and the Decline of American Civilization, ed.
  N. Stock (Chicago : Henry Regnery, 1960).
  (quoted as *Impact*).

Jefferson and/or Mussolini : L'Idea Statale, Fascism as I Have Seen It (Stanley
  Nott, 1935).
  (quoted as *Jefferson and/or Mussolini*).

The Letters of Ezra Pound : 1907–1941, ed. D. D. Paige (Faber and Faber, 1951).
  (quoted as *Letters*).

Literary Essays of Ezra Pound, ed. T. S. Eliot (Faber and Faber, 1954).
  (quoted as *Essays*).

Patria Mia and the Treatise on Harmony (Peter Owen, 1962).
  (quoted as *Patria Mia*).

Pavannes and Divagations (Peter Owen, 1960).
  (quoted as *Pavannes*).

The Spirit of Romance (Peter Owen, 1952).
  (quoted as *Spirit*).
  For books only occasionally used see Notes.

CRITICISM

Commentaries on the Cantos

Edwards, John H. and Vasse, William W. *Annotated Index to the Cantos of
  Ezra Pound* (Berkeley and Los Angeles : University of California Press,
  corrected edition, 1959).
  (quoted as *Index*).

The Pound Newsletter, ed. John H. Edwards (Berkeley : University of California, 1954–1956). 10 issues (mimeographed).

One of the main purposes of this series was to obtain information for the *Index*.

The Analyst, ed. Robert Mayo (Evanston : Northwestern University, 1953–). (mimeographed).

The following issues contain detailed guides to Cantos I–XI :

Nos. I (March 1953) and VIII (June 1955) : Cantos I–IV.

Nos. II–V (July 1953, etc.) : Cantos V–VIII.

No. VI (Jan. 1955) : Addenda to Cantos I–VIII.

No. VII (April 1955) : Canto IX.

No. XI (July 1956): Canto X.

No. XIII (July 1957) : Canto XI.

A number of students of Prof. N. H. Pearson, Yale University, have prepared notes on the following Cantos : III, IV, V, XIII, XVI, XXIII, XXX, XXXIII, XXXVII, XXXVIII, XLV, XLIX, L and LXXV.

(quoted as *Yale Notes*).

Books on Pound

Amdur, A. S. *The Poetry of Ezra Pound* (Cambridge, Mass. : Radcliff Honors Theses in English, No. 5, 1936).

Dekker, George. *Sailing After Knowledge : The Cantos of Ezra Pound* (Routledge and Kegan Paul, 1963).

Dembo, L. S. *The Confucian Odes of Ezra Pound : a Critical Appraisal* (Faber and Faber, 1963).

Eliot, T. S. *Ezra Pound : His Metric and Poetry* (New York : A. A. Knopf, 1917).

Emery, Clark. *Ideas into Action : a Study of Pound's Cantos* (Coral Gables, Fla. : University of Miami Press, 1958).

(quoted as Emery).

Espey, John J. *Ezra Pound's* Mauberley : *a Study in Composition* (Faber and Faber, 1955).

Fraser, G. S. *Ezra Pound* (Edinburgh : Oliver and Boyd, 1960).

Kenner, Hugh. *The Poetry of Ezra Pound* (Faber and Faber, 1951).

(quoted as Kenner).

Leary, Lewis, ed. *Motive and Method in* The Cantos *of Ezra Pound* (New York : Columbia University Press, 1954).

(quoted as *Motive & Method*).

Contains essays by Hugh Kenner, Guy Davenport, Sister M. Bernetta Quinn and Forrest Read, Jr.

de Nagy, N. C. *The Poetry of Ezra Pound : The Pre-Imagist Stage* (Berne : Francke, 1960).

181

Norman, Charles. *The Case of Ezra Pound* (New York : The Bodley Press, 1948).

Norman, Charles. *Ezra Pound* (New York : Macmillan, 1960).
(quoted as Norman).

Rosenthal, M. L. *A Primer of Ezra Pound* (New York : Macmillan, 1960).

Russell, Peter, ed. *Ezra Pound : a Collection of Essays* (Peter Nevill, 1950).
(quoted as Russell).

Stock, Noel, *Poet in Exile : Ezra Pound* (Manchester : The University Press, 1964).

Watts, H. H. *Ezra Pound and the Cantos* (Chicago : Henry Regnery, 1952).

Williams, Barbara M. 'The Development of Ezra Pound as a Poet, with special reference to his preoccupation with the theme of the artist in society' (unpublished M. A. thesis, Victoria University, Manchester, April 1957).

Yeats, W. B. *A Packet for Ezra Pound* (Dublin : The Cuala Press, 1929).
Reprinted in *A Vision* (Macmillan, 1937).

Books with Sections about Pound

Blackmur, R. P. *Language as Gesture* (1954).

Bogan, Louise. *Achievement in American Poetry 1900–1950* (Chicago, 1951).

Bowen, Stella. *Drawn from Life* (1941).

Brooks, Van Wyck. *The Confident Years 1885–1915* (1952).

Cunliffe, Marcus. *The Literature of the United States* (revised edition, 1961).

Ford, Ford Madox. *Thus to Revisit* (1921).
- *Return to Yesterday* (1931).
- *It was the Nightingale* (1934).
- *The March of Literature from Confucius to Modern Times* (1939).

Goldring, Douglas. *South Lodge* (1943).
- *The Last Pre-Raphaelite : a Record of the Life and Writings of Ford Madox Ford* (1948).

Graves Robert. *The Common Asphodel* (1949).
- *The Crowning Privilege* (1956).

Gregory, Horace and Zaturenska, Marya. *A History of American Poetry 1900–1940* (New York, 1946).

Highet, Gilbert. *The Classic Tradition : Greek and Roman Influences on Western Literature* (Oxford, 1949).

Hughes, Glenn. *Imagism and the Imagists* (reprinted, 1960).

Hunt, Violet. *The Flurried Years* (1926).

Kreymborg, Alfred. *A History of American Poetry : Our Singing Strength* (New York, 1934).

Leavis, F. R. *New Bearings in English Poetry* (1932).

Lewis, Wyndham. *Time and Western Man* (1927).

Matthiessen, F. O. *American Renaissance : Art and Expression in the Age of Emerson and Whitman* (New York, 1941).
Pound's opinion on Whitman discussed on pp. 579 f. & 592.

May, Henry F. *The End of American Innocence : a Study of the First Years of Our Own Time, 1912–17* (1959).

Miner, Earl. *The Japanese Tradition in British and American Literature* (Princeton, 1958).

O'Connor, William Van. *Sense and Sensibility in Modern Poetry* (Chicago, 1948).

Read, Herbert. *The Tenth Muse : Essays in Criticism* (1957).

Spiller, Robert E. and others. *Literary History of the United States*, vol. II (New York, 1949).

Straumann, Heinrich. *American Literature in the Twentieth Century* (revised edition, 1962).

Viereck, Peter. *Dream and Sensibility* (Washington, 1953).

Yeats, W. B., ed. *The Oxford Book of Modern Verse* (1936), Introduction.

The Letters of W. B. Yeats, ed. A. Wade (1954).

Articles and Reviews

Of the formidable bulk of critical writing on Pound in periodicals only those items are included here which were found most useful and, above all, obtainable in Europe. Comprehensive lists are given, for example, in :

Millett, Fred B. *Contemporary American Authors* (New York, 1944).
Up to 1940.

Leary, Lewis. *Articles on American Literature Appearing in Current Periodicals 1920–1945* (Durham, N. C., 1947).

Spiller, Robert E. and others. *Literary History of the United States*, vol. III (New York, 1949).
Up to 1947, carried on from 1948 to 1958 in its *Bibliographical Supplement*, ed. R. M. Ludwig (New York, 1959).

Alvarez, A. 'Ezra Pound : The Question and Limitation of Translation-Poetry', *Essays in Criticism*, VI (April 1956), 171 ff.
— 'Two Faces of Pound', *Observer* (March 6, 1960).

Bergman, Herbert. 'Ezra Pound and Walt Whitman', *American Literature*, XXVII (March 1955), 56–61.

Bradbury, Malcolm. *Twentieth Century* (June 1956), 604–606.

Brooke-Rose, Christine. 'Ezra Pound : Piers Plowman in the Modern Waste Land', *Review of English Literature*, II, 2 (April 1961), 74–88.

Conquest, Robert. 'Ezra Pound', *London Magazine* (April 1963), 33–49.

Davie, Donald. 'Adrian Stokes and Pound's "Cantos"', *Twentieth Century* (Nov. 1956), 419–436.

Duncan, Ronald. 'Pull Down Thy Vanity', *Sunday Times* (Feb. 11, 1962).

Eliot, T. S. 'Isolated Superiority', *Dial*, LXXXIV (Jan. 1928), 4–7.

Fitzgerald, Robert. 'Gloom and Gold in Ezra Pound', *Encounter* (July 1956), 16–22.
  — 'A Note on Ezra Pound, 1928–56', *Kenyon Review*, XVIII (Autumn 1956), 505–518.

Hall, Donald. 'The Cantos in England', *New Statesman* (March 12, 1960).
  — 'The Art of Poetry V: Ezra Pound', *Paris Review*, 28 (Summer/Fall 1962), 22–51.

Häusermann, H. W. 'W. B. Yeats's Criticism of Ezra Pound', *English Studies*, XXIX, 4 (1948), 97–109.

Honig, Edwin. 'That Mutation of Pound's', *Kenyon Review*, XVII (1955), 349–356.

Hynes, Samuel. 'Pound and the Prose Tradition', *Yale Review*, LI (Summer 1962), 532–546.

Kenner, Hugh. 'Gold in the Gloom', *Poetry*, 81 (Nov. 1952).
  — 'As of Wind and of Water', *Poetry*, 85 (Dec. 1954).
  — 'Plea for Metrics', *Poetry*, 86 (April 1955).

Merchant, W. Moelwyn. 'Featuring : Ezra Pound', *Critical Quarterly*, I (Winter 1956), 277–287.

Nänny, Max. 'Ezra Pound's Visual Poetry and the Method of Science', *English Studies*, XLIII (Oct. 1962), 426–430.

Pearce, Roy Harvey. 'Toward an American Epic', *Hudson Review*, XII (Autumn 1959), 362–377.

Read, Forrest, Jr. 'The Pattern of the Pisan Cantos', *Sewanee Review*, XLV (1957), 400–419.

Times Literary Supplement. 'His Name in the Record' (June 10, 1960), 368 (Review of *Pavannes and Divagations* and *Thrones*).
  For all further reviews of Pound's books and of books on Pound see the Indices to *T. L. S.*

Miscellaneous

Gerhardt, Rainer M. 'Die Pisaner Gesänge', a Radio Feature. (Frankfurt : Property of Hessischer Rundfunk, March 1952).
  An important part of it is quoted in translation by Emery, pp. 79–81.

For all other material used and referred to see Index and Notes.

NOTES

1. Published by Alfred A. Knopf, New York, Nov. 12, 1917, barely three months after the last part of 'Three Cantos' in *Poetry* (August 1917). Concerning the reception of 'Three Cantos' Pound wrote to Harriet Monroe : 'Eliot is the only person who proffered criticism instead of general objection.' (*Letters*, p. 173.).

2. 'Isolated Superiority', *Dial*, LXXXIV (1928), 4–7.

3. The works of the writers mentioned are as follows : F. R. Leavis, *New Bearings in English Poetry* (1932); Edith Sitwell, *Aspects of Modern Poetry* (1934), the pertinent part of which is reprinted in Russell, pp. 37–65; R. P. Blackmur, 'Masks of Ezra Pound' (1934), now reprinted in *Language as Gesture* (1954), pp. 124–154; A. S. Amdur, *The Poetry of Ezra Pound* (Cambridge, Mass., 1936). For Yeats's judgment implied in *A Packet for Ezra Pound* (Dublin, 1929) see H. W. Häusermann, 'W. B. Yeats's Criticism of Ezra Pound', *English Studies*, XXIX (1948), 97–109.

4. See *The Common Asphodel* (1949) and *The Crowning Privilege* (1956); cf. G. S. Fraser, *Ezra Pound* (Edinburgh, 1960), pp. 109–112.

5. For 'avowal — disavowal' see Harold H. Watts, *Ezra Pound and the Cantos* (Chicago, 1952), especially pp. 56 ff.

6. Charles Norman, *Ezra Pound* (New York, 1960), 493 pp.

7. Written in 1936, included in Russell, p. 72.

8. See Robert Browning, *Sordello*, ed. A. J. Whyte (1913), Introduction.

9. *A Packet for Ezra Pound*, p. 1.

10. See Eliot's Introduction (1928) to the *Selected Poems of Ezra Pound* (reissued 1948), p. 9.

11. *The Oxford Book of Modern Verse 1892–1935*, chosen by W. B. Yeats (1936), Introduction, p. xxv.

12. Caedmon TC 1122 (1960).

13. See Appendix, p. 175.

14. Kenner, pp. 318 & 317.

15. *Motive & Method*, pp. 83 & 85.

16. *Language as Gesture*, p. 147.

17. *Language as Gesture*, p. 146.

18. *Aeneid* III, 3.

19. Cf. *Purg.* XII, 61 : 'Vedea Troia in cenere e in caverne'; 'caverne' is annotated as 'ammassi di macerie sotto e fra le quali restano vani a mo' di grotte o caverne' in the *Divina Commedia*, ed. G. Vandelli (Milan, 1955), p. 404.

20. *The Waste Land*, I, 21–22.

21. *Aeneid* III, 2.

22. *Purg.* XII, 61–63.

23. Cf. 'Troy in Auvergnat' (5 : 18/22) and Troy at the court of Niccolò d'Este in 20 : 90/94.

24. *Iliad* III, 154–160.

25. See Ovid, *Metam.* III, 582 ff.

26. Cf. 84 : 116/573 and the whole of the *Pisan Cantos*.

27. *Agamemnon* 685–690, in *Aeschylus*, vol. II, Loeb Classical Library (1926) p. 61.

28. Gilbert Murray, *Aeschylus : The Creator of Tragedy* (Oxford, 1940), p. 200.

29. The compiler of Appendix A : Greek of the *Index*.

30. Quoted by John J. Espey, *Ezra Pound's Mauberley* (1955), p. 88; Espey also gives a summary of Pound's views on Pindar on pp. 86–88.

31. Translation as given in the *Index* under 'Anaxiforminges'.

32. *Personae*, p. 226; cf. 'ingenium nobis ipsa puella facit' (Propertius, *Elegies* II, i, 6).

33. See *Metam.* III, 95 ff.

34. See Emery, p. 91.

35. See 27 : 131 f. / 136 f. : a powerful but somewhat obscure chant.

36. Emery, p. 125.

37. 77 : 46 / 498; cf. *Metam.* III, 106 ff.

38. Cf. 74 : 8 f. / 457, where the two merge.

39. Cf. *Metam.* III, 35 & 46.

40. *Les Phéniciens et l'Odyssée*, vol. I (Paris, 1902), p. 224. An indirect approval of Bérard's scholarship is found in the *ABC of Reading*, p. 43 f.; the passage is discussed in Part Two.

41. See D. H. Tritschler in the *Analyst*, II (July 1953), 2.

42. Kenner, p. 319 and *Motive & Method*, pp. 14, 19 & 11.

43. Cf. 'Arnold Dolmetsch', *Pavannes and Divisions*, pp. 256 ff.

44. See Kenner, *Motive & Method*, p. 13.

45. *Motive & Method*, pp. 5 & 6.

46. From the 'We have seen thee, O Love' chorus of *Atalanta in Calydon*.

47. Beginning of the poem entitled 'Itylus', originally published in *Poems and Ballads : First Series* (1866).

48. The ND text has : 'Et ter flebiliter, Ityn, Ityn!'.

49. *Odes* IV, xii, 5–8; translation from C. E. Bennett, *Horace : The Odes and Epodes*, Loeb Classical Library (1914), pp. 330–333.

50. The tradition is anything but fixed, however. In *Odyssey* XIX, 518–523 it is indeed the nightingale who is the child's mother; the same is assumed by Matthew Arnold in his poem 'Philomela'. But Eliot's Philomel in *The Waste Land* (II, 99 ff.) is the sister and the nightingale. In Swinburne's 'Itylus', with which Pound is no doubt very familiar, the mother is the swallow. Ovid (*Metam.* VI, 424–676) leaves it open.

51. Pound mentions this story in *The Spirit of Romance* (p. 44) and dis-

approvingly refers to the 'alas, all too scholarly' treatment of it by A. de Langfors (footnote 4).

52. Kenner, p. 243.

53. Hugh Kenner and Sister Bernetta Quinn have compared certain Poundian devices to the art of the film. Kenner illustrates the analogy by referring to and quoting from Eisenstein (see Kenner, pp. 60 f., 113 f. & 260–262). Quinn makes the comparison in the course of defining Pound's notion of metamorphosis (see *Motive & Method*, p. 74). Cf. also Max Nänny, 'Ideogramm und Montage : Bemerkungen zur Beziehung zwischen Ezra Pound und Sergei Eisenstein', *Neue Zürcher Zeitung* (March 25, 1962).

54. Modern spelling 'Rodez', the nearby Provençal town (see *Index*).

55. See 'Vorticism', now in *Gaudier*, pp. 86 ff.

56. Why Pound put 'Ityn' and not simply 'Itys' is explained by Sister B. Quinn as 'also a union of Itys and Cabestan' (*Motive & Method*, p. 86). It is better to avoid pinning too many uncertain implications to a single word, not least because Pound may revise the text once more.

57. See her *Ezra Pound : Dichtung und Prosa* (Zurich, 1953); the book contains a German translation of Canto IV.

58. *Language as Gesture*, p. 147.

59. Cf. the chapter 'Psychology and Troubadours' in *The Spirit of Romance*, pp. 87–100.

60. Cf. : 'Speaking aesthetically, the myths are explications of mood' (*Spirit*, p. 92). See also the similar conception in 'RELIGIO or, The Child's Guide to Knowledge' (*Pavannes*, pp. 96–98).

61. Emery, p. 108.

62. Cf. *Metam*. III, 141.

63. Cf. : 'The valley is thick with leaves...' (l. 35) with 'vallis erat piceis et acuta densa cupressu' (*Metam*. III, 155). For the pines and cypresses Pound substitutes deciduous trees; he may have had in mind Ovid's description of Lake Pergusa, at the same time (see *Metam*. V, 385 ff.).

64. Russell, p. 60.

65. See Herodotus I, 12.

66. From 'Merciles Beautè', attributed to Chaucer; these lines are quoted in the *Pisan Cantos* (81 : 98/555).

67. Emery, p. 121; see 30 : 147/152.

68. See Geoffrey of Monmouth, *Histories of the Kings of Britain*, I, ll. Cf. also Emery, p. 156.

69. Kenner, p. 201.

70. See 80 : 79/535 and Kenner, pp. 200 ff.

71. The poem was first published in *Poetry* (March 1915) and specifically called a 'war poem' (see Norman, p. 158), now in *Personae*, p. 177.

72. Cf. : 'Aurum est commune sepulchrum. Usura commune sepulchrum.' (47 : 28/245).

73. O. Seyffert, etc., *A Dictionary of Classical Antiquities* (1908), under 'Actaeon'.

74. From Pound's description of the 'Artemis pose' in *Patria Mia*, p. 39 f.
75. Cf. :   '... victum spoliare parabat :
        arma relicta videt; corpus deus aequoris albam
        contulit in volucrem, cuius modo nomen habebat.' (*Metam.* XXII, 143–145).
76. Terms coined and discussed in Earl Miner, *The Japanese Tradition in British and American Literature* (Princeton, 1958), pp. 135–155. The basis of Miner's theorizing is Pound's article 'Vorticism'.
77. See : 'Tching prayed on the mountain and
            wrote MAKE IT NEW
        on his bath tub
            Day by day make it new' (53 : 10 f. / 274 f.).
    In the margin we find the Chinese, which also appeared on the title page of Pound's 1934 volume of essays, entitled *Make it New*.
78. E. M. Glenn in the *Analyst*, I (March 1953), 1.
79. See Miner, p. 4 (on the oriental gold).
80. See *The Waste Land* II & III.
81. Pound seems to have conceived of this symmetry only in later versions. The repetition of 'beneath the knees of the gods' is not in that of 1921.
82. See 74 : 7/455 where the ming[2] character should be replaced by hsin[3] : 'the tensile light' (cf. Emery, pp. 10 & 15). The hsin[3] ('hsien' with Pound) appears, however, in 91 : 72, and there the word 'tensile' beside it is appropriate, but not so in 74 : 7/455. In 98 : 45 the ming[2] and the hsin[3] are brought together; cf. also *Impact*, p. 44, where the term 'undivided light' is used.
83. In his Cavalcanti essay (*Essays*, especially pp. 160 ff.) Grosseteste and Cavalcanti are seen to complement each other, and in 55 : 44/311 both are placed side by side with Confucianism. The only indication of Cavalcanti's presence is, however, the Italian word 'risplende'. Yet this is the very word from the 'Canzone' line which Pound annotates in the essay by quoting Grosseteste. This 'equation' has so far escaped Poundian criticism.
84. 93 : 88; cf. 'plura diafana' quoted in 83 : 108/566 and 'per plura diafana' in 100 : 74, where Grosseteste is brought together with Plotinus.
85. Plato, *Phaedrus* 247 c, quoted by Pound in *The Spirit of Romance*, p. 140.
86. Cf. : ' "sunt lumina" said Erigena' (74 : 7/455) and 'omnia, quae sunt, lumina sunt, or whatever' (83 : 106/563), which is translated in 74 : 7/456 as : 'all things that are are lights'.
87. Ra-Set is the 'daughter of the Egyptian solar deity', who 'like Danaë, represents a fruitful god-man relationship' (Emery, pp. 156 & 112).
88. See Forrest Read, 'The Pattern of the Pisan Cantos', *Sewanee Review*, LXV (1957), 400–419.
89. Emery, p. 156.
90. From 'The Tree' (*Personae*, p. 17); they appear in 91 : 65 : 'Baucis, Philemon'.
91. According to Glenn (*Analyst*, I, 5).

92. *Translations*, p. 246; first pointed out by Espey in the *Analyst*, III (Dec. 1953), 11.
93. This phrase, like 'nimbus of gold flame', is from Earl Miner's interpretation in the *Japanese Tradition*, p. 148.
94. Gourdon : 'city in Provence, N of Toulouse; associated with troubadour poetry' *(Index)*.
95. See 26 : 121/126 and 29 : 141, 146/146, 151.
96. See 47 : 30 ff. / 246 ff. (Greek cult of Adonis) and for the same in China, e.g. 91 : 72.
97. There are several other passages in the *Cantos* which show Pound recalling his hiking tours in Provence.
98. *Carmen* LXI, 9–10, as translated by F. W. Cornish in *Catullus, Tibullus and Pervigilium Veneris*, Loeb Classical Library (1913), p. 69.
99. That it *is* a pondering over his translation can be assumed in the light of 23 : 107 f. / 111 f., where Pound also records the actual translating.
100. See C. R. Haines, *Sappho : The Poems and Fragments* (n. d.), p. 159.
101. Miner, p. 149.
102. In *170 Chinese Poems* (second edition, 1918), pp. 24–26.
103. Pointed out by Achilles Fang, together with the reference to Waley's translation, in the *Analyst*, II (July 1953), 8.
104. Herodotus I, 96 ff., translation from A. de Sélincourt, *Herodotus : The Histories*, Penguin Classics (1954), pp. 54 f.
105. Cf. : 'city of patterned streets' (5 : 17/21).
106. Cf. 'in the turn of the stairs' (1. 100) with Eliot's 'At the first turning of the second stair' etc.
107. Erigena, quoted in 36 : 29/185 and elsewhere.
108. *Motive & Method*, p. 21.
109. Cf. Kenner, pp. 318 f.
110. Achilles Fang, in the *Analyst*, II, 9, points out that the Chinese call these spirits *Hsien-jen*, Sennin being the Japanese, and that 'Rokku is not a mountain. The correct name should be Tai haku (Japanese for *T'ai-po*).' This is the name found in 56 : 47/315.
111. See Herodotus I, 88 ff.
112. See Barnefield's poem 'Philomel' and *The Waste Land* III, 206.
113. See 74 : 5,7/453,455 and 80 : 79/534 for the paraclete and 76 : 38/489 for 'Eurus as comforter'.
114. Cf. : 'Voices of the procession' (21 : 99/103); this appears to be something that haunted Pound for a long time.
115. Cf. 'thick like paint' (1. 120) with :
    'a great brute sweating paint said Vanderpyl 40 years later of Vlaminck' (74 : 13/462).
116. If it can be said that Pound adopted much of the Pre-Raphaelites' interest in Early Italian poetry and art, it must be added at once that Pound manages to recapture the mood of Early Italian culture to a degree denied to the romantically sentimental members of the Pre-Raphaelite Brotherhood.

117. Cf. Emery, p. 14.

118. From the 1921 version of Canto IV.

119. How fond Pound was of it is brought out again in : 'The ant's a centaur in his dragon world' (81 : 99/556).

120. See 29 : 145/150, 78 : 59/512 and also 91 : 74.

121. *Analyst*, I, 6 f.

122. The title of Part Two is derived from 24 : 111/116 : 'And he in his young youth, *in the wake of Odysseus*', where it applies to Niccolò d'Este. For the purpose of this study the phrase is understood in the widest sense.

123. Forrest Read, 'A Man of No Fortune' in *Motive & Method*, p. 101.

124. When the passage was first published it was part of Canto III, printed in *Poetry* (August 1917).

125. This is from a letter to his father dated April 11, 1927. It is probably the earliest general statement of the poem's theme. A year or so later Pound told Yeats much the same thing (see *A Packet for Ezra Pound*).

126. Above all from Catullus, *Carmen* XXXIV and the *Pervigilium Veneris* I : 'ver novum . . . canorum'.

127. See *Motive & Method*, pp. 78–79; Tate's comment is from his 1936 review of *A Draft of XXX Cantos* (Russell, p. 70).

128. *Motive & Method*, p. 108.

129. Donald Davie, 'Adrian Stokes and Pound's "Cantos" ', *Twentieth Century*, 160 (Nov. 1956), 422.

130. Cf. : 'stone knowing the form which the carver imparts it' (74 : 8/457).

131. Espey, *Ezra Pound's Mauberley*, p. 110.

132. See V. Bérard, *Did Homer Live*, transl. Brian Rhys (1931); this book is a summary of his theories.

133. Note that Pound invariably alters the term to 'periplum'.

134. The sources of this line in 78 : 60/514 are mentioned in *Essays*, pp. 247 & 255; the Greek from *Odyssey* I, 3 occurs in 12 : 54/58 and in 89 : 60.

135. Contained in the *Codex Heidelbergensis* 398, as pointed out in R. Hennig, *Terrae Incognitae*, vol. I (Leiden, 1944), p. 86.

136. Published in 1558. The word 'carroch', from Italian 'carrocchio', may indicate that Pound had this book to hand when making his adaptation.

137. Bérard, *Did Homer Live*, p. 151.

138. For the line numbering see the Hanno passage (40 : 49–51/207–209). The count starts with 'PLEASING . . .'.

139. Thomas Falconer, *The Voyage of Hanno*, transl., Greek text, etc. (1797); the two other translations, found less concise, are that of M. Cary in Cary & Warmington, *The Ancient Explorers* (1929), pp. 47 ff. and that of E. H. Warmington in his *Greek Geography* (1934), pp. 72 ff.

140. This is a direct transliteration from the title, 'Hannonos Karxedonion Basileos Periplous'; hence, wrongly, in the genitive.

141. *Did Homer Live*, p. 99.

142. The comment on Joyce is perhaps less a personal reminiscence than a result of Pound's study of the last section of *Ulysses*, where Gibraltar is

the most frequently recurring place. It is mentioned 9 times, and Molly Bloom says near the end : '...and Gibraltar as a girl where I was a Flower...' (Bodley Head ed., p. 742). The sailor she met there was her first lover; he, Pound seems to imply, sailed with her beyond the Pillars of Herakles.

143. See *Odyssey* IX, 480 ff. and X, 120 ff.
144. See *Odyssey* IX, 88–89 and X, 101.
145. Hennig (p. 89) speaks of 'schwunglose Nüchternheit'.
146. To show that Pound is not the only one who is fond of such metaphors when speaking of the light of heaven, this is quoted from E. G. Gardner, *Dante's Ten Heavens* (second edition, 1904), p. 218.
147. It is interesting to note that Hennig specifically calls his translation 'Hannos Westafrika-Fahrt zum "Götterwagen" '.
148. Emery, p. 126.
149. See the New Jerusalem as described in Rev. xxi and Blake's *Jerusalem* I, 13 : 'And every part of the City is fourfold...'.
150. From 'An Introduction to the Economic Nature of the United States' (1944), reprinted in *Impact*, p. 15. The Italian is borrowed from *Inf*. IV, 131, where the line : 'vidi 'l maestro di color che sanno' (I saw the master of those who know) refers to Aristotle. Pound's plural, 'maestri', is a significant misquotation.
151. Emery, pp. 101 & 102.
152. See *Odyssey* IX, 62–63, 565–566 and X, 133–134.
153. Only once does Homer make Odysseus imagine what his companions must have uttered (*Odyssey* X, 38–45). This passage may indeed have influenced Pound's presentation.
154. *Odyssey* X, 552 f. All English quotations from the *Odyssey* are from E. V. Rieu, *Homer : The Odyssey*, Penguin Classics (1946).
155. *Odyssey* XII, 261.
156. See *Odyssey* XII, 418.
157. See 74 : 21/470 f. and 77 : 42/493.
158. Kenner, pp. 278–280.
159. Quoted in this form by Emery, pp. 19 f. For the full text see *Essays*, pp. 212 f.
160. W. B. Stanford, *The Ulysses Theme* (Oxford, 1954) records no instance of a special emphasis on this event in the whole tradition.
161. *Odyssey* IX, 52–53.
162. *Homer : Odyssee* (Munich, 1955); cf. with this 'Wagnerian' version the quieter, pietistic version of J. H. Voss :
 '... Da suchte Gottes Verderben
 Uns Unglückliche heim, und überhäuft' uns mit Jammer.'
163. Cf. Pound's own use of the German 'Schicksal' in 56 : 54/321 and in 62 : 91/361, where it stands, however, more for 'destiny' and 'providence'.
164. *Odyssey* I, 31–43.
165. *The Ulysses Theme*, p. 179; cf. *Inf*. XXVI, 63.

166. *Letters*, p. 155. He repeats the thought in *Guide to Kulchur* : 'The play Kagekiyo has Homeric robustness.' (p. 81).

167. *Odyssey* XI, 543 ff.

168. See the commentary to *Inf.* XXVI, 94–96 by G. Vandelli.

169. *The Ulysses Theme*, p. 181. Stanford adds in a note : 'No satisfactory source has been found for this innovation of making Ulysses go from Circe to his death. Perhaps Dante had heard some confused account of Ulysses' voyage to the Land of Ghosts after leaving Circe . . .' (p. 273).

170. *Inf.* XXVI, 107–109.

171. *The Ulysses Theme*, pp. 180 & 182.

172. Cf. : ' "I am noman, my name is noman" ' (74 : 4/453).

173. 74 : 3/451, echoed in 74 : 9/457 and 76 : 30/480.

174. 74 : 8/456, recurring in 74 : 9/458.

175. 80 : 91, 92/548; see also : ' "and with a name to come" / εσσομένοισι' (74 : 24/473). The Greek indicates the Homeric source of Pound's 'and with a name to come' (already in 1 : 4/8) : *Odyssey* XI, 76.

176. Cf. 'magna Nux animae' (74 : 14/463) and 'nox animae magna' (74 : 15/464); see also the more explicit reference to St. John of the Cross in 74 : 16/465.

177. See *Par.* XIX, 46–48. Why Pound makes Lucifer fall in N. Carolina, is difficult to explain : the indication of a definite place gives it the kind of immediacy which Pound admires in Dante. On the other hand, Pound may be scorning the Americans in general for their Miltonic hebraic morals (?).

178. William Henry Denham Rouse (1863–1950), co-editor of the Loeb Classical Library and advocate of the direct method in the teaching of the classical languages, first made a children's version of the *Odyssey*, *The Adventures of Ulysses*, which Pound read 'straight through with gt. enjoyment' (*Letters*, p. 349). He then started on an adult version, instalments of which Pound recommended to the editor of the *New English Weekly* to be serialized. Rouse received a substantial number of letters from Pound, with comments and suggestions on the translation in progress (see *Letters*, pp. 356 ff.), and Pound hints that 'perhaps [this] private correspondence wd. show that [Rouse's] latest stimulus to know more of [the *Odyssey*], has not come from greek scholars' (*Guide*, p. 145), but from him. The finished work appeared with Nelson in 1937 as *The Story of Odysseus : A Translation of Homer's 'Odyssey' into Plain English*.

179. Liddell & Scott.

180. 78 : 60/514; cf. *ABC of Reading*, p. 44.

181. *The Ulysses Theme*, pp. 13 & 75.

182. *The Ulysses Theme*, p. 29.

183. See Emery, p. 132.

184. See Virgil, *Georg.* IV, 246, where Minerva's hatred of the spider is referred to.

185. 25 : 119/124; cf. 23 : 109/114 : 'and saw then, as of waves taking form' (ND), as against 'and I saw then, . . .' (F), the 'I' pertaining to Anchises.

186. 78 : 56 f. / 510. The passage is a reproduction, from memory, with comment, of Gavin Douglas' translation of *Aeneid* I, 5 f. Douglas' version, as printed by Pound in 'Notes on Elizabethan Classicists', is :

> 'Or he his goddis, brocht in Latio
> And belt the ciete, fra quham of nobil fame
> The Latyne peopil, taken has thare name.' (*Essays*, p. 245).

This and other quotations from *The XII Bukes of Eneados* are also found in *ABC of Reading*, pp. 115–123.

187. See *Impact*, p. 58; *Guide*, p. 191 and 74 : 13/461. In 91 : 70 and 106 : 106 the goddess is imagined to be there again, 'looking seaward'.

188. Cf. e.g. *Odyssey* II, 173. See also what Pound has said about Bloom in Joyce's *Ulysses* : '. . . he is *polumetis* and a receiver of all things' (*Essays*, p. 404).

189. See Emery, p. 36.

190. 9 : 36/40. 'Poliorcetes', 'taker of cities . . . was applied to Sigismondo Malatesta by Pisanello' (*Index*).

191. See *Odyssey* X, 50–53.

192. Pound derived the Greek from *Odyssey* I, 4 : 'and his heart experienced many sufferings upon the sea'.

193. See *Odyssey* X, 472 ff.

194. 77 : 45/497; cf. : '. . . this phrase brings us ultimately both to Confucius and Dante' (*Jefferson and/or Mussolini*, pp. 15 f.). The phrase, 'directio voluntatis' is from Dante's *De Vulgari Eloquentia* II, 2.

195. See *Odyssey* IX, 98 f.

196. 28 : 138/143; cf. 21 : 97/101 and 22 : 101/105. Further information about Pound's grandfather, lumberjack and Congressman, in Norman, pp. 232 ff.

197. *Jefferson and/or Mussolini*, p. 33. Pound's grandfather is, in effect, brought together with Mussolini here.

198. See *ABC of Reading*, p. 18. The manuscript of what Pound published as *The Chinese Written Character as a Medium for Poetry : an Ars Poetica* by Ernest Fenollosa was turned over to him by Fenollosa's widow as early as 1913 (see Norman, pp. 99 f.). Cf. in this connection Max Nänny, 'Ezra Pound's Visual Poetry and the Method of Science', *English Studies*, XLIII (1962), 426–430.

199. *The Ulysses Theme*, p. 210.

200. *American Literature in the Twentieth Century* (revised edition, 1962), p. 193.

201. *Paris Review*, 28 (Summer-Fall 1962), 39.

202. When Pound was interviewed on May 8, 1945, during his detention in Genoa, he told a reporter : 'Mussolini was a very human, imperfect character who lost his head.' (given in Norman, p. 396).

203. See Kenner, p. 249.

204. Of the two allusions to Aristotle's *Nicomachean Ethics* made in 74 : 19/469, the one relevant to our discussion comes from VI, xi, 4. Before quoting this in *Guide to Kulchur* in Greek and translating it as 'rules are based on

particular cases', Pound wrote that it 'might be advantageously written with letters of fire, a platitude never sufficiently grasped' (p. 329).

205. This is what Pound gives as the fourth of the four senses in which the *Divina Commedia* is written, in *Spirit*, p. 127.

206. See Appendix, pp. 176–178.

207. Cf. these two passages from *Jefferson and/or Mussolini* : 'This is not to say that I "advocate" fascism in and for America . . .' (p. 98). 'The challenge of Mussolini to America is simply : Do the driving ideas of Jefferson, Quincy Adams, Van Buren, or whoever else there is in the creditable pages of our history, FUNCTION actually in the America of this decade to the extent that they function in Italy under the DUCE?' (p. 104).

208. For a detailed discussion of the Wagadu legend and its implications see Guy Davenport, 'Pound and Frobenius', *Motive & Method*, pp. 33–59, particularly pp. 53 ff.

209. 80 : 77/533. Note that the ND text does not give the Chinese character; hence the 'if the bloke in the' is unintelligible there.

210. See Paul Demiéville, *Matériaux pour l'enseignement élémentaire du Chinois* (Paris, 1953).

211. 78 : 55/508; cf. 77 : 53/505 and 79 : 63/517.

212. *A Packet for Ezra Pound*, p. 6.

213. Printed in the *Paris Review*, 28, 17, as a facsimile. For the names of 'most of the early presidents' cf. 'and all the presidents / Washington Adams Monroe Polk Tyler' (74 : 14/464).

214. Cf. : 'a man on whom the sun has gone down' (74 : 8 & 9/456 & 457).

215. Norman, p. 397.

216. 74 : 12/461; cf. 76 : 35/486 and 78 : 60/513 f.

217. For the kind of 'metempsychosis' involved here cf. Quinn, *Motive & Method*, p. 69 and Pound's early poem 'Histrion' quoted there.

218. Norman, p. 397.

219. 79 : 63/517. The dog in question may be the one seen in 77 : 48/500 : 'till the dog Arlechino makes his round'.

220. 74 : 12/461, from I Cor. 13, 13. As Pound was, of course, given a bible in the camp, he started comparing some of it with Confucius' *Ta Hio*, the original of which was the only book that accompanied him to Pisa, where he went on working on its translation. He mentions the two texts when talking to a 'prowling night-puss' : 'you can neither eat manuscript nor Confucius / nor even the hebrew scriptures' (80 : 76/532). At Pisa part of 'the Jewish law receives the Poundian compliment of Confucian analogy', because 'it itself condemns the usurers and the counterfeiters' (Kenner, p. 328).

221. See the *Lustra* poems 'Commission' or 'Further Instruction' (*Personae*, pp. 97 & 103).

222. 'The Cantos as Epic', in Russell, p. 147.

223. 74 : 27/477 and recurring in 77 : 50/501.

224. 77 : 44/495; cf. the lines occurring one Canto earlier :

194

'nothing matters but the quality
of the affection –
in the end – that has carved the trace in the mind
dove sta memoria'   (76 : 35/485).

225. See Norman, p. 399.

226. See Norman, p. 398. The racquet was 'an old broom handle'.

227. A microfilm (No. D 731. U 457) was made of 'Ezra Pound : Broadcasts in
Federal Communications Commission Transcripts of Short Wave Broadcasts. Rome (approximately 122 broadcasts from 1941 to 1943)'. It can be
consulted in the British Museum.

228. *Money Pamphlet No. 2* (1951), p. 9. Due to Noel Stock's editorial policy
the opening sentence is suppressed in *Impact*, p. 108. Paterson's words
appear e.g. in 46 : 27/243. Pound actually broadcast Canto XLVI on Feb. 12,
1942.

229. Russell, p. 13.

230. From the letter of Feb. 3, 1909 to William Carlos Williams.

231. From the memorial poem on Swinburne in the *Athenaeum* (April 17, 1909).

232. Cf. : 'I have been praised by the greatest living poet.' (*Letters*, p. 44 f.).

233. See John Masefield, *So Long to Learn* (1952), p. 160.

234. The *Academy* was probably the only notable negative voice : 'The "Song
of the Sirens" was lovely, though it brought destruction ... one likes to
think of him [Swinburne] as one sent "out of season" with a message the
world would not hear – because it must not.' (April 17, 1909). Such words
might very well be applied to Pound once, by certain critics.

235. As this ode has been out of print since 1917 most critics do not even know
of its existence. The first to call proper attention to it again is Christoph
N. de Nagy in *The Poetry of Ezra Pound : the Pre-Imagist Stage* (Berne,
1960), pp. 69 ff.

236. E. Gosse, *The Life of A. C. Swinburne* (1917), p. 21.

237. First published in *Poetry* (March 1918) as a review of Sir Edmund Gosse's
Swinburne biography.

238. *Swinburne : a Selection* (1960), Introduction, p. 12.

239. As pointed out in the *Index*, p. 331.

240. Cf. : 'Even Tennyson tried to go out / through the fire-place' (80 : 86/543).
Pound seems to have this from Ford as well.

241. *Impact*, p. 246; cf. : '... virtuous as these things go in a world of Gosse,
Royal Acc., etc.' (*Letters*, p. 419). It was Gosse, however, who finally
secured Joyce a government grant (see A. Wade, *The Letters of W. B. Yeats*
[1954]).

242. H. Hare, *Swinburne : a Biographical Approach* (1949), pp. 195 & 187.

243. Gosse, *The Life*, p. 244.

244. *Swinburne*, p. 187.

245. See 'No. 2, The Pines', in *And Even Now* (1921), pp. 57–88.

246. Quoted in Kenneth Young, *Ford Madox Ford* (Writers & Their Work,
1956), p. 10.

247. J. Lewis May, *John Lane and the Nineties* (1936), pp. 35, 121, 35 & 38.

248. See Emery, p. 129.

249. *The End of American Innocence* (1959), p. 271.

250. *The March of Literature from Confucius to Modern Times* (1939), pp. 827 f.

251. Pound was aware of this in *Mauberley* :
     '. . . but seeing he had been born
   In a half savage country, out of date' (*Personae*, p. 197).

252. *The Ulysses Theme*, p. 14.

253. F. M. Ford, *It was the Nightingale* (1934), pp. 273 & 308.

254. Espey, *Ezra Pound's Mauberley*, p. 82.

255. Stella Bowen, *Drawn from Life* (1941), p. 143.

256. See *ABC of Reading*, p. 185; cf. Emery, p. 149.

257. Formulation as used by Emery, p. 148.

258. F. M. Ford, *Return to Yesterday* (1931), p. 417.

259. *Drawn from Life*, p. 144.

260. 80 : 79/535. These words are from *Twelfth Night* IV, ii, 44 f., and are spoken by the Clown, masquerading as Sir Topaz the curate, to Malvolio in prison. They are not found on the pedestal, as an inspection in London proved, but on the scroll held by Shakespeare. For Bellotti see also the *Lustra* poem 'Black Slippers : Bellotti' (*Personae*, p. 121).

261. *Impact*, p. 48. Adams' statement is, of course, also in the *Cantos*, e.g. in 52 : 3/267.

262. 74 : 4/452. We note, in passing, that he also said : 'I think an alliance with Stalin's Russia is rotten.' (Jan. 29, 1942).

263. Cf. Abraham Lincoln's comment which Pound put in his *Introductory Textbook* : '. . . and gave to the people of this Republic THE GREATEST BLESSING THEY EVER HAD — THEIR OWN PAPER TO PAY THEIR OWN DEBTS.' (now in *Guide*, p. 354). Pound believes, incidentally, that Lincoln was assassinated because of such a view of banking.

264. 'The Pattern of the Pisan Cantos', *Sewanee Review*, LXV (1957), 401.

265. See 80 : 94/551 :
   'Tudor indeed is gone and every rose,
    Blood-red, blanch-white that in the sunset glows',
this beginning being a variation of 'Iram indeed is gone with all its Rose' (*Rubáiyát* 5, pointed out in the *Index*).

266. See *The Life*, pp. 178 f. and *Portraits and Sketches*, pp. 22 ff.

267. *Return to Yesterday*, p. 16.

268. *Portraits and Sketches*, p. 25 : 'Ivy should have grown up the masts and the sound of flutes been heard in the forecastle, as when Dionysus boarded the pirate vessel off Naxos.' Pound, however, does not appear to connect Swinburne's swimming accident with this myth, although it is the myth which first introduces the theme of metamorphosis into the *Cantos* (V. 2 : 7–9/11–13).

269. *The March of Literature*, p. 828.

270. See *Portraits and Sketches*, p. 25 f. and *The Life*, pp. 178 f.

271. *Essays*, p. 291. Gosse says, however : 'He was never a powerful swimmer...,
but he was ... accustomed to relieve his limbs by frequent floating.' (*The
Life*, p. 178).

272. See *Odyssey* V, 333 ff.

273. See 91 : 75,76; 93 : 83; 95 : 104,105,106,107; 96 : 3,6; 98 : 36,37; 100 : 68,69;
102 : 80,81; 109 : 126. *Section : Rock-Drill* ends with it, and *Thrones* both
starts and practically ends with it.

274. *Par.* II, 1; used thus as early as 7 : 26/31, translated as 'You in the dinghy
(piccioletta) astern there!' at the very end of *Thrones* (cf. 93 : 91).

275. *A Study of Swinburne* (1926), p. 204.

276. See pp. 46 f., which is a slight extension of what is said in 'How to Read'
(*Essays*, p. 27).

277. This is a corrected text.

278. H. Weir Smyth's translation in the Loeb *Aeschylus*.

279. *Iliad* I, 225 (W. H. D. Rouse's translation); see *Analyst*, VI, 1.

280. *Analyst*, VI, 1. Cf. : ' "for my bitch eyes" in Ilion' (102 : 82).

281. *Agamemnon* 1404–1406 (Weir Smyth).

282. See *Essays*, p. 270, where Pound quotes Browning's *Agamemnon* :
' – this man is Agamemnon,
My husband, dead, the work of this right hand here,
Aye, of a just artificer : so things are'.

283. This was written in 1919, which would mean that Pound was seventeen
when his enthusiasm for Browning was kindled.

284. Cf. : 'and there was also Uncle William / labouring a sonnet of Ronsard'
(80 : 83/540). This is Yeats trying his hand at recreating Ronsard's 'Quand
vous serez bien vieille'.

285. *Agamemnon* 685–690; cf. Part One.

286. See 2 : 6/10 and 7 : 24,25/28,29.

287. Cf. :
'Every bank of discount is downright corruption
taxing the public for private individuals' gain.' (71 : 162/438).
This statement by John Adams is frequently echoed in the later Cantos.

288. Cf. :'The mystery of economics has been more jealously guarded than
were ever the mysteries of Eleusis.' (*Impact*, p. 185).

289. Emery, p. 20.

290. Gilbert Murray, *Aeschylus*, pp. 185, 186 & 193.

291. See *Odyssey* III, 229–312. Cf. P. Mazon, *Eschyle*, vol. II (Paris, 1949), p. iv :
'La teinte dominante est la teinte "mycénienne". Elle est à fond d'or ...'.

292. *Odyssey* III, 305.

293. 77 : 49/501. Jefferson Davis (1808–1889) was the president of the Con-
federate States of America (1861–1865).

294. Murray, *Aeschylus*, p. 200. Cf. Part One.

295. 78 : 55,60/508,514; cf. 77 : 53/505.

296. Cf. Mazon, *Eschyle*, p. iii : '*Agamemnon* est le drame de l'angoisse.
L'angoisse y va croissant de scène en scène.'

297. The *Index* suggests for 'brother Percy' Shelley, as for 16 : 70/74, but this helps neither here, nor, properly, in Canto XVI.

298. See Lady Emily Lutyens, ed., *The Birth of Rowland : an Exchange of Letters between Robert Lytton and his Wife* (1956), pp. 67, 78 n, & 78 f.

299. From the Preface to the single vol. ed. of W. S. Blunt, *My Diaries : Being a Personal Narrative of Events, 1888–1914* (1932), p. ix.

300. See J. Hone, *W. B. Yeats* (1942), pp. 272 f.

301. See 30 : 148/153 f.; for the identification see *Yale Notes* to Canto XXX.

302. Cf. : 'And he talked down the anti-Hellene' (9 : 34/38).

303. *ABC of Reading*, p. 48. Of Erigena Pound also says that he 'put greek tags in his excellent verses' (83 : 106/563).

304. 71 : 166/442. What Adams had published was Otis' *Rudiments of Latin Prosody* (1760). The direct source of these passages is *The Works of John Adams*, ed. C. F. Adams (Boston, 1852–65), vol. X (*Correspondence, General*, cont.), pp. 262–266 & 274–277.

305. *Works*, X, 274 & 265.

306. *Works*, X, 208.

307. Title of an essay written in 1937, printed in *Impact*, p. 166.

308. Whether Pound wants the phrase 'marble men' to allude to a particular poet is hard to say. Keats, of course, is very fond of it; see *Endymion* I and the 'Ode on a Grecian Urn' : '... with brede / Of marble men ...'.

309. *Letters*, p. 130. It was *The Rainbow* which had just been tried.

310. *Essays*, pp. 373, 55 & 388. The French is from Stendhal's famous dictum about poetry being much below prose, with all its prescribed ornaments (quoted in full in *Essays*, p. 54). Pound refers to it in various ways and contexts (e.g. *Essays*, p. 371).

311. Listed in dictionaries, e.g. in the *Concise Oxford*.

312. Perhaps his *Love of the Angels* (1823).

313. Emery, p. 123.

314. See 77 : 42/493. Cf. *Jefferson and/or Mussolini*, p. 84 : 'When one *beau monde* gets too ditheringly silly or too besottedly ugly, a new and different *beau monde* rises to replace it.' See also *Impact*, p. 50 and the Epilogue below.

315. 74 : 11/460. Cf. *Guide*, p. 83, where 'Kokka' is called 'my most prolific Urquell'.

316. Violet Hunt, *The Flurried Years* (1926), p. 74.

317. See A. Wade, ed., *The Letters of W. B. Yeats* (1954), p. 574 n.

318. *Richard Ellmann, Yeats : The Man and the Mask* (1947), p. 12.

319. Hone, *W. B. Yeats*, p. 269.

320. See his *Some Memories of W. B. Yeats* (New York, 1940) and *So Long to Learn*, pp. 137–147.

321. Pound is wrong in calling it 'metaphysical'; see Ellmann's *Yeats*, p. 197.

322. Douglas Goldring, *South Lodge* (1943), p. 49.

323. From *D. H. Lawrence : a Composite Biography*, quoted by Norman, p. 51.

324. *A Packet for Ezra Pound*, p. 3.

325. *The Letters of W. B. Yeats*, p. 543.

326. Kenner, p. 209.

327. See Pound's 1938 article, 'This Hulme Business', reprinted in Kenner, p. 309. From this article we may see that T. E. Hulme did not have such a decisive influence on Pound as the historians of Imagism would make us believe.

328. Goldring, *South Lodge*, p. 48. For the following see also Norman, pp. 51 ff.

329. Quoted by Young, *Ford Madox Ford*, p. 10 (without source).

330. Kenner, p. 271.

331. Young, *Ford Madox Ford*, p. 15.

332. See Kenner, pp. 269, 268, 257 ff., 256 & 253.

333. See e.g. the story of the sailor who was taught to read Virgil and who, when asked about the hero, said that he had thought Aeneas was not a hero, but a priest (given in the *ABC of Reading*, p. 44).

334. *Experiments in Autobiography* (1934), p. 622.

335. *Ford Madox Ford*, p. 10.

336. *Experiments*, p. 615.

337. 'This Hulme Business', in Kenner, p. 307.

338. *Experiments*, p. 622.

339. *South Lodge*, p. 205.

340. See *Mauberley* : 'Beneath the sagging roof / The stylist has taken shelter' (*Personae*, p. 204). Kenner believes that 'it was the spectacle of Ford's disillusion that animates these three extraordinary stanzas' (p. 174). Ford was farming down in Sussex at the time (cf. Norman, p. 220).

341. *Drawn from Life*, p. 164.

342. Kenner, p. 216.

343. Cf. : 'Clearly what they translate virtue is the greek *arete*', and having given the character jên[2] he continues, 'it is not medieval *virtu*, though it is radically *virtus* from *vir*. It is, in chinese, the whole man and the whole man's contents.' (*Impact*, p. 124). Cf. *Confucius*, p. 22 and *Index*, p. 274.

344. *The Lost Childhood* (1951), p. 91.

345. This rather odd document was translated into English by Olga Rudge, a musician-friend of Pound's, and printed in *Pavannes*, pp. 153–155.

346. Cf.: 'Tard, très tard je t'ai connue, la Tristesse,
        I have been hard as youth sixty years' (80 : 91/548).

347. In 76 : 34/485; 80 : 89/546 and 84 : 116/573.

348. Thus in the light of Landor's comment on this and another epigram : 'Here are two pieces of verse for you. That on Dirce was sent me by Pericles; to prove that his Athenians can sport with Charon even now.' (*Pericles and Aspasia* in *The Complete Works of W. S. Landor* [1927–28], X, 241). The relevance of this is rather doubtful.

349. The line 'Be glad, poor beaste, love follows after thee' is listed in the *Index* as 'poss. variation on Chaucer, *Balade de Bon Conseyl*, translated by Henry Van Dyke in Speare, *Pocket Book of Verse : Therefore, poor beaste...*'. For Speare's anthology see below.

350. Cf. : '... the power over wild beasts' (47 : 33/249 and 49 : 39/256).

351. Eliot, *Waste Land* I, 22–23.

352. Emery, p. 132.

353. From the peace-seeker poem, 'Innisfree'.

354. See Norman, pp. 400 & 403. Cf. : 'see Time for June 25th' (74 : 12/460) and 84 : 115/572.

355. Kenner, p. 329.

356. Cf. Angus Fletcher, *Yale Notes* on Canto LXXV, p. 2.

357. *Motive & Method*, p. 96. The line is found in *Letters*, p. 449. It must be said in passing that neither the figures used in Canto LXXIX nor the letters in our Canto make sense as musical notation, a deplorable fact when we consider that Pound was a composer himself in his Paris years (see the sample of his opera *Villon* printed in *Guide*, pp. 361 ff.). But, together with so many other minor obscurities, this is better disregarded in an appreciation of the major implications.

358. Sinologists are inclined to doubt Kung's authorship and argue that Mencius must have been referring to another work now lost (see H. G. Creel, *Confucius : The Man and the Myth* [1951], pp. 113 f.). The title, 'Spring and Autumn', a literal translation of the Chinese characters used, denotes the two seasons merely because they are a 'compendious expression for all the four' (James Legge, *The Chinese Classics*, vol. V [1872], p. 7). Pound appears to be untouched by these intricacies.

359. *Paris Review*, 28, 44.

360. See A. Ponsonby, *Falsehood in War-Time* (New York, 1928), especially the Introduction, pp. 13–29.

361. See e.g. 81 : 96/553 and 87 : 34.

362. See *If This Be Treason* (Siena, 1948), p. 27 : 'The word Eleusis is used to recall the Mysteries of that place...' (from the manuscript of Pound's broadcast on Canto XLV). To Carlo Izzo, who was translating Canto XLV, he explained : ' "Eleusis" is very elliptical...' (*Letters*, p. 397).

363. See *Select Epigrams*, p. 197.

364. See 39 : 45/203 and 74 : 13/461. Although Wissowa, in W. H. Roscher, *Ausführliches Lexikon der griech. und röm. Mythologie*, vol. VI (instalment publ. Jan. 10, 1925), p. 202, informs us that these remains were found in 1894, encyclopaedists still continue to mention only the ruins of the Jupiter temple discovered there. Hence we also find this misleading information in the *Index*. Pound would call such negligence typical of the state of reference-book making in our 'usurocratic' times, in which the correlation of knowledge is often strangely hindered.

365. Kenner, *Motive & Method*, p. 17.

366. How the image of such eyes is always present in Pound's mind can be seen not only in *Thrones* – 'By Circeo, the stone eyes looking seaward' (106 : 106) – but also in 'Peregrinations', where he says about Gaudier's 'Hieratic Head' representing him : '... and the stone eyes gazed seaward' (*Gaudier*, p. 146, added in 1960).

367. *Guide*, p. 191. Cf. also : 'To replace the marble goddess on her pedestal at Terracina is worth more than any metaphysical argument.' (*Impact*, p. 58).

368. Cf. Pound's aphorism : 'Literature is news that STAYS news.' (*ABC of Reading*, p. 29). The statement also occurs in *Jefferson and/or Mussolini*, p. 8.

369. Henry Thornton Wharton, *Sappho : Memoirs, Text, Selected Renderings and a Literal Translation*, apparently only published in his year of death, 1895.

370. Kenner, *Motive & Method*, p. 15.

371. C. R. Haines' translation in his *Sappho*, p. 84.

372. 74 : 22–24/472–474 : echoed four times, and another twice in 80 : 89/545 f.

373. 74 : 24/474; inaccurate for 'I have seen . . . the most loving knight lie dead'.

374. 80 : 89/546. This is the opening line of 'Modern Beauty'. Cf. the observations made about the Nineties, etc. in the *Cantos* by Kenner, pp. 229–232 and again by Kenner in *Motive & Method*, pp. 15 f.

375. 76 : 40/491; cf. 76 : 39/490, where the same line about the butterfly is preceded by Sappho's 'who wrongs thee', from the same hymn.

376. 'Ode to Psyche'. It is hard to say, however, whether Pound, who has always seemed to despise the Romantics, had Keats in mind.

377. Printed at the end of Herbert Bergman's fairly comprehensive study, 'Ezra Pound and Walt Whitman', *American Literature*, XXVII (March 1955), 59–61.

378. 'What I Feel About Walt Whitman', p. 59.

379. Cf. : '(the silly quotation third-truth from Whitman)' (*Letters*, p. 210). See Bergman's article, pp. 56 f. and May's *The End of American Innocence*, p. 274.

380. 'What I Feel About Walt Whitman', p. 61.

381. Cf. : 'I thought I was fighting for a Constitutional point.' (*Paris Review*, 28, 44).

382. 'What I Feel About Walt Whitman', pp. 59 & 60.

383. Denmark first heard about the poet of American democracy in an article by Schmidt in February 1872 (as pointed out in G. W. Allen, *The Solitary Singer : a Critical Biography of Walt Whitman* [New York, 1955], p. 441). That Whitman had 'arrived' in Denmark, not merely as a medium for political propaganda, but as a poet, may be seen from the fact that it was a Dane who wrote one of the best books on him : Frederik Schyberg, *Walt Whitman* (Copenhagen, 1933), translated into English by E. A. Allen (New York, 1951).

384. Cf. : 'It is cheering to reflect that America accepted Whitman when he was properly introduced by William Michael Rossetti, and not before then.' (*Patria Mia*, p. 28). See also Whitman's own comments in his letters to Rudolf Schmidt (Jan. 16 & 20, 1872), printed in Horace Traubel, *With Walt Whitman in Camden : March 28 – July 14, 1888* (Boston, 1906), pp. 406 f.

385. *Democratic Vistas*, in *The Complete Prose Works of Walt Whitman* (Philadelphia, 1897), p. 225.

386. Pointed out in the *Index*. Thanks to Speare, too, Richard Lovelace, otherwise never mentioned by Pound, also appears :

  'I had not loved thee half so well

  Loved I not womankand' (79 : 62/516),

which is adapted from 'To Lucasta, Going to the Wars' : 'I could not love thee, Dear, so much, / Loved I not Honour more.' The line 'at my grates no Althea' (81 : 97/555) is, of course, an allusion to the other poem by Lovelace printed in Speare, 'To Althea, from Prison' (see *The Pocket Book of Verse* [new edition, 1960], pp. 59–60). There may be further borrowing from this anthology.

387. See Leo Spitzer's most illuminating article, ' "Explication de Texte" Applied to Walt Whitman's "Out of the Cradle Endlessly Rocking" ', *Journal of English Literary History*, XVII (Sept. 1949), 229–249.

388. In Whitman it is : 'O troubled reflection in the sea!' and it refers to 'the moon, drooping upon the sea' (see *The Pocket Book of Verse*, p. 253).

389. 24 : 113/118. Cf. E. G. Gardner, *Dukes and Poets in Ferrara* (1904), p. 44, where the passage from the *Diario Ferrarese* Pound adapted in Canto XXIV is rendered as : '. . . and he was interred bare without any pomp'.

390. In the *ABC of Reading* Pound has defined 'melopoeia' as 'inducing emotional correlations by the sound and rhythm of the speech' (p. 63).

391. Andrew Lang, *Theocritus, Bion and Moschus* (1892).

392. J. M. S. Tompkins, *The Art of Rudyard Kipling* (1959), pp. 214 f. & 206. The line 'Wisdom of the Grave' is from Kipling's poem 'The Sacrifice of Er-Heb'.

393. *The Odyssey : a Modern Sequel*, translated into English verse by Kimon Friar (1958), Bk. I, 848–849.

394. *Complete Prose Works*, pp. 229 & 253.

395. *Leaves of Grass* (Philadelphia, 1900), p. 136.

396. Forrest Read, *Sewanee Review*, LXV, 416.

397. See *Index*, p. 263; it should be ἔφατο.

398. i. e. 'kai philoteti' (*Odyssey* X, 335) as employed in 39 : 44/202.

399. See Emery, p. 5.

400. 52 : 4/268 and 53 : 18/283.

401. J. C. Lawson, *Modern Greek Folklore and Ancient Religion* (Cambridge, 1910), p. 545.

402. S. Angus, *The Mystery-Religions and Christianity* (1925), p. 112.

403. Pound's use of 'ΧΘΟΝΟΣ', genitive of 'χθών', is hard to explain. F has 'ΧΘΟΝΙΟΣ' in l. 119.

404. Definition of 'ἰχώρ' in the abridged Liddell & Scott.

405. In 'Out of the Cradle Endlessly Rocking'.

406. From *Inf.* XXVII, 63 (cf. *Index*).

407. 80 : 91/548; cf. Villon's 'Epitaphe' : 'REPOS ETERNEL DONNE A CIL' in A. Longnon, ed., *François Villon : Oeuvres* (4th ed., Paris, 1958), p. 73.

408. Kenner, p. 329.

409. See *Odyssey* V, 83–84, 152–158.

410. Cf. : 'and tovarish blessed without aim / wept in the rainditch at evening' (74 : 8/456).
411. From Venice for example (see 83 : 110/567). To indicate tears he mostly uses, as in our Canto, the Greek 'ΛΑΚΡΥΩΝ', either present participle or possibly gen. pl. of the noun for 'tears' (cf. *Index*).
412. *Sewanee Review*, LXV, 411.
413. *Journal of English Literary History*, XVII, 230 & 244.
414. *Paris Review*, 28, 49.
415. Kenner, p. 312; cf. his whole Appendix 2, 'Second Thoughts', pp. 310–313.
416. The title of the Epilogue is from 80 : 71/526, where we also find, reiterated : 'senesco sed amo'. The motto occurs twice in the *Rock-Drill* Cantos (92 : 79 and 95 : 105). It may be a quotation, perhaps from an Elizabethan writer.
417. From 'Ezra Pound : Readings and Recollections, 2. The Cantos', broadcast by the BBC (my own transcript), and from *Paris Review*, 28, 42.
418. See Max Nänny, *English Studies*, XLIII, 426–430; Watts, *Ezra Pound and the Cantos*, pp. 90 f.; Samuel Hynes, 'Pound and the Prose Tradition', *Yale Review*, LI (June 1962), 532–546.
419. *Poet in Exile : Ezra Pound* (Manchester, 1964); see the review in *T. L. S.* (May 28, 1964).
420. *Paris Review*, 28, 23–27.
421. *Poet in Exile*, pp. 220, 225 & passim.
422. See e.g. M. L. Rosenthal, *A Primer of Ezra Pound* (New York, 1960), p. 50.
423. See Stella Bowen, *Drawn from Life*, p. 96.
424. *Poet in Exile*, p. 254.
425. 86 : 28, continued, from the second line, in 87 : 29; cf. the echoes in 88 : 39, 88 : 41 and 100 : 65 f. Stock used this modified form as the motto of *Impact* : 'Bellum cano perenne, between usura and the man / who wants to do a good job'.
426. *Paris Review*, 28, 47; *Impact*, p. 142.
427. Cf. : 'But in his general criticism of the present age, especially in his attacks on "the present accounting system" and on "monetary inflation", there is little more than a smartly expressed indignation at the relationship between culture and money.' (Straumann, *American Literature in the 20th Cent.*, p. 197).
428. 77 : 47/498. It was Dr. Henry Slominsky (see *Index*) who said this to Pound, judging by the mimicry, with a heavy German accent. Cf. : 'Slovinsky [sic] looked at me in 1912 : "Boundt, haff you gno bolidigal basshuntz?" ' (*Impact*, p. 88).
429. *Paris Review*, 28, 41.
430. 98 : 37; cf. 102 : 80. The Chinese character indicates incompleteness. See Pound's obituary, 'In the Wounds : Memoriam A. R. Orage', in *Impact*, pp. 157–165. Cf. also : 'Thus Orage respected belatedly' (104 : 94).
431. *Impact*, p. 65. On the dubiety of his grandfather's paper scrip money used by his own Union Lumbering Company see Norman, pp. 234 f. & 351.

432. 100 : 69. Stock writes : 'After many years of study he came to the conclusion that monetary manipulation could be reduced to variations on the following "rackets" : (1) the lending of that which is made out of nothing; and (2) the alteration of the value of the monetary unit.' (*Poet in Exile*, p. 192).

433. Cf. : 'Can't move 'em with / a cold thing like economics' (78 : 59/512; cf. 103 : 87, etc.). This records an observation made by the Sinn Feiner leader, Arthur Griffith (cf. Stock, *Poet in Exile*, p. 251).

434. *Paris Review*, 28, 48. For 'jury trial in Athens' see Part Three.

435. *London Magazine* (Aug. 1959), p. 41. From the controversy between H. Read and C. P. Snow over the latter's Rede Lecture, *The Two Cultures and the Scientific Revolution*, continued in the issues for October (pp. 57 f.) and November (p. 73).

436. 52 : 3/267. See the founding of the Monte dei Paschi, treated in Cantos XLII–XLIV and e.g. in *Impact*, pp. 46 & 147; cf. also *Guide*, p. 194, where Pound calls it, after the Malatesta Cantos, 'the second episode'.

437. The line in *The Merchant of Venice* I, iii, 95 occurs in Antonio's reply to Shylock's account of Jacob's thriving on sheep. Shylock answers : 'I cannot tell : I make it breed as fast.' Cf. *Guide*, p. 149.

438. 13 : 60/64. The phrase actually refers to 'the blossoms of the apricot', but implied is the Confucian rectification of the heart.

439. Pointed out by Quinn, *Motive & Method*, p. 85.

440. *Impact*, pp. 57 & 74, the second time immediately before the already mentioned palindrome :   'R O M A
                     O   M
                     M   O
                 A M O R'.

441. *Paris Review*, 28, 28.

442. *Confucius*, p. 29; cf. 77 : 43/494.

443. Meant are, of course, the poems in the *Shih Ching*, translated by Pound as *The Classic Anthology Defined by Confucius*. 'Kung's insistence on the ODES', Pound holds, 'lifts him above all occidental philosophers.' Moreover : '... people need poetry; ... prose is NOT education but the outer courts of the same. Beyond its doors are the mysteries. Eleusis. Things not to be spoken save in secret.' (*Guide*, pp. 127 & 144 f.).

444. This pattern was emphasized by Forrest Read (*Sewanee Review*, LXV, 400–419).

445. For such a list see George Dekker, *Sailing After Knowledge* (1963), p. 203.

446. Kenner, p. 326.

447. Printed in *Agenda* (London), 3 (Dec.–Jan. 1963/4), 3. The version given in *Paris Review*, 28, 13, is without the first 5 lines quoted here.

448. Norman, p. 335.

449. See the newspaper comment quoted by T. S. Eliot in *Ezra Pound : His Metric and Poetry* (New York, 1917), p. 23.

450. *Paris Review*, 28, 49.

451. From Canto 116 (*Paris Review*, 28, 16).
452. See Grazia Livi, 'Io So Di Non Sapere Nulla', *Epoca* (Milan, March 24, 1963), 90–93. For the echo in the press see *New York Herald Tribune* (Paris, March 23–24, 1963) and *Daily Express* (March 23, 1963).
453. *Paris Review*, 28, 16 & 47.

INDEX

Note : Complete indexing has not been attempted, but fairly full reference is made to writers on Pound, including those quoted in the text, but only identified in the Notes. Italic figures refer to the Notes which are consecutively numbered.

207